How to
Start and Run
Your Own
Advertising
Agency

How to Start and Run Your Own Advertising Agency

Allan Krieff

McGraw-Hill, Inc.

New York   St. Louis   San Francisco   Auckland   Bogotá
Caracas   Lisbon   London   Madrid   Mexico   Milan
Montreal   New Delhi   Paris   San Juan   São Paulo
Singapore   Sydney   Tokyo   Toronto

Library of Congress Cataloging-in-Publication Data

Krieff, Allan.
    How to start and run your own advertising agency / Allan Krieff.
       p.   cm.
    Includes index.
    ISBN 0-07-035219-4 :
    1. Advertising agencies—Management.   2. New business enterprises—
Management. I. Title.
HF6178.K75 1993
659.1'068—dc20   92-23940
                                                    CIP

1 2 3 4 5 6 7 8 9 0 DOH/DOH 9 8 7 6 5 4 3 2

ISBN   0-07-035219-4

The sponsoring editor for this book was Karen A. Hansen, the editing supervisor was Jane Palmieri, and the production supervisor was Suzanne W. Babeuf. It was set in Garamond Light by McGraw-Hill's Professional Book Group composition unit.

Printed and bound by R. R. Donnelley & Sons Company.

Thanks to my parents, Anne and Ben, for not getting too upset when I decided on advertising instead of dentistry. Otherwise, this might have been a book on molars.

Thanks to my beautiful wife, Beth, for listening to all those ideas that seemed so brilliant at 3 o'clock in the morning.

Thanks to Laureen Plake, God's gift to advertising, for helping to make those brilliant ideas feasible at 3 in the afternoon.

And thanks to all my clients, who for 35 years made every day but one enjoyable. Wait till you read that book.

About the Author

Allan Krieff, a graduate of New York University with a B.S. in marketing, is a veteran of more than 35 years in the advertising business. Starting in the research department of Young & Rubicam in late 1956, he moved on to major account management at Weiss & Geller Advertising, a medium-sized New York agency known for its then revolutionary use of motivational advertising.

In 1962, Mr. Krieff moved to Florida and opened a one-man ad agency with modest billings. Krieff Advertising, based in Hollywood, Florida, grew to a full-service advertising/marketing agency with complete in-house creative and production facilities, and for many years has been among the top 10 agencies in billing in south Florida. The agency was responsible for introducing many innovative marketing techniques which are now commonly used in the business, and prides itself on its ability to produce effective, fairly priced advertising and marketing campaigns for its clients, which has resulted in client, employee, and media loyalty uncommon in the business.

This book is the result of years of helping other people start and run their own successful agencies.

Contents

Part 4. Record Keeping and Accounting

Part 7. Production and Printing

Part 8. Toward a More Perfect Agency-Client Relationship

Part 12. Conclusions

34. Some Final Words About Creativity, the Advertising Business Today, and What the Future Holds

Foreword

On April 15, 1983, two writers and an art director who worked for me at Ogilvy & Mather San Francisco, the advertising firm I started in 1977, announced they were quitting to open their own agency. Their names were Jeff Goodby, Andy Berlin, and Rich Silverstein. I wished them well and promised whatever support I could provide. Less than nine years later they sold their company to Omnicom for $20 million.

It sounds easy, but for every such success story there are probably 50 failures. At least one reason why is the fact that most new agencies are started by creative people. And creative people are uncomfortable with, or don't give a damn or know much about, business.

That includes me. I started in advertising in 1956 as a mail boy for Batten, Barton, Durstine & Osborne. Over the next 30 years, at BBDO and other agencies, I became a market researcher, an account executive, an art director, head art director, copywriter, creative director, and eventually managing director of an agency. And at no time did I have the slightest desire to start my own business.

I was, I thought, well paid—overpaid, in fact. And with some nice stock options, a comfortable severance agreement, and a reasonable retirement plan, I couldn't imagine why I should risk going out on my own. Besides, while on one hand it's nice to get credit for the agency's successes, it's also nice to have someone else—like Ogilvy & Mather or BBDO—take the blame or financial risk when something goes wrong.

Ironically, it was my own insecurity that delivered an advertising agency into my lap. In 1984, seven years after I founded their San Francisco office, Ogilvy & Mather suggested that we become a subsidiary under my name. Our agency had grown dramatically, and with advertising for such accounts as Gallo, Alamo, and Bartles & Jaymes, we'd earned a national reputation. And it was Ogilvy's belief that we could grow even faster without the client conflicts we suffered as the smallest office of one of the world's largest advertising firms.

I dug in my heels. I was 52 and had no desire to see my name on the agency door. Especially if someone else owned the door. Besides, beyond the resolution of conflicts, I could see few benefits for me, our employees, or our clients.

We wrangled with the concept for almost a year and a half—Ogilvy proposing mysterious and complicated stock option agreements, and I pleading uncertainty and confusion. Ogilvy eventually lost patience with me and accepted an account in New York which was in direct conflict with our largest client in San Francisco. I had no choice. I was stuck with an agency, whether I liked it or not.

We were able to make a most reasonable deal with Ogilvy & Mather for their interests and today own the agency outright. We are five or six times as large as we were when we separated. And I am just as scared as I ever was.

But I'm also a lot richer. And so are many of the people who work here. I'm also a lot wiser, at least in some respects. For despite my fears, I now realize that if there is any chance to start your own business rather than simply being an employee, you'd be a fool not to give it a shot.

But I would suggest that before you do, you read this book. I wish I'd had it to read. My life would have been infinitely easier, and probably considerably more successful. It is too late for me, but not for you.

Anyway, I wish you well in your new venture. At the very least it will be exciting. If you're lucky, as I have been, you may get to sell cars, ice cream, candy, beer, tractors, and even an occasional President, in addition, of course, to living well, having fun, and working with a lot of talented and interesting people.

As for me, I'm going to lunch. Some guy wants to talk to me about buying the advertising agency.

Hal Riney
San Francisco

Preface

There is no feeling in the world quite like the feeling of starting your own business. And there are few businesses that are as rewarding, stimulating, satisfying, and exciting as advertising.

Statistics show that eventually nearly every business will advertise in one way or another. It could be a commercial on network television, an ad in the local yellow pages, or something as simple as handing out a business card. Whatever the medium may be, creating the proper message, directing it to the proper target market, and following through with an effective advertising and marketing plan are essential. Most knowledgeable advertisers recognize that the best way to accomplish these goals is to use the services of a professional advertising agency or a professionally trained in-house advertising department.

Each year, advertisers direct myriads of messages to the public through magazines, newspapers, posters, television, radio, car cards, direct mail, telemarketing, and a long list of other media, from skywriting to calendars and T-shirts. It is no wonder that the advertising industry has grown to be one of the largest service industries in the world.

Establishing your own advertising agency means you are entering a prestige business—a business without inventory, that sells service and creativity, earning its income from media commissions, professional service fees, and production and outside purchase markups. With proper financial management and an active clientele it is possible for the new agency owner to reap handsome rewards from the very outset. In this business, profit margins can be high, the cost of entering the field can be relatively low, and there is a readily available supply of talented, experienced help—if the agency owner knows where to look.

If you like excitement, a touch of glamour, and daily challenges, this is the business to be in. Your clients will be businesspeople like you, who want to make money. And if your agency can help them accomplish this goal, your profits will rise in direct proportion to theirs—because as they make more money, they will spend more money with you.

Not every advertising agency handles multimillion-dollar clients. Most are small firms (one or two people), serving small and medium-size accounts. Yet many of these agencies are billing seven figures per year—some even in their first year.

Advertising, as it is practiced today, is a highly technical profession that involves many specialized skills. This book is written from the point of view of the person who will be responsible for coordinating the efforts of these specialists—you, the president of your own agency.

Advertising is one of the few businesses that welcomes the generalist and the specialist. Both can work side by side in the fascinating process of creating ideas and finding new ways of communicating them.

You belong in your own advertising business if:

- You have had some experience with an ad agency, house agency, ad department, or art/production studio

- You're looking for a career at the core of business, where the end product of your work will help people live better

- You enjoy working with other imaginative people in a variety of stimulating jobs that call for creative, selling, analytical, marketing, and management talent

- You have a knack for developing ideas, solving marketing problems, and working under pressure

- You'd like to get ahead, both in terms of responsibility and earnings, and understand that for you to succeed, so must your clients

- You have the ability to put yourself in your client's shoes, focus on your client's customers, and make important decisions as though the client's business were your business

- You are able to both give direction to others and are willing to listen, learn, and communicate with others

- You have the stamina and emotional strength to meet strict deadlines, deal with employees and vendors who may disappoint you, and put in long working hours, often 7 days a week and maybe even on holidays

- You are aware of the many risks associated with starting a new business and are prepared to earn less income in the first years of your new venture

If this sounds like you, welcome to the business.

Oh yes, advertising sometimes fails. The brightest advertising idea in the world won't sell an inferior product—more than once. Actually, advertising helps drive such products out of the marketplace by informing people about better or less expensive competitive products.

This book was developed as a practical step-by-step guide to help you establish and operate your own advertising agency to serve business clients in your community. It is really many books in one, based on experience that has worked for others and can work for you. As you go through the various chapters, you will be exposed to nearly all the situations that you will encounter in your day-to-day operations. You will see the different forms, contracts, and layout ideas typically used by agencies. You will learn how to handle the day-to-day problems that affect agency-client relationships throughout the country.

Though there is no guaranteed formula to running a successful agency, if you follow the ideas and counsel contained within these pages, use your own good common sense, and take advantage of opportunities when they present themselves, your ad agency could become a profitable, enjoyable, long-running business for you.

It takes courage to open your own advertising agency. There will be long hours, short deadlines, vendors that are late with deliveries, clients that are late with payments, ads that work and ads that don't, good times and bad times.

It is my sincere hope that this book will help increase the good times, and make money, lots of money, for you.

Allan Krieff

Part 1

An Introduction to the Advertising Agency Business

1

Overview of Advertising and What an Agency Does

When most people think of the advertising business, they think of the advertising agency. While the agency is just a part of the total advertising picture, it is a vital part. Hollywood has created a "glamorous" impression of the ad agency business. Though it is glamorous in a sense, it is also creative and an ever changing business. It deals with art and writing and research and financing and buying media and many other functions.

For every client and product, the agency is always striving to create an advertising theme that is provocative, arresting, believable, convincing, and memorable. Advertising that is fresh, original, and effective. Advertising that moves the consumer. Most clients will agree there is little other point for an advertising agency's existence.

When that kind of theme has been found, it is up to various people within the agency to present and "sell" that theme to the client, to physically produce the materials needed by the media, to place the idea in one or more media, and to perform the various financial and accounting functions necessary to pay for and bill for services.

Agencies are people—of all sorts—who put in a full workweek and frequently something extra. People who have desks and telephones and word processors, and who, if they are fortunate, have offices of their own. As a service business meeting the needs of its clients, a successful agency must overcome daily frustrations arising from the unpredictability of creative work and the pressure of deadline schedules. But when a creative effort put out by the agency proves successful for the client, there is no greater feeling of satisfaction and accomplishment.

What Is an Advertising Agency?

Simply stated, advertising agencies are in business to create advertisements that deliver their clients' messages to prospective customers. Their success hinges on their creative and business skills. The agency is responsible for understanding clients' objectives and for conceiving the ideas to fulfill those objectives. It is responsible for writing the words or copy that will appear in the ad or be spoken by an actor. It is responsible for designing the layout for the print ad or collateral piece or the shooting of a film or video sequence for a television commercial. In the case of a small agency just starting out, some of these responsibilities can be "farmed out" to freelancers who specialize in creative services such as writing, layout, illustration, photography, and voice-over.

The agency, however, is responsible for contracting for these services on behalf of its clients, providing direction concerning the end product and controlling the process until that product is finished.

The finished advertisement should accomplish the following:

- It should create a need and desire for the client's products or services or educate the public about new products.
- It should convince the potential customer that the client's products or services are the best.
- It should attract customers to purchase the client's products or services.

An effective ad should have these elements:

- It should tell in sincere, easily understood language who, what, when, where, how, and why.
- It should be truthful.
- It should be eye appealing and, if possible, entertaining.
- It should be directed (targeted) to the right audience through the most cost-effective media that reach that audience.
- It should be forceful enough to cause response (traffic, sales, or inquiry).

There has been a tendency to divide agencies into two categories: marketing and creative. The marketing-oriented advertising agency, in addition to creating advertisements for clients, also acts as a consultant to the client with regard to the total marketing plan and is often deeply involved in the formulation of those plans. The creative agency, on the other hand, tends to work from marketing plans provided by the client and limits its activities to the creation of advertisements.

In recent years there has been an increasing recognition that advertising cannot be created in a vacuum—that it is a part of the whole marketing strategy. Therefore, before an advertising agency can create advertisements, the whole marketing plan must be developed. For that reason, more and more agencies are becoming involved in planning marketing strategy.

In order to create advertising to sell a client's goods or services, an agency should follow certain procedures.

1. Study the client's product or service in order to determine the advantages and disadvantages inherent in the product itself, and its relation to competition.
2. Analyze the present and potential market to which the product or service is adapted:
   a. As to location
   b. As to extent of possible sale
   c. As to season
   d. As to trade and economic conditions
   e. As to nature and amount of competition
3. Study the factors of distribution and sales and their methods of operation.
4. Know all the available media and means which can profitably be used to convey the interpretation of the product or service to consumer, wholesaler, dealer, contractor, or other factor. This knowledge covers:
   a. Character
   b. Influence
   c. Circulation:
      (1) Quantity
      (2) Quality
      (3) Location
   d. Physical requirements
   e. Costs

Acting on the analysis and knowledge as explained above, the agency makes recommendations and the following procedures ensue:

5. Formulate a definite plan and present this plan to the client.
6. Execute this plan:
   a. Writing, designing, and illustrating of advertisements or other appropriate forms of the message
   b. Contracting for the space, time, or other means of advertising
   c. Proper incorporation of the message in mechanical form and forwarding it with proper instructions for the fulfillment of the contract
   d. Checking and verifying of insertions, ad positioning, ad reproduction, and so on
   e. Auditing and billing for the service, space, and preparation
   f. Arranging for the media to return all client materials
7. Cooperate with the client's sales force to ensure the greatest effect from advertising

Advertising Classifications

Some agencies provide clients with specialized services such as media planning and placement, design and art services, marketing, and research. Others provide a full gamut of agency services and are known as "full-service agencies." They prepare art-work, graphics, and copy for print and broadcast, as well as direct-mail pieces, out-door advertising, and the like. They plan and purchase media, produce final materi-als, and deliver to the media for insertion. They also negotiate contracts, follow up with billing verification, collect cooperative funds (if any), bill for media and produc-tion, and pay outside vendors and media.

A full-service advertising agency is concerned mostly with the following types of commonly used advertising.

Print Advertising

Print ads appear in newspapers, magazines, trade journals, yellow pages, and pe-riodicals. There are a number of different types of print ads but the two that will concern most agencies are display ads and direct-response ads. Ads are usually cate-gorized by size. They are measured in column-inches or agate lines in newspapers and by page segment (full, ½-page, ¼-page, etc.) or by column-inches in magazines.

Display Ads.   Display ads usually have illustrations, borders, or photographs as part of the overall graphics. They can be black and white, black with a second or third color added for special emphasis, or full-color.

Direct-Response Ads.   A direct-response ad usually tries to accomplish a sale or other kind of immediate response. It will carry a coupon or telephone number or both as well as complete information about the product or service. Such ads are most often used by mail-order companies. They usually run in magazines, catalogs, trade journals, and newspapers. Direct response is covered in more depth in Chapter 31.

Printed Collateral

Collateral includes preparing and printing catalogs, newsletters, mailing pieces, flyers, hang tags, specialties such as key chains and printed pens, mail stuffers, and merchandising aids. Chapter 23 covers printing in greater detail.

Broadcast Commercials

Broadcast includes both radio and television. Commercials are measured by their length—usually 60, 30, 20, or 10 seconds. It is possible to purchase 2-minute and 5-minute spots from some stations. It is also possible to purchase 15-minute to 60-minute or more "infomercials." Broadcast spots can be aired on a local basis, through a regional hookup, or on a national scope via a network.

The role of the agency in broadcast includes creating the commercial; supervis-ing the recording and production of the spot through an outside audio or video pro-duction company; selecting and hiring actors, models, announcers, and other talent; then planning and purchasing schedules on radio and TV stations. Commercials for television can be videotaped, filmed, or done live. Commercials for radio can be done on audiotape or live.

Direct Mail and Telemarketing

In the direct-mail category, the agency will write, print, and distribute advertising through the mail to a targeted list. The agency will usually purchase the mailing list from a mailing house, which can provide other services such as addressing, stuffing, stamping, bundling by zip codes, and mailing. Some mailing firms also act as fulfillment houses. That means they will respond to inquiries from direct mailings by sending brochures, products, or additional information about the product.

Telemarketing is selling through direct phone contact. Agency functions in this area include creating the selling approach or "canned script" used by the caller, hiring the people who will make the calls, and creating the follow-up procedures. There are companies that specialize in live and computerized phone campaigns and fulfillment. See Chapter 31 for an in-depth look at telemarketing.

Outdoor Advertising

Outdoor includes billboards, posters, and bus benches that appear on highways, roadsides, and building sites, as well as cards, posters, and dioramas which may be seen on buses, on taxicabs, in airports, and in other transportation terminals. Outdoor advertising can also include such abstract media as skywriting, balloon advertising, and stadium computerized graphics.

Specialty Advertising

Specialty advertising includes putting a client message on items such as matchbook covers, calendars, shopping bags, keychains, sun visors, and T-shirts. There are vendors that specialize in these items and can provide the agency with catalogs that describe the various companies and products they represent. The agency will prepare the materials needed to produce the message on the specialty item according to the specifications given by each manufacturer.

Public Relations and Publicity

Though public relations is separate from advertising, the agency may, from time to time, be called upon to produce news releases, publicity photos, and promotional materials that do not fall under the "paid advertising" category.

The specific functional areas within an advertising agency are examined in the following chapter.

2

Overview of the Functional Areas of an Advertising Agency

Unless your agency specializes in a particular service, such as media buying, your company will perform a number of services and functions for your clients. In large agencies, these functions are very clearly delineated, because each function is the responsibility of one individual or group. In the small agency, on the other hand, one individual may be responsible for several of these functions. We will examine them here, not necessarily in order of importance, but with a view toward their integration and coordination. In addition to those functions which are essential to the minimum needs of an advertising agency, some of the functional areas which have been added as agencies increase the scope of their operations will be noted.

In broad terms, the functions of an agency fall into four categories: consultation, production, media, and administration. These categories can be further broken down to show that consultation, for instance, can include research and planning as well as marketing and merchandising.

The division of labor in one agency may be different than in another. An account executive in one firm may solely call on and service clients. The same position in another agency can have the account executive involved with creative and consulting functions.

The creative person or persons in one agency may consult with clients and create ideas and illustrations. In another agency, they may also be involved with other aspects of production such as printing and production billing. In a small agency, responsibilities may vary and overlap. If yours is a one-person shop, you'll be wearing all the hats. And knowing which hat is which is very important.

An advertising agency has many more parts of course: administration, office services, fashion, traffic, production, data processing, research, and even psychology. Some agencies have people who handle sales promotion, merchandising, public relations, home economics, typesetting, photography, and personnel. And like other firms, agencies need comptrollers, secretaries, general office workers, bookkeepers, and billing clerks. The list goes on and on. But as a small agency, you will be most concerned with the major functions needed for basic operation, as described below.

Organizational Structure

The organizational structure of any service business will be only as good as the people in the company. More than anything else, your clients will be buying the talents and skills of your people.

There are probably as many possible organizational structures as there are agencies. The organization depends on the size of the shop, the functions it performs, the clients it serves, and the managerial planning of its executives.

Among ad agencies, there are three broad kinds of organizational structure. The first two are most often found in large or medium-size agencies.

- In a group arrangement, each client is dealt with by its own group of personnel—account executive, copywriter, art director, media and traffic, and so on. These people work together to plan the advertising strategy and create the campaigns for a client or group of clients.

- In a departmental arrangement, each department in the agency serves all clients, with the possible exception of the account executive, who serves only his or her own accounts. The account executive calls on the copy chief for copywriting, the art director for layouts, and so on.

- In a smaller agency, the duties, interests, and responsibilities of every key person often dovetail. Thus, the account executive may come up with creative ideas, and a creative person who works closely with a client may develop a better flair for billing than the account manager.

In the beginning, you must plan on running the business yourself, and look at it as a full-time, 7-day-a-week job to get the company off the ground. An advertising agency is not a business that grows without your active involvement.

Basic Job Descriptions
President and CEO

The president and chief executive officer (CEO) or chief operating officer (COO) is responsible for planning, implementation, and control of the agency's objectives and may also have responsibility for creative direction. The president provides leadership in establishing policies and plans; develops and maintains organizational structure, competent personnel, and plans for management succession; approves budgets and appropriations; and studies and evaluates company operations.

Operations Manager

The operations manager has responsibility for overall administration and coordination of office functions and responsibility for matters pertaining to day-to-day business activities. The manager may also be responsible for developing and implementing policies, plans, and programs; for financial activities such as accounting, budgets, audits, taxes, and preparation of government reports; and for systems and procedures necessary to maintain efficiency.

Account Manager

The account executive or account manager is the liaison between client and agency. The account executive may also be responsible for getting new clients. This person receives and supervises client requests and serves as the channel through which agency work and recommendations flow to the client.

The account executive functions very much like a building contractor, helping to develop an advertising program for clients on the basis of an understanding of client needs. He or she then guides, oversees, and continues to monitor the program, suggesting improvements along the way and working with clients and agency specialists to prepare additional efforts.

The account executive must understand the client's business and business needs and desires. This enables the account executive to provide the most valuable contribution to the agency solution: posing the right problem. The thinking and insight for problem solving, known as strategy, becomes the true contact between client and agency. By posing the right problem, the account executive ensures that the talent and resources of the agency will result in solutions that the client will recognize as valuable.

Tackling the right problem enables the talents of the agency to be unleashed to provide solutions. This is an interactive process. The account executive naturally must have some creative ability and marketing knowledge and know-how—although, of course, he or she will seldom be expert in all these areas and will work closely with the agency specialists in each field. The account exec's facilitation skills are truly tested within the agency. While guiding the process, the executive must remain open to the ideas and solutions that develop from the agency's team effort.

Creative Director

The creative side of the advertising agency—that is, the areas responsible for the creation and execution of advertisements and commercials—consists of four major functional areas: art, copy, print production, and television and radio (broadcast) production. Today there is a tendency to merge some of these functional areas into one creative department, on the assumption that creativity is a total process frequently stemming from the collective thinking of persons in several of these areas. Such creative departments are headed by a creative director.

In general, the creative director has overall responsibility for guiding the direction and the development of creative concepts; for establishing graphic standards and designs; and for directing creative personnel such as illustrators, copywriters, production personnel, and photographers.

Major Functional Areas

New Business

The lifeblood of an advertising agency is, of course, its clients. For an agency to grow, it must secure new business. In some instances, the agency is approached by an advertiser; in other instances, the agency takes the initiative in soliciting new business. This activity is handled in a variety of ways by different advertising agencies. In some, the task is left to the top executive personnel; in others it is done by account managers. Some agencies have special "new business" departments whose sole task is to attract and secure new clients. See Chapters 24 and 25 for an in-depth look at getting and servicing clients.

Traffic

As an advertising agency grows in size, there is an increasing need for coordinating the activities of the various departments and centering the responsibility for meeting schedules and closing dates (deadlines for submitting advertisements and commercials to media). This is the task of the traffic department. Traffic is the nerve center of the advertising agency and its role is to channel the many elements necessary to complete every individual job to the proper places within the agency as well as to outside vendors.

Traffic must coordinate each phase of each job opened, making sure that as one part is completed, the job moves on the to next phase. It may also fall upon the traffic department to price out various elements needed to complete a job. In Chapter 18 traffic is covered more completely.

Art Department

The art department, usually headed by an art director, is responsible for the creation of the pictorial element in the advertisement (artwork) and for the design of the whole advertisement, which is called a layout. In the case of a television commercial, the layout is known as a storyboard. In general, the art director and assistant artists are responsible for the visualization of artwork, the execution of layouts and storyboards, the preparation of mechanicals (blueprints for the production of advertisements), and the specification of type. Because some finished artwork may be produced outside of the agency, it must be purchased from free-lance artists and photographers. Consequently, the art department may have an art buyer, who is responsible for locating suitable artists and photographers and purchasing finished artwork from them. Chapter 20 is devoted to a detailed profile of the art department.

Copy Department

Where separate copy departments exist, they are headed by the copy director, who supervises various copy chiefs. They, in turn, have copywriters working for them.

Copy chiefs and copywriters may be assigned to a particular account or group of accounts.

Most ad production begins with the copy. The copywriter writes the display lines (headlines and subheads) and body copy (text) used in print and copy for broadcast commercials as well as other kinds of advertising and collateral materials. The copywriter may work with the artist, who will often contribute new ideas as well as constructively criticize unfeasible ideas.

Because creative activity is not narrowly confined, the copywriter may prepare a rough or visual layout of the advertisement in addition to writing the copy, just as the art director may develop copy ideas. In any case, the copywriter functions as part of a team effort and seldom works alone.

A good copywriter is creative. You cannot make a noncreative person creative. There are principles that can help creative people realize their full potential. See Chapter 19 for more on copywriting.

Print Production

After the copy and layout have been approved, the artwork completed, and the mechanicals prepared, advertisements for print media must be put into production. If the physical production of advertisements is not done by the agency, the production department acts as a sort of purchasing department which is responsible for developing all specifications. For this reason, the production department must have a thorough knowledge of the graphic arts, as well as the negatives, film positives, and photoengravings which must be ordered. Production personnel also assist the copywriter and artist by delineating the limitations of the various graphic arts techniques, so that what they prepare will be practical for reproduction in the various media.

Television and Radio Production

In the early years of television, advertising agencies not only prepared the commercials but frequently originated the format of programs and prepared their content. Today this latter activity has been taken over almost entirely by the networks and individual stations and by independent specialists known as producers, leaving the radio and television production departments of advertising agencies responsible in most instances only for the production of the commercials. Using the storyboard as a guide or script, the agency TV production department will cast the commercial, secure the necessary props, and usually have the commercial taped or filmed by an outside studio under its supervision. In the case of a radio commercial, a voice-over cassette is recorded using talent selected by the agency (with or without music), special effects, and the like. In the case of live commercials, of course, there is no filming or recording, and the agency's television and radio production department simply supervises the commercial portion of the program.

Media Department

The proper selection, purchase, and use of the many communication media can be crucial to the success of an ad or campaign. The task of determining which medium or media to be used in a particular advertising plan is the job of the media department. Decisions must be made as to which of the major media classifications should be included to meet the goals set for the client in the most productive and cost-efficient manner. For example, should the plan make use of television, magazines, newspapers, or a combination of these? Then decisions must be made regarding the individual media within these broad classifications. For example, should *Time* or *Newsweek* be used? With the myriad choices of media available, a tremendous amount of statistical work is necessary in order to discover a vehicle that will best deliver the advertising message at the lowest cost to the advertiser. The responsibility for the operation of this department is delegated to the media director.

The activities of the media department may be divided into two broad areas: broadcast media and print media. For radio and television there are broadcast buyers; for print media there are space buyers. In addition to selecting and recommending media to be used in specific campaigns, this department is responsible for contracting for space and time with the media and for establishing the advertising media schedule. These and other areas of media are discussed in depth in Chapter 21.

Printed Collateral Buying Department

Print media buying should not be confused with the buying of printing. One of the most lucrative functions of an agency can be the purchase of printed matter needed by clients. In some agencies, the purchase of printed matter is handled by the traffic or production departments. A good printing buyer should understand the various methods of printing and the different kinds of stock (paper) available, and have a general knowledge of agency production procedures. Each of these areas can be critical in pricing out a print job. The less work a printer has to do on a print job before it goes on press, the lower the cost to both agency and client. The more work that is done in house, the greater the agency's production charges.

Reprinting of collateral materials can mean lots of money with little work attached. Usually, reprinting a piece without copy changes involves only a phone call to the printer that did it last. Chapter 23 covers just about everything you'll need to know about printing.

Accounting

It goes without saying that getting paid for the creativity and production work your agency does and for the media and outside purchases it places for clients is the reason you are in business in the first place.

Because the advertising agency deals with numerous media and suppliers on behalf of its clients, there is a considerable amount of bookkeeping work involved. This is the task of the accounting (or billing) department, whose work involving agency compensation and billing, when priced correctly, will hopefully make a profit for the agency.

It is always important for the accounting department to check with the account executive, since many clients require estimates of costs before contracting for work. Client quotes and actual costs can differ greatly.

Always keep billing current. If possible, bill your clients in advance of your having to pay media or vendors. The subjects of agency compensation and billing are examined in Part 4 of this book.

Research

Research is indispensable to the successful operation of the agency. Before any effective advertising can be prepared, information must be gathered. The job of the research department or outside research firm primarily involves gathering the facts necessary to provide the basis on which to build effective advertising strategy. This involves not only advertising research but also more basic analysis and marketing research (feasibility studies, focus groups, product pretesting, etc.).

Although the in-house research department may prepare a good many of its own research studies, smaller agencies can make use of the numerous specialized research organizations and frequently will farm out work to independent research firms.

Other Functions

All the functions described above are found in some manner in all advertising agencies. Over the years, however, some advertising agencies have expanded their activities beyond the realm of advertising per se in order to serve the needs of their clients. Some of these areas involve merchandising, sales promotion, and telemarketing. In an effort to improve their advertising, many agencies have established departments to serve clients in these areas. These departments are staffed by personnel who are well versed in sales management.

See Chapter 17 for more issues regarding personnel. We turn next to the critical task of developing a business plan.

3

Your Business Plan and Agency Policies

Making and keeping to a business plan is essential to the success of a business, but it is of crucial importance to any new business starting up. In making a business plan you should consider your basic objectives, policies, and, of course, resources.

In addition to helping you set reasonable goals for your business, a business plan makes you think like a businessperson and work along with other businesspeople. And, by outlining orderly management procedures, a business plan can provide assurance for other employees, whose personal stake in your company may be far less than yours. In short, it can be your "manual for survival" in a ruthless, competitive business world.

Planning Control

The basic reason for making a business plan is for planning control of your new operations. Such a plan will be instrumental in providing you with information you can use in making important managerial decisions.

When creating a plan, decide first on how long a time period you want it to cover. A 6-month or yearly period would be ideal for a small or recently organized company whose fortunes can change quickly. Once the plan is launched, it can then be broken down into quarterly segments. Plans that are designed for longer periods tend to serve more as planning tools than as day-to-day management tools.

No matter how talented or innovative you may be in your area of expertise, your new business may not survive if the services you provide are not treated as a busi-

15

ness. A good business plan helps you focus on the business and the objectives you strive for.

The First Steps

In preparing a business plan, start by writing down and analyzing all your reasons for wanting to be in business for yourself. Be aware of the risks involved with starting a new business. Speak with people who have started their own businesses and find out the pros and cons as they see them.

Next, prepare a budget. Estimate your start-up and continuing costs for the period of the plan. Determine the number of employees you can afford, the kind of office you need, and the equipment (phones, faxes, furnishings, supplies, etc.).

Try to determine your sales projections. To do this you will also have to estimate your billing charges for the various services you will provide, as well as the volume of business you will need to cover your expenses and make a profit. Of course, a mature business can more easily project future sales much more closely on the basis of past experience. A budget is really just a simple way to track your company's income and outgo. It lets you see how much your sales are for a given period compared to your expenses. It may be the quickest way—other than receiving a bounced check in the mail—to find out if you're spending more than you're taking in. Using the budget, you can decide what level of production capabilities and what level of staffing you need.

Forecasting sales (in the case of an ad agency, getting new clients) is the beginning point for all budgeting. If acquiring new clients turns out to be less than what was forecast, you will have to revise your budget or take other actions to reduce your overhead, possibly even lay off employees.

In determining your budget, be sure to include all your sources of cash. If you've been putting spare money in a money-market account, be sure to include the interest when tallying up the take.

As for expenses, start with the known costs (payroll, rent, taxes, etc.). Be sure not to miss expenses such as commissions paid to selling agents (account executives), professional dues, insurance, advertising, stationery and business card costs, and any loan payments.

If you plan to extend credit to your clients, you'll need to make some assumption regarding the collection of accounts receivable as well as what percentage of bad debt you're possibly going to have. Timing is critical in terms of cash receipts. You need to make assumptions correctly.

Consider what you want your income to be as opposed to what your income projections are. Since "time is money," you can overextend your time on lots of small clients to produce the income you need. But it may be better to have fewer accounts that pay higher billing charges, giving yourself more time to devote to other areas and needs.

Never make "blue sky" projections. Rather, try to be conservative when forecasting potential billing and gross profits. Plan each client separately. Your judgment, based on the client's sales volume and sales forecast, will provide a great deal of guidance. And after you come up with what you think is the most conservative of billing and gross profit forecasts, *reduce it by 15 percent.*

In planning your operating expenses, always remember that you can't spend more than you take in—at least not for very long. Your gross profit represents 100 percent of all the funds available to pay all your operating expenses and return a reasonable profit. In planning your operating expenses, try to use the standard allowances mentioned in Chapter 15 as your guide. If every item is planned per the allowance, and operating expenses are held to 80 percent of your projected gross profit, the agency should realize an operating profit of 20 percent.

Creating a successful advertising agency business can be the most exciting and rewarding of experiences, and the business plan can be instrumental in making this happen. Every business plan should be reviewed for accuracy and revised accordingly each year. With a year of experience under your belt, your projections in future plans will be more accurate.

When reviewing your business plan, also examine the level of service provided by those who are instrumental to the efficient running of your business. If you are not satisfied with your banker, attorney, or accountant, do not hesitate to discuss your problems with them. If you can't get the satisfaction you want, replace those services quickly.

Finally, every business plan should include one very important element: enjoyment. The plan is a formula not just to achieve success, but to have fun while doing it—with clients and vendors and staff you enjoy working with, often well into the night, and sometimes during weekends and holidays. Too many people in this world are not happy in their jobs, and it would be a shame to put time, money, and hard work into a venture that did not provide enjoyment along with the benefits of success. There is no better feeling than waking up each morning and looking forward to going to work.

Agency Philosophy and Policies

Aside from its personnel and organizational structure, what really sets one agency apart from another is its character, which includes its philosophy and policies. Thus, some agencies have a character of reserve, whereas others are innovative and aggressive. Some emphasize copy; others, visualization. Some subordinate advertising to a role in the total marketing mix, while others look at advertising as being independent of other marketing activities. Like most businesses, your company will have growth and profitability plans for the future. There is insufficient space here to develop all the pertinent inputs and influences. However, there are ten crucial corporate goals an agency should consider to be successful.

"The Ten Commitments"

1. *You Succeed Only When Your Clients Succeed.*   Their bottom line is ultimately your bottom line. So you must take the initiative and treat their business and money as if it were your own. The sense of ownership means you expect to be held accountable for results.

2. *Your Focus Must Be on Your Client's Customer.* Serving the customer is why both your client and you exist. So you must make it a point to be in close touch with your client's customer. That's where the most creative ideas really begin and where they must ultimately be tested.

3. *You Will Use Only Two Principles in Your Charging Practices.* Competitiveness and flexibility.

4. *Excellence Is a Team Concept.* Advertising is a collaborative business, between client and agency and among agencies. So you must expect your staff to be team players, to be contributors, and to be motivated by a sense of accomplishment. When everyone is allowed to contribute, the client and the team will always win.

5. *No Guts, No Glory.* To do great work you must be willing to reject the expected, to trust your intuition, and to dare to reach for inspired solutions.

6. *Successful Relationships Are Built on Trust.* Your goal is to have long-term clients and associates whom you respect and who let you contribute to their growth. But if you can't build and maintain a climate of trust, these relationships won't work and won't last.

7. *Communications Is 90 Percent Listening.* You are in the persuasion business; so everything you do depends upon how well you listen to and communicate with clients, customers, and other agencies.

8. *There Are No Shortcuts to Quality.* Discipline is more fundamental to success than brilliance; so the true spirit of an organization lives in its sense of discipline and its attention to details. You must do your homework and take pride in doing things right the first time.

9. *Your Agency Is Primarily a Business.* It should always be conducted as such. Don't cover yourself with a "professional" or "creative" mystique, even though your business employs professionals and sells the services of creative people.

10. *You Have to Feel Good About What You Do.* If you do all the above you can take pride in your company, yourself, and what you do for a living. You can look in the mirror and feel proud about how you got where you are—and good about where you are going.

Your Company and Its Purpose

Your company, XYZ Advertising Inc., is a full-service advertising agency which provides marketing communications services to fill the needs of industrial, business, and corporate advertising clients. Your typical agency services might include:

- Marketing consultation and planning
- Market and advertising research
- Design and production of advertising and collateral materials (including direct-mail pieces, sales literature, catalogs, displays, audiovisual presenta-

tions, package design, corporate brochures, technical bulletins, product manuals, advertising novelties, corporate stationery, and news releases)

- Media planning and execution
- Publicity
- Public relations
- Special promotion and execution
- Special-event planning (press conferences, plant openings, etc.)

These services are provided in full or in part to XYZ clients depending upon their individual requirements.

Agency Recognition

A large part of the compensation for an advertising agency comes in the form of commissions from advertising media. However, media will pay commissions only to those advertising agencies they recognize. For an agency to receive recognition, media generally require that the agency be completely independent, without control or ownership by a medium or a client, and that it have the financial capacity to meet its obligations. Individual media reserve the right to recognize an advertising agency, and in reaching a decision on this matter they usually will use the data provided by the various media associations which investigate advertising agencies for their members.

Part 1 Action Checklist

- ✔ The advertising agency is a vital part of the total advertising and marketing picture. It deals with creativity in art and writing. It also deals with planning and buying media, production of advertising materials, research, and other functions. As part of the total marketing strategy, it is important for the agency to understand the total client marketing plan.

- ✔ Your agency is in business to create fresh, original, and effective advertisements that deliver your client's messages to the correct prospective customers in the most effective and efficient manner.

- ✔ As a full-service advertising agency, your company will deal with the creation and placement of many different kinds of advertising including: print and direct-response ads; printed collateral and sales promotional materials; broadcast commercials; outdoor, direct-mail, and telemarketing approaches—and possibly public relations and publicity.

- ✔ The functions of an advertising agency fall into four broad categories: consultation, production, media, and administration. The responsibilities of employees within these categories may vary from agency to agency.

- ✔ Operating under the direction of the president and CEO and/or operations manager, the departments of a typical advertising agency would include: account management; new business; traffic; creative (art and copywriting); production (print and broadcast); media; accounting; and others such as merchandising, sales promotion, and so on, depending on the size of the agency.

✔ Developing a business plan is essential to the success of any start-up agency. Such a plan should outline your business and creative objectives, policies, and resources.

✔ In preparing an operating budget for your agency, estimate your start-up and continuing costs for the period of the plan. Determine the number of employees you absolutely need, as well as the office facilities, furnishings, and equipment needed to provide the services you will offer your clients.

✔ Try to estimate your sales projections. To do this you will have to first determine what you will charge for your services, and the volume of business you will need to cover your estimated expenses plus a profit. Be sure to include all your sources of cash and all your expected expenses—even down to the costs of your stationery, insurance, and loan payments.

✔ If you expect to extend credit to your clients, your business plan must also include accurate assumptions regarding collection of accounts receivable and a bad debt allowance. Never make "blue sky" projections. Always be conservative when forecasting billing and gross profits. Consider each client separately in your projections, then reduce those projections by 15 percent.

✔ You might want to add an additional 15 percent to whatever operating expenses you project to cover unforeseen costs that may come up. Remember, your gross profit represents 100 percent of all the funds available to pay your operating expenses and return a reasonable profit.

✔ The corporate and creative goals you set for your company will set your agency apart from the competition and help make it successful. Your agency plan should include "The Ten Commitments."

✔ If you expect any part of your agency compensation to be in the form of media commissions, your agency must qualify for and get agency recognition. Briefly, it means the agency must be independent of control or ownership by a medium or client, and of course, it must be able and willing to meet its financial obligations to media.

Part 2

Setting Up
Your Company

4

Getting Started: An Overview

Your Market

Regardless of their size, organization, or location, all advertising agencies are service businesses composed of creative and business people who develop, prepare, and place advertising in advertising media for clients, which are other businesses. The agencies' purpose is to provide the buying public with information regarding the products and services sold by their clients in ways that will persuade consumers to respond and hopefully to buy. Beyond this, advertising agencies may do work in public relations, marketing strategy, research, merchandising, and other specialties.

Some agencies may be more marketing oriented than others and, in addition to creating advertisements, may act as consultant to the client with regard to the total marketing plan. In fact, an advertising agency is one of those rare businesses that has two markets to consider. The first is made up of its own clients—business firms, civic or political organizations, mail-order companies, and the like. The second market comprises the various target markets its clients want to reach.

An advertising agency soliciting business from prospective clients must know each clients' target market in order to obtain advertising accounts. In order to keep those accounts, the agency must also know how to reach its clients' markets.

Advertising is considered a highly professional and specialized industry. This fact is important because there are many aspects of the advertising business which advertising agencies are far better equipped to handle than the clients. A well-run advertising agency performing professional services to the business community will always be in high demand.

Those who work in the media in which advertising appears prefer to deal with advertising agencies who "speak their language," rather than with the advertisers directly. Advertising agency personnel are creative and experienced professionals who know the ins and outs of placing ads correctly. Ad agency personnel have access to the media and to the creative pros who execute promotional ideas in a way that the advertisers themselves cannot. In any case, smart advertisers are more interested in running their own business than in becoming experts in the ad game.

The process of creating and placing advertising through an ad agency is advantageous to all concerned. The ad person is the go-between for advertiser and advertising media. He or she is the account executive and frequently the creative force behind an advertising campaign. The account exec knows how to reach the advertiser's market and provide the services needed to reach that market.

In today's fast-paced, highly competitive business environment, most companies have neither the capital nor the opportunity to rely totally on advertising produced by their own personnel. Instead, they make use of the expertise of professional marketers to tell their story to the public. They use their ad agency in much the same way as they use their legal firm, their accounting firm, and the services of other business professionals.

Many smaller companies consider a full-time, on-staff advertising manager a luxury. Most don't need one because they have no need for an employee whose sole function is to make their company look good. Advertising agencies, on the other hand, are considered not luxuries but necessities. Ad agencies perform creative and productive work which keeps the advertiser's name and products in front of the market. Operations personnel at a small ad agency will deal mainly with top people in the client company—president, executive vice presidents, and so forth—instead of middle management.

Advertising Defined

The American Marketing Association defines advertising as "any paid form of nonpersonal presentation and promotion of ideas, goods, or services by an identified sponsor." The key words here are "paid," "nonpersonal," and "identified." Advertising differs from the related field of publicity primarily in that advertising is paid for directly and its sponsorship is almost always clearly identified. Advertising can be distinguished from personal selling because it is a nonpersonal presentation.

Frequently, the terms *advertising* and *sales promotion* are confused. Used in a broad sense, sales promotion refers to those sales activities which supplement advertising and personal selling, such as exhibitions, displays, demonstrations, and other nonrecurrent selling activities. Difficulty arises in distinguishing between advertising and sales promotion because business firms vary in their methods of classifying their own activities.

The advertising that you prepare for your clients will be customized to the markets to which it is addressed. Different kinds of advertising are used for different markets. Following are some of the most frequently used kinds of advertising, classified by markets at which the advertising is aimed and the kinds of clients that employ that kind of advertising. Various media may be used in each area, although some media are more commonly used for certain kinds of advertising than others.

Classifications of Advertising

National Consumer Advertising

The most common kind of advertising is consumer advertising, which features nationally distributed products such as cosmetics, appliances, automobiles, and fast food. These items are advertised in nationally distributed magazines and newspapers as well as on network radio and television. Often, nationally distributed products sponsor programs and become identified with nationally known celebrities. It is unusual for a local advertising agency to have a number of clients that sell consumer products on a national basis. By and large, this function is fulfilled by the much larger advertising agencies.

Local Retail Advertising

Local merchants use area print and broadcast media to promote specials in their retail outlets. Local service businesses such as banks, insurance agents, lawyers, hospitals, and local franchises also advertise in this manner.

Mail-Related Advertising

Mail-related advertising can be divided into mail-order advertising and direct-mail advertising. In mail-order advertising (direct-response advertising), the product or service ad is accompanied by a coupon or other response vehicle, such as a toll-free telephone number. Some ads are more complex than others. Newspapers, magazines, catalogs, and electronic media are used in mail-order advertising.

Mail-order advertising is directed at a more or less general audience. Anyone can watch TV or pick up a newspaper or magazine; mail-order houses frequently do mass mailings of their catalogs to the public. When mail-related advertising is aimed at and mailed to a specific person, or a person who falls into a specific customer category, it is more properly referred to as direct mail.

In direct-mail advertising, a solicitation letter and frequently a brochure are used to sell products or services. The difference between direct mail and mail order is that direct mail advertising targets a specific market directly. Typically, direct mail is used in conjunction with mailing lists which narrow the market sharply. Direct-mail advertising occurs *only* through the mail. There is no use of another medium (such as a periodical) to help make the sale. Mailing-list brokers maintain exceptionally good, computerized lists. For example, they can tell a list renter how many doctors in a certain age group earning between $100,000 and $200,000 per year are within 10 miles of a particular location.

Direct mail can be used to advertise any number of products or services. Mail-order companies use direct mail to advertise items that may be ordered through the mail. Retail outlets use direct mail to advertise special sales. Virtually any kind of business, from small service firms to banks, can make use of direct mail to advertise or promote what it is selling.

Trade Advertising

Company-to-company display ads are placed in professional, association, or industrial publications. For example, well-drilling equipment manufacturers advertise their products in *Oil and Gas Journal.* Restaurant supply houses advertise their food-service equipment in *Restaurant Business* or *Restaurant News.*

Small manufacturers and wholesalers make frequent use of trade advertising, and do relatively little traditional advertising. Most lines of wholesaling—large and small firms alike—spend 10 to 20 times as much on personal selling as on advertising.

Catalogs, price lists, sales letters, and dealer-aid material, usually furnished by the manufacturer, constitute the principal forms of advertising used by wholesalers. The object is to pave the way for personal selling and to minimize time spent on sales calls. Almost no direct merchandise advertising is undertaken by the wholesaler personally.

Corporate Advertising

Major corporations use various media to tell their story to the public or to the business community. One example of such advertising in magazines and on television is the institutional-type ad of oil companies extolling their commitment to ecology.

Of the above, a small, local advertising agency will be likely to use national consumer advertising *least.* To varying degrees, and depending totally on the needs of the client, the other types of advertising will be used. Each client company's advertising program will develop a life of its own. Your choices of media and method will vary according to your clients' goals.

Types of Advertising Agencies

Specialist Agencies

Some advertising agencies have highly specialized knowledge in specific fields. Medical, high tech, and financial are examples of areas in which legal considerations, technical knowledge, and extreme accuracy are essential. A relatively new specialty area is classified display advertising.

With few exceptions, advertising agencies do not handle competitive accounts (for example, two automobile accounts or two soft drink accounts). Thus, there are advertising agencies specializing in women's fashions, others specializing in children's wear, and so on. Generally, an advertiser uses such an agency when it needs special skills but is too small to be handled by a general agency. The specialist agency, unlike the general agency, can spread the cost of such skills over a number of accounts.

International Advertising Agencies

Many American businesses sell their products abroad as well as in the United States and, consequently, wish to advertise internationally. Domestic agencies may handle foreign advertising in several ways: they may place it directly with foreign media; they may affiliate with and use the services of foreign agencies; or they may use the services of export agencies that specialize in placing advertising abroad and act as a sort of export division for the domestic agency.

Because of translation problems, foreign regulations, and different customs of buyers in foreign markets, it is always safer for a domestic agency to rely on the knowledge of an ad agency in the foreign market to be reached. Working with an international agency on a shared compensation basis can save time, avoid problems, and usually end up being less costly than if the domestic agency operated on its own.

House Agencies

From time to time, a few large advertisers have attempted to set up their own subsidiary advertising agencies. These agencies may handle only one account or may supplement it, usually with a group of much smaller accounts. The advantage claimed by advertisers who own the house agencies is the prospect of saving money by cutting overhead expenses and receiving rebates on a portion of the media commissions. Such advertisers also believe they will get more attention from the agency when they are the major or only client of the house. However, some media will not give commissions to house agencies, arguing that these are not bonafide advertising agencies. From the client's point of view, there are several drawbacks to a house agency. To begin with, a dissatisfied client can quickly replace a regular agency, but is a captive of a house agency. In addition, the advertiser loses the value of independent advertising agency objectivity; the house agency often loses vitality and incentive from lack of competition; and such agencies tend to lack the versatility, experience, and diversity of talents which an independent agency with many clients can provide. Still, there apparently have been some successful house agencies and there has been a recent renewal of interest in them, especially during recessionary times. History has shown, however, that most advertisers who try such an arrangement sooner or later abandon it. See Chapter 33 for an in-depth look at house agencies.

Boutiques and Media Buying Services

With the high demand for creative talent, a type of limited-service advertising agency has emerged that sells only creative work. Advertisers using such a creative boutique must still seek other sources for the additional advertising services they need.

Independent Media Buying Services

Some companies specialize in buying media for both advertisers and ad agencies. Their major selling point is the claim that they can save money for advertisers through volume buying, bartering, or the ability to negotiate.

Defining Your Office Location

Choosing the proper location for your business can be a major factor in its success or failure. A good location may allow a mediocre business to survive, but a bad location may spell failure for the finest of businesses. There are certain basic facts to consider, depending on the needs of your particular venture and your intentions and goals.

Both deciding on the particular community and then choosing a site within that community are important. Your choice of a particular community should be based on the level of business activity going on there in general, plus the level of ancillary advertising services—commercial art, printing, and so on—readily available to you. Your choice of a site within a community should be based on what it will do to enhance your image within the business community as a whole and with respect to the image you want to cultivate with your prospective clients and advertising industry colleagues.

Evaluating a Community

Most of the activity in the advertising business takes place in major metropolitan centers. However, there are also quite successful agencies in small cities. The key to success for an advertising agency is the amount of business activity in a particular area, not necessarily the number of people living there.

The measure of business activity will vary tremendously from market to market. In some areas, there may be a great amount of retail trade going on. If so, it is likely that your clients would include a number of retail outlets. In other areas, there may be manufacturing companies producing equipment and selling nationwide. Yet the degree of retail trade in the area may not reflect the national scope of the company. Your client may be the manufacturer and the account a national one. Yet you might represent only a very few local merchants. This is common with local franchises of national firms. The national "image" advertising is done by a large agency. The local promotions, mailings, couponing, and so on are done by a local agency.

Because smaller agencies generally produce such advertising pieces as catalogs, specification sheets, trade ads, direct-mail pieces, and other collateral material, you can readily see that it is possible for an independent agency to thrive outside major metro markets. Banks and savings and loan associations, insurance agencies, real estate brokers, and small manufacturers are in towns and cities of all sizes.

For example, banks and savings and loan associations frequently advertise in local newspapers. In addition, they might advertise in regional glossy magazines, in trade magazines catering to businesses that are customers of the banks, or on television stations serving the area in which they are located. Insurance agencies or real estate companies may wish to do a mailing to a set of prospective customers. In such a situation, they might need help in preparing a brochure, writing copy for a pitch letter, and so forth.

A mail-order company might start up in any area. In such a case, an advertising agency might prepare ad copy and artwork for a mail-order catalog. That same company might wish to advertise in relevant mail-order trade publications.

One point of interest is the fact that your agency need not necessarily be located in the same city as your client. In today's modern world, overnight mail services and new electronic technology make it possible for you to service clients thousands of miles away and fax them visual layouts, artwork, photographs, and other documents in minutes.

In order to determine whether an advertising agency business is viable in your area, you have to find out the degree of economic activity going on there. If there is plenty of business being done, and if you can help increase it, then you can probably make a good start. There are certain techniques you can use to research your local area to determine your prospects if you are in a marginal situation.

A community's economic base determines to a great extent the opportunities that exist for the small business owner in a particular place. To evaluate a community's economic base, find out:

1. The number of people employed and the trend in employment
2. Total payrolls and the average wage or family income
3. The amount and trend of bank deposits
4. Per capita retail sales
5. The proportion of home ownership and home values

As a prospective business owner, you can obtain this information by studying available census data and other business statistics. However, you can also learn a great deal about a community by looking and listening.

Some danger signals are:

- The necessity for high school and college graduates to leave town to find suitable employment
- The inability of other residents to find jobs locally
- Declining retail sales and industrial production
- An apathetic attitude on the part of local business owners, educational administrators, and other residents

Favorable signs include:

- Opening of chain or department store branches
- Branch plants of large industrial firms locating in the community
- A progressive chamber of commerce and other civic organizations
- Good schools and public services
- Well-maintained business and residential premises
- Good transportation facilities to other parts of the country
- Construction activity accompanied by an absence of vacant buildings and unoccupied homes or houses for sale

Area Demographics

The market you wish to serve must be carefully defined. The advertising agency business caters to the business, professional, and commercial markets. What are the factors to consider in examining the business firms in the area? If you do your research, you will be able to see whether there is enough commercial activity in your area to support your agency. You will also be able to determine to a certain extent the kinds of advertising you can expect to do.

If there is a good deal of retail trade in the area, you can expect to get business from merchants. Accordingly, your media would include newspapers, consumer magazines, the radio, and perhaps some television advertising on local stations. If you are in an industrial or mining area, you would probably deal with trade publications of one sort or another, plus brochures, direct-mail pieces, and the like. Then, of course, there are the banks, insurance companies, and other such institutions which make use of both consumer and commercial avenues of trade from time to time.

Evaluate your area in terms of advertising dollar potential in the business community as a whole, the kinds of local businesses which tend to advertise, their means of advertising, their longevity in the community, and their public image. Also, once you are established in your location, you must remain aware of these same client characteristics, for as the business community changes you must be prepared to change your market or the definition of the market you wish to serve.

Conducting Your Own Market Survey

A market survey determines a reasonable sales forecast. It will seek to estimate the number of customers in the market area who may become clients for your planned business. Take the following steps:

1. Determine the limits of the market or trading area.

2. Study the business firms in the area to determine their potential advertising needs.

3. Determine the purchasing power of the area.

4. Determine the present volume of money spent on advertising by various potential advertiser-clients.

5. Estimate what proportion of the total advertising accounts you can reasonably obtain.

The last step is particularly important. Opening a new business within a given trade area does not necessarily generate additional advertising volume; it may simply redistribute business already there.

As an advertising agency owner, you need to help your clients redistribute existing business incorporating their favor and to create new business and new markets for them with innovative ad campaign ideas.

Data Sources

Where can you find out how many new business firms have opened in the past 5 to 10 years in your market area? The city license bureau or county clerk's office will have on file the names and addresses of businesses which have filed fictitious name or dba (doing business as) statements. A corporation commission or similar agency in your state has names and addresses of corporations which have filed appropriate documents for incorporating their companies. The number of such filings can indicate a trend of business activity in your area.

Contact publishers and ad managers of newspapers and magazines in your area. Find out the financial situations of the companies that are your potential clients. Local editors will know just how much your prospective clients are spending to advertise in their publications. Do the same thing with the broadcast media managers in your area. This kind of research will give you an idea of whether there is a valid market for the services you want to provide.

All the media keep up-to-date information and business profiles of the community to use in their sales efforts. These are available free when you contact the sales departments. Other sources of information include the yellow pages and Dun & Bradstreet listings (you can buy mailing lists from them, too).

Collect names from every source you can find at this stage; names of business owners are crucial to your own in-house marketing program. You should be able to get the names of businesses from the local chamber of commerce, media salespeople, yellow pages, and Dun & Bradstreet without too much trouble. Also collect the names of new businesses by watching the license listings in your local paper. These leads will be solid gold—as you will discover later in this book.

Study print and broadcast media serving the area you want to cover. Count the ads; measure their size; time the radio and TV commercials (10, 30, 60 seconds). Evaluate the quality and content of the advertising and figure out how you can improve it and hustle business for yourself.

Call up typesetters, commercial artists, and print shops in your area. From them you can find out how much and what kind of advertising is going on and which types of businesses are doing the most advertising in the area you want to cover. These people can also give you an idea of how your potential competitors in the ad agency business pay their bills; it is a complaint of printers and artists that ad agencies sometimes don't pay on time. If you can do better, they will be happy to welcome you as a client.

Reports and studies published by various government agencies are also useful and readily accessible sources of information.

United States Census of Business

U.S. census data include information on total volume of business done in a particular line. Numbers of firms in each line of business are reported for towns down to 2500 people. Larger city reports are more detailed. Your own state census of business is also very valuable in this regard.

Chambers of Commerce or Business Development Departments

Chambers of commerce in major cities have the important job of encouraging the development of new business firms in their communities. They will gladly supply all types of information regarding population studies, income characteristics of the community, trends, payrolls, industrial development, and so on. Such information is usually free for the asking.

Industry Sources

Study the industry of the area under consideration. One good source is the *Dun & Bradstreet Directory,* which lists financial and other information regarding various companies. The key is to determine the level of permanence and growth of industries in your area in order to see whether a particular company is worth pursuing as a client.

Finally, two extremely important sources of information on area businesses that are potential clients of your agency are the local media and your prospective colleagues.

Choosing the District and Site

Once you are satisfied that the community or trading area you plan to serve has the qualities to support your business, you must choose the district and site where you will locate.

The following factors are of importance: (1) accessibility, (2) proximity to other businesses, (3) restrictive ordinances, and (4) parking facilities.

Accessibility of the Business

Profits in this business depend in part on client and agent contact, and some clients will visit your offices. For this purpose, you will need to make it easy for them. Accessibility is thus mainly a question of the ease with which customers can reach your office.

A site in a high-rise with valet parking is ideal, except that the rent may be beyond your means. Accessibility to clients will be influenced by distance from other upscale service businesses, terrain, and dangerous street crossings or other hazards. The nature of the entrance may be important if it is even slightly above sidewalk level, or if you have an off-the-street location, such as an upper floor.

Proximity to Other Businesses

Like an individual, a business should keep the right company. In this business, your neighbors will be attorneys, secretarial services, accountants, and other office-oriented businesses. One strong advantage of the advertising business is that you aren't dealing with "consumers" in the regular sense. So you needn't spend precious start-up capital on fancy headquarters in a high foot-traffic location. You will find advertising agencies located in out-of-the-way office buildings, industrial parks, and even in private homes.

Even though you don't need the fanciest of offices, stay away from the "seedy" part of town. To a degree, you're selling your clients an image, and you've got to convey the best. The concept of an advertising service is easier to sell to local businesses if you maintain a professional image.

Restrictive Ordinances

Restrictive delivery or traffic ordinances may make an otherwise ideal site less desirable than another. You aren't running a retail store, requiring constant loading and unloading of merchandise, but you may have semiregular deliveries of art and stationery supplies, or messenger-service vehicles coming and going quite a bit, so you must consider any restrictive ordinances which might cause problems.

Zoning regulations may also cause difficulties if you attempt to open your office in an area restricted against your type of business. You may be using chemicals in your art department that are restricted by zoning regulations. Check it out.

Before signing a lease, ask neighboring businesses about drainage and other potential area problems. Also consider your location in reference to how far your employees will have to travel to get to work.

Parking

Does the particular site provide easy parking and access and other comforts for clients, for free-lance personnel who come to your office to deliver and pick up jobs, and for messenger-service vehicles?

Leasing Your Office

Real estate leases are as varied as the types of space available. However, there are certain points that are common to all leasing negotiations. It is important to know how to bargain over these various points—a process that, though nerve-wracking, can save you substantial dollars in the long run.

Generally speaking, the longer the lease on your office space, the better its terms. However, leases are usually very strong contracts. If you sign a lease for $1000 per month for a period of 1 year, for example, you are agreeing to pay $12,000 regardless of what happens to your business. Therefore, it is wise when starting out to get the shortest-term lease possible until you can see where you are going. Of course, it will all depend on your near-term cash needs, in which case you may also want to consider a flat fee for the term of the lease or gradual increases annually.

Always check out local vacancy rates and negotiate accordingly. When vacancy rates are high in an area, bargains usually exist. Ask for free rent. Many landlords offer 1 year free if you lease for 5 years. All they can say is no. In a competitive area, building owners make whatever deals they can just to keep their space filled.

A 1- or 2-year lease with an option on renewal for 5 years at an agreed rental is a desirable target for most beginning agencies. In certain businesses, however—especially office-oriented businesses—it will be safer to arrange for a month-to-month rental at the beginning. Then, if your business outgrows its original location after 6 months of operation, you won't be faced with the problem of having to sublet the first office when you move to more spacious premises. Unlike most retail or service businesses, office-oriented businesses such as advertising agencies have found outgrowing their space to be a problem.

Percentage Leases

Many leases require lessees to pay a percentage of their gross receipts in addition to a fixed minimum monthly rent. This guarantees the landlord a definite base rent plus additional amounts as your business prospers. Regardless of whether you negotiate a flat-rate or a percentage lease, the objective is to stay in line with the standard rent ratio or to compensate for any deviation by more or less advertising, superior managerial ability, or similar considerations. Consequently, the standard ratio for the particular line of business should be known, and the rental demanded for any site under consideration should be appraised in terms of the site's potential volume of sales and the volume necessary to achieve this ratio.

Other Terms

The lease usually provides for many other important points, such as cost-of-living increases, any remodeling to be done and who is to pay for it, liabilities and duties assumed by each party, subletting, and permission or authority for the tenant to erect certain external signs, engage in additional lines of business, or make alterations to the premises in the future if needed. If the landlord owns adjacent property, it is sometimes possible to incorporate in the lease provisions governing the kinds of businesses to which these sites will be rented. A lease is an important legal document, and you should always seek competent legal counsel before entering into a formal agreement.

Negotiate Before You Sign

The point, of course, is that the lease prepared by the lessor is negotiable. This offer is not engraved in stone, but is extended to you for your consideration. If you accept it without discussion, you have met the lessor's conditions entirely. It may not be necessary to do so. You may be able to negotiate something much better for yourself, especially with respect to the length of the lease, by simply asking. If the lessor's answer is no, you still haven't lost anything. You can always look elsewhere for what you want, and if you don't find it, you can come back to the first location.

Determine your own requirements thoroughly. When negotiating with the landlord, ask for inclusion of anything that will be an expense for you.

Leasing Guidelines

After choosing your site, check the following points before you sign the lease.

- Is there sufficient electrical power and are there enough outlets?
- Is there enough parking space for customers and employees?

- Is there sufficient lighting, heating, and air conditioning, especially in the art department?

- How large a sign, and what type, can you erect on the building?

- Will the building and zoning department of your city allow your business to operate in the building?

- Does your city or county health department require one or two restrooms if you have both male and female employees?

- Will the landlord allow any alterations that you deem necessary for your business?

- Must you pay for returning the premises to their original condition when you move out?

- Does the office meet requirements for the handicapped?

- Will the delivery and shipping of material and goods from the building be easily accomplished?

- Is there any indication of roof leaks? (A heavy rain could damage your equipment, fixtures, and artwork.)

- Is the cost of burglary insurance high in the area? (This varies tremendously.) Can the building be made secure against the threat of burglary at a low cost?

- Is there a water heater?

- Will the fire department approve the operation of your business at this location?

Buying Versus Leasing

When first starting any new business, you will probably find it advantageous to lease facilities rather than buy. There are so many variables, risks, and monetary outlays you will encounter in the first years of your new profession that the fact that you are not tied to a long-term mortgage and did not have to lay out a large down payment will give you a little more peace of mind and loose cash which can be put to better use.

For those who can afford to think about purchasing office space—namely, a condominium office or building—there are many pluses to consider. As most people have learned through home ownership, real estate is an investment which provides tremendous appreciation potential as well as significant tax write-offs. Unfortunately, because of a lack of suitable investment vehicles and ignorance about the full financial ramifications, most business owners have not availed themselves of the opportunity to own their place of business.

Look at the facts. The reasons to own commercial real estate rather than residential are even more pronounced because the owner may deduct depreciation expenses as well as taxes, mortgage interest, insurance, and maintenance costs. Considering appreciation potential, tax benefits, and the owner's ability to control office occupancy cost, the leasing alternative does not compare.

The commercial condominium has been a primary mode of real estate investment in Europe and Latin America for decades. Basically, the concept permits the small and medium-size business to purchase the precise amount of office space needed or, if growth is anticipated, additional space to provide for expansion.

Aside from the immediate financial advantages of owning your space, you also benefit from being able to freeze the cost of your office space. Business owners who have been paying cost-of-living increases or have observed the escalating office rents of new buildings understand the implications of this fact.

Furthermore, office condominium owners can reasonably expect their real estate to appreciate in value. If the condominium is purchased in the owner's personal name and leased back to the business, the appreciation provides a couple of benefits. First, as prevailing market rents inflate over time and office condo costs remain the same, a "rent gap" will be created. The owner can then increase the rent to his or her business and, in doing so, take cash from the business and avoid double taxation. Second, the growing value of the real estate becomes an investment nest egg that accumulates with no out-of-pocket costs.

Now let's take a look at your new office.

5

The Facility

A Simple Office Is Adequate at First

You should be able to start with 500 to 1000 square feet of office space. Rents should be competitive and in line with similar space in the area. If you set up shop at home at first, this expense will be eliminated.

An office at home can be quite professional if it has a separate outside entrance and is attractively furnished. Many one- and two-person advertising agencies have been started from home offices. But look at your own marketing efforts just as you look at the efforts of your clients. How would you best go about reaching and getting prospects for them if you could not convey a proper image on their behalf? Similarly, how can you best go about reaching and getting clients if you do not convey a totally professional image of yourself?

Most ad agency owners think that to achieve authentic growth they must get out of the house and into a proper office as soon as possible. You have to tell your public that you are in full operation. You want to look successful, and an office location will help you do this.

Naturally, you want to keep overhead as low as possible when starting out. Don't invest too much in fancy fixtures and decor, but do plan for expansion later on, as volume and image requirements warrant.

Layout

In the beginning you will be running the business yourself, whether you act as creative director, account executive, office manager, or all of the above. There are three major procedures to plan for: record keeping, solicitation, and production. You may want an office for your own use, and perhaps a second one for the creative director or a copywriter. Day to day, the account executive will be handling record-keeping chores and promoting new business. The creative director may need an office but can also use the production room for this purpose. Keep in mind that the account executive will be out on the road as well as in the office; you can't make this business work without personal visits.

Client records should be readily accessible to the account executive. He or she will be on the phone dealing with client inquiries, logging production transactions, and the like. So set this up for maximum efficiency.

The final area to consider is production, which involves artwork, layouts, design, updates, sales materials, copywriting, and so forth. A convenient storage area rounds out layout needs. Look at the sample floor plan in Figure 5-1 and modify it to suit your needs.

Decor and Atmosphere

Your decor can be in just about any style you like, as long as you aim for an image of professionalism and vitality. Choose furnishings and interior design that enhance this image.

Furniture should be functional and does not have to be expensive. Typically, modern-style, carefully chosen furniture is found in advertising shops. To keep start-

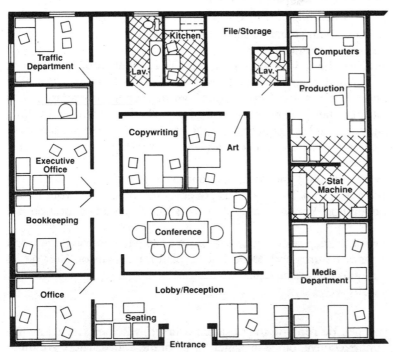

Fig. 5-1. A sample layout of an advertising agency office with a space of 2700 square feet. Note the tiled floors for areas where chemicals are used.

up costs down, begin with good-quality used office furniture. Many good pieces can be bought used for a fraction of the cost of new if you shop carefully.

Desks, chairs, filing cabinets in the right place, hanging plants, a few prints on the wall—together with a good coat of paint—are about all you need in the opening phase. If you can afford them, the services of a professional decorator can help you develop a decor that is tasteful and that has a look of quality about it. However, try to avoid going overboard when you're in the start-up phase. For example, don't spend money hanging expensive lithographs in back offices that clients will never enter.

Phone and Utilities

In the starting phase of your new business, it is best to lease your phone equipment.

Telephone and utility companies throughout the nation have different policies concerning deposit requirements for businesses. Some do not require a deposit if you own real estate or have established a payment record with them. Others base deposit fees on how many phones and what type of service you require.

In this business, you will need a good-quality phone system geared for heavy use. One approach is to arrange for a multiline rotary system in which incoming calls are automatically routed to the next available inbound line. You can reserve up to 10 lines while only installing 3 to begin with, allowing for expansion while trimming start-up expenses.

Plan to spend some time with a representative of the local phone company to get the kind of system suited to your needs. As a convenience, some owners install an incoming toll-free number, but unless you have a lot of out-of-town clients this should not be necessary.

Invest in a call-forwarding system or an answering service that will track you down if your clients need to get hold of you. You might want to consider a portable cellular phone. Some advertising agencies make use of answering machines, but in this kind of operation a service is more desirable. Try to insist on the service answering on the second ring, if possible. One piece of equipment that is a must is a fax machine. The superb image-quality reproduction with halftone (photograph) transmission capabilities allows you to send art, layouts, contracts, copy, and other documents anywhere in the world for approval in minutes. Nearly every business uses a fax today, and costs for basic machines are relatively small. You may also need a dedicated phone line, depending on the equipment you buy.

Electric and gas utility deposits (when required) will vary according to your projected usage. It is possible to lower them somewhat by not mentioning any equipment that uses a lot of electricity.

Buying Used Equipment

Equipment for almost any type of business may be bought secondhand or even thirdhand for a fraction of the cost new. Businesses that have failed, merged, or grown to the point where they require larger, more modern equipment are often good sources of used items.

You'll save considerably by shopping wisely for secondhand furniture, equipment, and fixtures. Judicious shopping can turn up some excellent bargains. In the classified section of most newspapers you'll find a host of used furniture and equipment dealers. If you prefer buying new, most cities have discount stores where you can get very good buys on new office furniture and equipment.

Leasing Equipment

The advantage of leasing is that your initial cash outlay is considerably less than buying on an installment contract. Consult with your accountant on how the tax laws affect the purchase of equipment and whether or not current laws allow you to take investment tax credit. In considering these and other advantages, however, you should also recognize that the total cost of leasing over a number of years is likely to be greater than if the equipment is purchased. Often you may lease and still acquire the investment tax credit.

Two more important concerns remain in setting up your office: purchasing supplies and obtaining credit.

6

Supplies
and Credit

There is no inventory in the conventional sense in the advertising business, because what you are selling is a service.

Office Supplies

Business cards and stationery are necessities. They serve as important representations of you and your business and should be designed carefully, keeping image in mind. Don't skimp on the cost of having them printed. It's best to use engraving on top-quality paper stock.

A simple, businesslike, and conservative design is usual. The printer will have sample books available. Getting a free-lance graphic artist to design a format for you is a good way of checking out future employees. A decent artist won't take more than an hour or so to work up a design that will make a favorable impression.

Business forms you will need will include purchase orders, invoices, insertion orders, and printing orders. Some agencies use contract forms as well. A number of different kinds of forms are available. Samples of various kinds are provided later in this book. Modify the samples to suit your needs. One thing that may in large measure simplify your use of forms is to get the kind that require no carbon paper. These NCR forms are more expensive than standard forms with carbons, but they are also far less messy and cumbersome.

Art Supplies

For artwork and graphics preparation, you will be using a lot of art and drafting supplies. If you are an artist, you probably have a pretty good idea of what kinds of production supplies you will need. If you hire a creative director, he or she should have a handle on the supplies needed for artwork production. Of course, if you contract out your art to free-lancers or mechanical production houses, you will not have to invest in artists' supplies. But as your business develops, you will want to move a certain amount of production under your roof to save on subcontracting costs.

Most cities have at least one art supply store. Some art supplies can be ordered from direct-mail houses. Refer to the list below for companies that supply complete catalogs. A word of caution with respect to art supplies: Don't buy out the store. Try, as far as possible, to stick with those supplies that you can use over and over. It's easy to buy every little art gadget, and art directors are notorious for purchasing art supplies they never use. So get what you need.

Art Supply Mail-Order Houses

Artype Inc., Fort Myers, FL

Cello-Tak Mfg., Inc., Island Park, NY

Chartpak, Leeds, MA

Graphic Products Corporation, Rolling Meadows, IL

Letraset USA, Inc., Paramus, NJ

Dealing with Suppliers

Good, reliable suppliers are valuable assets to your business. They can "bail you out" many times when your own customers make difficult requests and demands upon you. Your suppliers are in business for the same reason you are: to make money. They will continue to serve you only so long as your business is profitable to them. If you go to the mat with them on every bill they send, if you try to get them to shave prices on everything they sell to you, if you put them in a highly competitive bidding situation every time you do business with them, if you fail to pay your bills within a reasonable time after goods or services have been delivered in good order, if you constantly badger suppliers when they are doing their best to provide you with a service or product you need at a price you can afford, don't be surprised when they stop calling, decline to do business with you, and leave you looking elsewhere.

As an executive in a competitive business, you should look for the best deal you can get on a consistent basis from those who want to supply you. But remember that suppliers and salespeople are human, and they are in business to make money. If they cannot make a fair profit by doing business with you, they will sever the relationship, just as you would do under similar circumstances.

As a small business owner, you cannot expect to command the same kind of attention a big company may be able to. However, developing excellent working relationships with suppliers will mean many dollars of profit to you over the years as these suppliers help you meet your obligations to your customers. No business arrangement that is worthwhile can continue for long unless something of value is rendered and received by all those involved. This is the basis for every continuing business relationship you will have, including your relationship with suppliers.

Be frank, open, courteous, and firm with your suppliers. Tell them what you need and when you need it, have at least a general understanding about the total cost, and expect them to deliver on schedule, just as your own customers expect the same from you.

Obtaining Credit

Arranging initial credit for supplies and services for your business is fairly easy. Most service organizations will bill you automatically without the need for credit references. Suppliers of materials are more cautious. Naturally, you will not be able to supply trade references, since you are just getting started, and your bank probably will not give you a credit rating, since your account is too new.

Honesty and a personal financial statement are the only answers. If your suppliers are small, the manner in which you present yourself personally to each owner will be very important to obtaining your initial line of credit. If your suppliers are large and the credit managers are protecting their position, you may find the going cold and impersonal. A personal visit when requesting credit, however, will always be impressive and will accelerate your acceptance.

Here is a technique that will impress even the coldest credit manager or owner. After presenting your financial statement and a dissertation of your prospects for success in the business you are starting, stress this line: "I have always honored my obligations, and any time you care to discuss anything with me, you may call me at my office or my home. My home phone number is _____ and my home address is _____. Please take them down, as they don't appear on my statement."

The important thing to remember is this: Whoever grants credit to you initially grants it strictly on gut feelings and impressions, since you do not have sufficient credit references. If you can convince suppliers that you are an honest, hard-working, bill-paying believer in the American system, they will assist you in many ways—through credit, advice, and encouragement—and may even tell others about you.

Never present grossly inflated financial statements to bridge your references gap when attempting to obtain credit. This practice is illegal and a felony. It's also easily detected by the sophisticated credit manager. Some suppliers will say, "All right, we will put you on a COD basis for a couple of months and then issue you a line of credit." Just say, "Thank you." They know that if you are underfinanced, you will have problems with COD shortly.

After 2 or 3 months, you will have some valid credit references that you can present to any new supplier, and it will be easy for you to obtain credit from there on—if you have paid your bills on time.

Always take discounts if offered. You will realize large savings and at the same time give your credit rating a big boost.

7

Important Publications and Professional Organizations

Publications

Information is one of the primary tools of your trade and there are various publications and reference books you will need. The larger the library of source information you can accumulate, the better you will be able to function. You should build an office business library with as much information in it as you can afford and do it as rapidly as possible.

The Standard Rate and Data Service

There is one major publishing company that provides the "bibles" of the industry: the Standard Rate and Data Service of Wilmette, Illinois. The SRDS will be mentioned often in this book; you *must* become familiar with its publications.

There are two classifications in the SRDS line of periodicals. The first consists of publications which list rates of print space or broadcast time in various media. In addition, some provide technical specifications with respect to size, art, screens, and photographic standards for advertisements which appear in various media.

The second publication category of the SRDS consists of industry directories, or

Red Books, used by publishers and broadcasters to check credit or other commercial information available on agencies or companies which place advertising with them. Some publications or broadcasters will not accept advertising from agencies or companies that are not profiled in the Red Books without first running an extensive credit check on them.

The Red Books are useful in checking out competing agencies, advertising agencies in other areas that you may want to develop professional cooperation with, companies that you may wish to acquire advertising business from, and so on. The books list names of key personnel who can be very important in developing promotions. All the following periodicals are published by Standard Rate and Data Service, Inc., 3004 Glenview Road, Wilmette, IL 60091; 800-323-4588 or 708-256-8333 in Illinois.

Classification I

Print Media Production Data.   Published quarterly. Gives production specifications (data) on magazines and newspapers around the country. It is sold by subscription only, and covers local and major markets.

Newspaper Circulation Analysis.   Published yearly. Gives information on readers of many newspapers. It is sold by subscription only, and covers local and major markets.

Newspaper Rates and Data.   Published monthly. Gives ad placement information (data) on newspapers around the country. It is sold by subscription only, and covers local and major markets.

Direct Mail List Rates and Data.   Published quarterly. Provides mailing-list names readily available for use in direct-mail marketing. All known opportunities for using mail-oriented advertising are given.

Spot Radio Rates and Data.   Published monthly. Gives ad placement information on commercial radio stations around the country. It is sold by subscription only, and covers local and major markets.

Spot Radio Small Markets Edition.   Published semiannually. Gives ad placement information on commercial radio stations around the country. It is sold by subscription only, and covers local (small) markets.

Spot Television Rates and Data and Cable Television Rates and Data.   Published monthly. Offers ad placement information on commercial TV stations around the country. It is sold by subscription only, and covers local and major markets.

Business Publication Rates and Data.   Published monthly. Gives ad placement information (data) on business magazines and newspapers around the country. It is sold by subscription only, and covers local and major markets.

Canadian Advertising Rates and Data.   Published monthly. Provides ad placement information (data) on broadcast and print media in Canada. It is sold by subscription only, and covers local and major markets.

Community Publication Rates and Data.   Published semiannually. Gives ad placement information (data) on local magazines and newspapers around the country. It is sold by subscription only, and covers local markets.

Consumer Magazine and Farm Publication Rates and Data.   Published monthly. Gives production specification (data) on magazines and newspapers read by the consumer market and by the farm market. It is sold by subscription only, and covers local and major markets.

Change Bulletin Newspaper Rates and Data.   Published weekly. Updates ad placement information (data) on newspapers around the country. It is sold by subscription only, and covers local and major markets.

Change Bulletin Spot Television Rates and Data.   Published weekly. Updates ad placement information (data) in broadcast media around the country. It is sold by subscription only, and covers local and major markets.

Classification II

Standard Directory of Advertisers (Advertiser Red Book).   According to the publisher, an advertiser that places $30,000 worth of national advertising or $50,000 worth of regional media advertising per year on a regular basis is listed in this particular Red Book.

Standard Directory of Advertising Agencies (Agency Red Book).   According to the publisher, an agency serving as the agency of record for at least one advertiser that qualifies for listing in the Advertiser Red Book is listed in this particular Red Book.

Magazines

To keep abreast of the latest trends and happenings in the business, you will want also to take out subscriptions to *Ad Age Magazine, Broadcast Magazine,* and *Ad Weekly Magazine.*

Professional and Trade Associations

It is not only the responsibility of the advertising agency to meet the consumers' needs for product information, it is also the responsibility of the agency to keep informed about what is going on in the advertising industry as well as the marketplace. As a member of professional and trade organizations, the agency will have current information on a myriad of subjects including: consumer attitudes and habits; federal, state, and local regulations and guidelines; and comparative advertising expenditures, new products, and other industry developments that concern agency operations and relations between agency, clients, and consumers. You may want to join the following advertising organizations.

Advertising Associations

Advertising Council

Advertising Research Foundation

Advertising Typographers Association of America

Advertising Women of New York

American Association of Advertising Agencies (AAAA)

American Marketing Association

International Advertising Association

Marketing Research Association

Promotion Marketing Association of America

Specialty Advertising Association International

Suburban Newspapers of America

Traffic Audit Bureau

Advertising Federations

Advertising Club of New York

American Advertising Federation

League of Advertising Agencies

Advertising Organizations by Business Specialty

Brand Names Trading

National Agri-Marketing Association

Retail Advertising Conference

Financial Analysts Federation

Advertising Associations by Media Specialty

Association of Independent Commercial Producers

Direct Mail/Marketing Association

Institute of Outdoor Advertising

Mail Advertising Service Association International

Radio Advertising Bureau

Television Bureau of Advertising

Part 2 Action Checklist

- ✔ What type of clients will your agency be servicing, and what services will your agency provide for these clients?

- ✔ What are the markets that your clients will want to reach? How do you reach them? Different types of advertising are used for different markets and various media may be used within those areas.

- ✔ When you select the location of your office, both the community and the actual site can be instrumental in the success or failure of your business.

- ✔ The community in which your office is located should offer a high level of commercial and professional business activity. Data on the communities you are considering is available at little or no cost.

- ✔ When you consider the site of your office within a community, accessibility, proximity to other businesses, restrictive ordinances, anticipated sales volume, and the terms of leasing or buying your facility are considerations of prime importance.

✔ What kind of image do you want to convey? Low-key professional? Highly visible creative? An image of success? All of the above? Your office decor can help convey that image. But remember, you are just starting out, so keep overhead and expenses to a minimum.

✔ When planning the layout of your office, you must consider the needs of the business. How much space will be needed for creative work and production? Will record keeping and new business departments need their own quarters? How much space will be needed for storage and filing of the art and client materials you will be creating?

✔ The furnishings you select should be both functional and enhancing to the image you want to convey.

✔ Before you rush out to purchase new equipment like telephones, computers, and copy and fax machines, consider leasing or buying used equipment.

✔ You will be needing office supplies. Business cards and stationery are essential. So are the various agency forms, such as purchase and insertion orders, invoices, and work orders, as well as fax and copy paper. Your art and production supplies depend on how much production your company will be doing in house. Have your production and creative personnel submit lists of what supplies they will need. Don't purchase more than you need unless there are substantial savings on larger quantities.

✔ Ask around about suppliers. Which ones are the most dependable? Which are the best pricewise? Establish your credit with suppliers at the outset. Your relationship with the trade is important.

✔ Since information is one of the primary tools of the advertising business, obtain the various trade publications and reference materials you will need to rely on in your day-to-day operations. These include rate books, mechanical requirements books, and reference materials you can use to help find and obtain new clients. Also join professional associations.

Part 3

Legal and Governmental Requirements

8

Types of Business Structures and Options for Financing

Types of Business Structures

Among the first decisions you will have to make when starting up your new business is the legal form under which it will operate. There are four legal forms to consider: (1) sole proprietorship, (2) partnership, (3) limited partnership, and (4) corporation.

Sole Proprietorship

The sole proprietorship has a single owner. No legal papers are required to set up this type of operation. You need only file a fictitious name with the county clerk (see below) and take out a business license.

The drawback of the sole proprietorship is your legal exposure to creditors of your company. They can sue you personally, even attach your personal property and bank accounts, and ruin your personal credit.

Partnership

Even more dangerous than the sole proprietorship is the partnership of two or more people. In this form of operation, each partner is liable for the other's actions.

In case of legal action against the partnership, each partner will be sued individually with property, bank accounts, and other property being attached. Should any of the partners not be available for legal action, the others are left "holding the bag," and the ones with the most to lose personally will probably bear the brunt of the loss. Finally, partnerships tend to breed conflict among the owners and often are a cause of a business breaking up or going under.

You should hire an attorney to form your partnership, rather than doing it yourself. Responsibilities of each partner should be set forth in writing so that there are no misunderstandings later. Attorney's fees for forming a partnership contract should be slightly higher than the fee for forming a corporation—depending on how involved the partnership arrangement is.

Limited Partnership

In this form of operation, the investors become limited partners and are personally liable for the amount of their investment. The partner who operates the limited partnership is known as the general partner. The general partner can be a sole proprietor or a corporation.

Attorney's fees for forming a limited partnership can be substantially higher than for forming a corporation, mainly because in many states limited partnerships come under security laws.

Corporation

You don't need to erect a downtown skyscraper or build an office park in the suburbs to start a corporation. In fact, in most states it's about as simple as sending a letter.

Why incorporate? The two most common reasons for incorporating your business are that it reduces your legal liability—the corporation is sued, not the shareholders—and that it may have tax advantages in many instances.

A corporate structure is the most common and safest way to operate your new business. The corporation operates as a separate entity apart from you personally, and the corporation, not you, is legally responsible for its actions and debts. You will in effect be an employee of the corporation, protected from legal action, even though you may own all or most of the corporation's stock.

When partners form a corporation, ownership is usually divided into shares. Responsibilities of each partner can be spelled out in the corporate minutes, and in the event of a partner split-up or a death, the business does not have to be dissolved.

There are many other executive privileges to be enjoyed that are easier to justify in a corporation than in a sole proprietorship or partnership. It is easier for a corporation to borrow. Corporate stock may be used as collateral. Profits can be deferred. Capital can be accumulated without taxation, and owners can borrow money personally from the corporation.

Because corporations must pay taxes on net income and owners must pay taxes on dividends received from the corporation, a double taxation situation arises. Often, owners increase their own salaries to reduce or wipe out corporate profits, thereby lowering tax liability. Double taxation can be avoided by filing a Subchapter S election, which allows profits or losses to go through the corporation to you and your partners personally. Corporate losses can be deducted against other income you may have, reducing or eliminating any tax liability you may have. In other words, under Subchapter S, corporations elect not to be taxed as corporations. Shareholders of such corporations include in their individual gross incomes their proportionate shares of the corporate profits and losses.

To qualify under Subchapter S, the corporation must be domestic, must not be a member of an affiliated group, must have one class of stock only, must not have more than 10 shareholders who are individuals or estates, and must not have a nonresident alien as a shareholder. Subchapter S election forms are available from the local IRS office or through an accountant.

Forming a Corporation

Even though you may set up a corporation in another state and pay your fees there, you will still have to file in the state where your business is actually located as well, and pay even higher filing fees than a "domestic" company.

Attorney's charges to file corporate papers vary depending on the complexity of the situation. Unless you have over 10 stockholders or a very complicated partner arrangement, you don't need an attorney to set up a corporation.

The easiest money an attorney makes is in setting up a simple corporation. The forms are simpler than the average credit application, and except in South Carolina the law doesn't require an attorney to apply for you. Do-it-yourself incorporation kits for every U.S. state are available at most stationery stores. Filled-out samples show you how to complete the blanks and where and how to apply.

Choosing a Fictitious Name

Business owners frequently like to choose a distinctive name for their business. If you are a sole proprietor or a partner and you want to operate your business under a name different from your personal name (e.g., John Doe doing business as "AEC Advertising"), you may be required by the county, city, or state to register your fictitious name. The procedure varies from area to area. In many states you are required only to go to the county offices and pay a fee to the county clerk for registering the name.

In some states you must first go to a local newspaper and order a fictitious-name ad. The newspaper will run a legal advertisement for your business name and file the necessary papers for you with the county clerk.

The simplest way to determine the procedure for your county or state is to call your bank and ask if you need a fictitious-name registry or certificate in order to open a business account. If so, inquire as to where you should go to obtain one.

The Business Bank Account

Every business needs a business or commercial bank account. This does not mean merely choosing the most convenient bank. Different businesses have different needs. Determine what your needs will be and then interview the managers of the banks in your area by phone.

This approach will put you at a psychological advantage with the bank manager with whom you plan to do business. It offers you the opportunity to establish a relationship. Normally, when you just walk in to open an account, you are handled by the new-accounts clerk and never come in contact with the bank executives.

The closer your relationship with the bank manager, the better your chances of obtaining loans and special favors. If you are in a branch-banking state, you may do business with a large bank with many branches, and the managers will change frequently. Watch for changes and introduce yourself to each new manager.

To obtain the most personalized service, find an independent bank with no branches, or the smallest chain able to fill your needs. In a small bank your account may be important, whereas in a large bank you may never be noticed.

Avoid moving your account from bank to bank. Your bank reference is an important key to obtaining credit from suppliers. Also, try not to display an aloof attitude toward bank employees. Become acquainted with as many of the employees as possible. Various situations may occur in the course of conducting business, and clerks and tellers who know you can be most helpful.

In the advertising business, good banking relations are important. The reason is that you may have to pay for the media advertising before your client pays you. Arranging to keep your cash flow alive before it gets into trouble can be extremely helpful.

Bankers handle money problems in the same manner that doctors handle medical problems. Don't be afraid to discuss your difficulties with your banker. No matter how small the problem, he or she may know how to handle it in a manner of which you may not be aware. Don't pretend you know everything to impress your banker.

Bankers are experts in their field. Learn to talk to them in their language. Not only will it help you in your present situation, but it will improve your position the next time you approach them.

Business Borrowing

Every new business experiences some rough financial periods or growing pains, and will require financing of some type sooner or later. Watch for signs of an upcoming problem and approach it as far in advance as possible—not after you find yourself in the midst of a crisis.

There isn't a business in existence that can survive without money. But whereas General Motors may quickly raise $100 million in a stock issue, the corner grocery may find it difficult to raise $5000.

As the saying goes, banks lend money only to those who don't need it. Although this may be an exaggeration, it sometimes appears that way to the person starting or operating a small business. It is a fact that the majority of new business owners have to dip into their pockets to finance their entrepreneurial dreams.

So what are the options for the others? Banks are a major source. But banks usually shy away from start-up loans. They're looking for a track record. If you decide to approach a bank for a start-up loan, keep several points in mind.

Plan your growth program and presell your banker. This will impress your banker that you are, indeed, a professional business manager who is on top of every situation. By showing your foresight, you will improve your chances of obtaining a loan under marginal conditions by at least 50 percent over the person who waits until the last minute to apply for a loan.

Some banks do not attempt to attract loan business from small firms but tend to go after the big money; other banks may be more attentive to small, growing concerns. You can usually judge them, to some degree, by their eagerness to obtain your banking account. Here are a few more questions that you might ask when interviewing bankers:

- Is it necessary to maintain certain balances before the bank will consider a loan?

- Will the bank give you a "line of credit" (the maximum credit allowed a borrower), and if so, what is the maximum amount and what are the collateral or other requirements?

- Does the bank have limitations on the number of small loans it will grant or the type of business to which it will grant loans?

- What is the bank's policy on the size or description of checks deposited to be held for collection?

- Will checks under that size be credited immediately to your checking account?

The last question is very important and you must press for a definite answer. In the advertising business, you as agent pay the media to run the ad and must collect your fees from your client afterward. In order to keep your cash flow alive, you must know for certain that checks you deposited will be credited immediately.

If you do not have a previous business account from which the bank may obtain a reference, a few banks may hold all checks for collection until they have developed experience with your account. This precaution may also be affected by your personal credit rating.

When you open your business account, the bank will need your Social Security number or your federal employer's identification number, your driver's license, and your fictitious-name certificate, if you are required to have one.

The Venture-Capital Road

Venture capitalists are looking for fast growth potential. But be warned. Venture capitalists will most likely want a piece of the pie in exchange for their dollars.

For the right company with the right prospects in the right industry, money might be available from a small business investment company (SBIC), which often will be part of a larger venture-capital group. Some SBICs will make straight loans, sometimes requiring that you pay back only the interest in the early years; others prefer to loan money in exchange for stock in the young enterprise.

Banks are probably still the best bet—and should always be considered after you've tapped your own pockets—for a small business in need of a loan.

Tips to Remember When Asking for a Loan

- Make your loan request in narrative form.
- Include a résumé with your loan application.
- Say how much you are prepared to invest yourself.
- Prepare a detailed financial statement and make an attempt to project the business earnings.

Once you have found the right banker, there are three other important professionals you will need.

9

Selecting
an Attorney,
an Accountant, and
a Business Consultant

Attorneys

Finding the right attorney (preferably one with a knowledge of advertising or advertising terminology) is one of the most important tasks you will face as an aspiring small business owner. There are several things an attorney must possess in order to meet the needs of a small business.

An honest attorney will tell you if what you are asking is far afield from his or her principal line of practice, and may refer you to another lawyer who can do a better job for you. But some attorneys, as is true of some of those in any field, are simply dishonest.

Unless the attorney you choose has the time and willingness to sit down and talk with you, or to discuss a legal problem with you on the telephone when you need advice, the attorney cannot be of much help to you, irrespective of how competent and honest he or she may be. If you keep calling your attorney only to be told that your call will be returned—and the attorney gets back to you days or weeks later— you should try to find another who appreciates your business and has the time to do justice to your needs. A great attorney you can't reach is worthless to you.

Remember: An attorney is selling a service, just as you and other business owners are. If, for whatever reason, your attorney cannot or will not provide that service to you when you need it, in a manner that meets your needs, and at a price consistent with the service, then you must find one who can and will.

Once you locate and establish a relationship with a good, honest, competent, available, and energetic attorney, you will doubtless agree that this is one of the most valuable tools in your possession as a business owner or manager. Chapter 12 presents more information on the legal aspects of the advertising business.

Accountants

A good accountant (also preferably one with a knowledge of advertising procedures) is the most important single outside adviser the small businessperson has. While the attorney's services may be vital during specific periods in the development of a small business or in times of trouble, and while the ability to get an attorney's advice from time to time on specific questions is necessary or desirable, it is the accountant whose role on a continuing basis has far greater impact on the ultimate success or failure of a small business.

Never settle for one who is not a CPA—a *certified public accountant*. CPAs are required to meet certain proficiency levels in order to be licensed by the state in which they practice. They must subscribe to certain standards of ethical behavior concerning their relationship with clients and fellow CPAs. While this does not ensure that the CPA will automatically do a good job for you, it does narrow your chances of getting some self-styled accountant who could likely foul up your books and records.

It is worthwhile to obtain the counseling of a CPA prior to starting your business. An experienced CPA will usually know the accounting problems peculiar to your business and will be able to advise and direct you wisely. If you have a sole proprietorship or partnership, it is wise to call in a CPA to organize you before the first tax year or calendar ends. If you are organizing a corporation, it is very important to have a CPA available for counseling while you are starting up to determine the best approaches for your tax situation.

Ideally, an accountant should help you organize the statistical data concerning your business, assist you in charting future actions on the basis of past performance, and advise you on your overall financial strategy with regard to purchasing, capital investments, and similar activities. In fact, however, much of the accountant's time will be taken up trying to keep you, the small business owner, in substantial compliance with the myriad of laws and regulations with which you must learn to live.

This is why you need an accountant—indeed, why you must have one—if you expect to succeed as a small business operator. Accountants specialize in keeping up with the requirements of the law and with shifting interpretations of proliferating regulations. Also, they either know or can readily find the answers to many of the perplexing questions which might take you hours to uncover yourself. As a businessperson, you should be spending your time managing, not doing your own accounting.

Where do you find a good accountant? Ask other ad agency owners or small business owners to recommend someone. Or perhaps your attorney or banker may be able to suggest someone.

Accountants' fees, like those of lawyers, doctors, and other professionals, vary widely. Small town accountants in business for themselves may charge less for their time than the large nationally known firms. Bring up the matter of fees very early in your relationship with any outside adviser and make sure there's a clear understanding of what services you will receive for the money. Part 4 examines record keeping and accounting in detail.

Business Consultants

When you have a medical problem you go to a doctor. When you have a legal question you see an attorney. But, most people jump headlong into a business venture, often pouring in their life savings and never for a second considering having their business plan (if they have one at all) analyzed by a competent business consultant. So enthralled are they by enthusiasm for their idea that, like a horse with blinders, they can only see straight ahead to their goal, and never once consider the possibility that they could fail or simply be wrong in some aspects of their plan.

Experienced business owners are as apt as the neophyte to overrate their own ideas. Enthusiasm is dangerous in business because it encourages people to rush ahead. Careful advance planning is a necessary evil in any business venture. Even more important is an unbiased analysis to uncover potential failure factors. Enthusiasm discourages such a logical and objective approach.

Business and management consultants are not restrictively licensed like doctors and lawyers. Anyone can hang out a shingle and claim to be a consultant. Because of this danger, you should demand proof of any consultant's expertise prior to retaining his or her services.

10

Licenses, Permits, and Taxes

Licenses and Permits

Most cities and counties require business operators to obtain various licenses or permits to show compliance with local regulations.

Business License

The majority of city business license departments are operated as tax-collecting bureaus and do not perform any public service. You simply pay a fee to operate your business in that city. Some cities receive a percentage of your gross sales in addition to the license fee.

When applying for a license, you will find that the most useful service is performed by the building and zoning departments of a city. If a building is not structurally suitable for your business, the license will be denied on the ground of public safety. Building and zoning departments will not allow anyone to operate a business in any area that is not zoned for commercial or industrial use.

Many license laws are ambiguous or complex, and license bureau employees often make informed (or uninformed) guesses. Ask the same question of three different license clerks and you may receive three different answers. If your business is a typical business in a typical location, you probably will not experience any difficulties. If there is anything unusual about it, expect trouble.

Sign Permit

Many cities have instituted sign ordinances that restrict the size, location, and sometimes the lighting and type of sign used. In addition, a landlord of a small shopping center will often impose other sign restrictions in the interests of aesthetic appeal, ignoring your business needs. Therefore, you must receive written approval of your proposed sign specifications and location.

County governments often require essentially the same types of permits and licenses that cities require for commercial enterprises located in the county but not the city. There are county ordinances that apply to particular types of business that need compliance.

Zoning Variance

If your new business is to be located in an already existing facility or was purchased from a previous owner, zoning regulations should not be a problem. However, if a new facility is to be constructed, if an existing building is to be used for a purpose different from that for which it was originally intended, or if extensive remodeling is required, local building and zoning codes should be carefully checked. If zoning regulations do not allow operation of the type business you wish to open, you may file for a zoning variance or a zone change. A zoning variance grants you permission to operate your business on a site not zoned for that purpose. The filing fee for a variance varies from city to city, and it may take months before you get a decision. The variance amounts to a permanent change in the way a particular area is zoned. It involves a lengthy procedure of filing a petition with the city planning commission, holding public hearings, and getting the city council to approve the change.

If the request for zoning is approved, a number of restrictions still apply. In addition to meeting all local building codes, you will probably still need to satisfy certain requirements for minimum setbacks at the front, side, and rear of the structure, minimum total area requirements, minimum provisions for parking space, maximum building heights, and other factors. There can be no generalizations on this subject, since each government entity has its own specific policies. However, in any situation, if the proper zoning conditions cannot be met, no business can be conducted. The overriding theory of zoning is that land must be zoned to its wisest and best use. Any restrictions considered unreasonable by the applicant for a zoning change must be appealed through the courts.

Other Regulations

Certain business practices are prohibited or restricted by federal and state legislation that is designed to encourage competition. These laws prohibit contracts, combinations, and conspiracies in restraint of trade; they prohibit discrimination in price between different purchasers of commodities similar in grade and quality that may injure competition; and they make unfair methods of competition and unfair or deceptive practices unlawful. The term *deceptive practices* refers to false advertising, misrepresentation, simulation of competitive products, and "bad mouthing" competitors.

Because of the complexities and implications of these various regulations and the penalties imposed for their violation, consultation with a lawyer is almost essential.

Taxes

As a business owner and employer, you will be responsible for collecting various state and federal taxes and remitting these to the proper agencies. In addition, you will be required to pay certain taxes yourself.

Employer ID Number

If you employ one or more people, you are required to withhold income tax and social security tax from each employee's paycheck and to remit these amounts to the proper tax-collecting agency.

The first thing you will need is an employer ID number. Call your local state and federal offices to apply for one. They will send you a number, together with quarterly forms; annual forms; W-2, W-3, W-4, and W-9 forms; tax deposit forms; and an instruction manual for filling out forms. They will also send you charts used for deducting taxes from payroll checks. No advance fees or deposits are necessary.

Income Tax Withholding

The deductions the employer is required to withhold from the wages of each employee depend upon the employee's wage level, the number of exemptions claimed by the employee on the withholding exemption certificate (Form W-4), the employee's marital status, and the length of the payroll period.

Social Security (FICA) Tax

The Federal Insurance Contributions Act, or FICA, requires that an employer match and pay the same amount of social security tax as the employee does. The table below shows typical increases that applied to the FICA tax in 1990–1992. The last column gives the maximum amount of tax payable both by employee and employer.

Calendar year	Maximum taxable wage	Tax rate percentage		Maximum tax on employee's wages
		Employer	Employee	
1990	$51,300	7.65	7.65	$3,924.45
1991	$53,400 (Social Security)	6.20	6.20	$3,310.80
1991	$125,000 (Medicare)	1.45	1.45	$1,812.50
1992	$55,500 (Social Security)	6.20	6.20	$3,441.00
1992	$130,200 (Medicare)	1.45	1.45	$1,887.90

Charts and instructions for federal income tax and social security deductions come with the IRS payroll forms.

Three different reports must be filed with the IRS district director in connection with the payroll taxes (relating to both FICA and income tax) that you withhold from your employees:

1. Quarterly return of taxes withheld on wages (Form 941)
2. Annual statement of taxes withheld on wages (Form W-2)
3. Reconciliation of quarterly returns of taxes withheld with annual statement of taxes withheld (Form W-3)

State Payroll Taxes

Almost all states have payroll taxes of some kind which employers must collect and remit to the appropriate agency. Most states have an unemployment tax that is paid entirely by the employer. The tax is figured as a percentage of the employer's total payroll and it is remitted quarterly. The actual percentage varies with the state and the employer.

Some states have income taxes that must be deducted from each employee's paycheck. The employer is responsible for collecting and remitting this tax to the state. A few states have a "disability insurance" tax that must be deducted from employees' pay; in some states, this tax may be split between employee and employer.

Most states have patterned their tax-collecting systems after the federal government's. They issue employer numbers and similar forms and instruction booklets for filling out the forms and making payroll deductions. You may apply for the employer number and various forms and booklets by calling your state office.

Independent Contractors

If you hire someone to perform a service as an independent contractor, you must file annually an "information" return (Form 1099) to report payments totaling $600 or more made to any individual in the course of trade or business during the calendar year.

This is an important point for you to bear in mind, since in the advertising business you will be dealing with quite a number of independents and free-lancers. It is important to get the name and address and social security number of a free-lancer for accounting purposes.

From time to time, you may run across a copywriter or pasteup person who wants to be paid "under the table." While some service businesses go along with this wish on the part of independent contractors, the practice is not recommended. If for some reason the IRS finds out about it, you face prosecution. The wisest course is for you to operate a completely aboveboard firm and not threaten your professional standing.

Personal Income Tax

If you operate as a sole proprietor or as a partner, you will not be paid a salary like an employee; therefore, no income tax will be withheld from money you take out of your business for personal use. Instead, you must estimate your tax liability each year and then make quarterly installments. Your local IRS office will supply the forms and instructions for filing estimated tax returns. When you apply for the forms, also request the *Tax Guide for Small Business.*

At the end of the year, you file an income tax return as an individual, and compute your tax liability on the profits earned in your business for that year.

Corporate Income Tax

If your business is organized as a corporation, you will be paid a salary like other employees. Any profit the business makes will accrue to the corporation, not to you personally. At the end of the year, a corporate income tax return must be filed.

Corporate tax returns may be prepared on a calendar- or fiscal-year basis. If the tax liability of the business is calculated on a calendar-year basis, the tax return must be filed with the Internal Revenue Service no later than April 15 each year. Most businesses, however, find it more convenient to report their income on a fiscal-year cycle.

Your tax year may end in any month you choose. Usually you choose it when you form the corporation. Discuss with your accountant the best time to end your fiscal year.

Sales and Use Taxes

Sales and use taxes are assessed by virtually every state in the country and even by some counties and cities. While the basic tax laws are essentially the same, interpretation by various tax enforcers varies sufficiently to warrant close adherence to the regulations governing your specific taxing region.

It is impossible to write a chapter covering sales and use tax as applied to every taxing agency. *Sales tax* refers to tax on items of tangible personal property sold at retail in intrastate commerce. *Use tax* refers to tax on items of tangible personal property purchased outside the state for use in the state and sold at retail.

The ultimate consumer pays the sales tax, which is collected and reported by the seller.

The use tax is paid by the consumer directly to the state. In some states the seller may be held responsible for collecting and reporting use tax.

The question that determines the capacity the agency acts in is "Which transaction was the retail sale?"

For the most part agencies are agents for the client, buying production items on the client's behalf.

If the agency sells tangible personal property to the client (e.g., finished art prepared by the agency), the agency becomes a seller and must add sales tax to the finished art cost, collect the tax, and report it to the state.

Different states and taxing authorities have specific criteria that must be met by the agency if the agency is going to act on behalf of the client. Generally, the authority to act as agent for the client is covered in the agency-client agreement. In the absence of such an agreement, the agency would be well advised to get the client to sign an agreement authorizing the agency to act on its behalf in the purchase of materials or services.

All purchase orders issued by the agency for materials and/or services being purchased on behalf of the client should clearly state the client's name and the job number when applicable.

The production cost being taxed to the client should be the same cost shown on the supplier invoice to the agency.

The agency cannot use any of the materials purchased on behalf of a client for its own use or charge more than one client for the same material.

The question of what is "tangible personal property" varies by states. Finished art is an example of tangible personal property produced by the agency. Yet the argument continues, in some states, that finished art is not tangible. Still other states maintain that even "rough layouts" are tangible if a charge is made for them.

In many states, wholesalers or manufacturers will not sell to you at wholesale prices unless you can present them with your sales-tax permit or number. You will usually have to sign a tax card for their files.

When conducting business across state lines, you are not normally required to collect taxes for any other states except those where you have offices or stores.

For those items that are subject to sales tax, you can get a resale-tax identifying number. When you receive such a number from a sales-tax collecting agency in your state, it allows you to purchase taxable goods from wholesalers without paying the tax at that time. The sales tax must be paid, of course, but it need be paid only once. When you buy, for example, typesetting, copy, or art from a typographer, copywriter, or artists, you pay only for the product itself. The typographer, copywriter, or artist records your sales-tax identification number, and you make note of the transaction and the amount of the tax. In effect, your vendors are your wholesalers.

You pay the sales tax to the collection bureau or state on a monthly basis, filing forms along with your tax remittance.

You are entitled to a percentage of the tax collected if you file your state sales-tax return on time each month. You will be charged a penalty plus interest on the sales tax you collected during a particular month if you file a delinquent return.

Become familiar with the sales and use tax regulations governing your state and comply accordingly. An audit by sales and use tax field representatives can be a costly experience to those agencies that have been careless in adhering to the regulations.

Professional Fee and Advertising Tax

Some states, in order to raise additional tax income, have or are considering imposing a tax on professional fees as well as production and media charges on advertising that originates within the state and on advertising that enters the state via national or regional media.

Check with your accountant or with your state revenue department to determine if these taxes, even if they are imposed by states other than your own, apply to you.

For example, suppose your state has a 5 percent advertising tax. If you prepare and run an advertisement for one of your clients in a newspaper within your state, you may have to collect 5 percent of the space costs payable to the state. It gets more complicated if the advertisement is regional or national in its coverage. You may then have to figure out the percentage of the total audience seeing your advertisement, determine how much that percentage represents of your total budget, and then collect 5 percent of that amount for your state. In addition, some of your fee and production charges may also be taxable.

Tax Reporting Summary

Every government entity, bureau, or agency that has any legal jurisdiction whatsoever over the business requires that something be submitted in writing, usually accompanied by a payment on a monthly, quarterly, or annual basis. Here's a list:

Federal

Income tax	FICA (Social Security) tax
Estimated income tax deposits	FICA tax deposits
Self-employment tax	FUTA (unemployment) tax
Income tax withholding	FUTA tax deposits
Income tax withholding deposits	

State

Income tax (state or residence)	Withholding tax
Income tax (state in which business is located)	Withholding tax deposits
	Sales tax
Estimated income tax (state of residence)	Conservation tax
Estimated income tax (state in which business is located)	Retail sales license (one-time payment when business starts)

County

Personal property business tax	Merchant's license
Merchant's inventory tax	

City

Sales tax	Earnings tax withholding
Transportation tax	Business earnings and profits tax
Earnings tax	Business personal property tax

These taxes don't apply in every state or city. Any other taxes that you may pay in your area will come automatically to you. In other words, the agencies doing the collecting will find you.

11

Insurance

Carrying the proper liability insurance and buying it right is an important aspect of good risk management. In making these determinations, you should consider (1) the size of the potential loss, (2) its probability, and (3) the resources that would be available to meet the loss if it should occur.

No firm can possibly eliminate or transfer all of the risks that it faces; it obviously must assume some of the risks. The most important factor in determining whether a particular risk should be transferred (to an insurance company) or assumed (by your firm) is the maximum potential loss that might result from the risk; if the loss would be likely to force your firm into bankruptcy, or cause it serious financial impairment, then you should not assume the risk.

There should be a reasonable relationship between the cost of transferring the risk (the cost of insurance) and the value that accrues to the insured firm. For example, the additional premium required to eliminate or reduce "deductibles" in many types of insurance is quite high in relation to the added protection. This rule also reinforces the first rule: The firm that neglects to purchase insurance against severe losses is risking a lot (the possible loss) for a little (the premiums paid).

Contrary to popular opinion, a high probability that a loss will occur does not indicate that the risk should be insured. In fact, the contrary is true: The greater the probability of occurrence, the less appropriate is the purchase of insurance for dealing with the risk. In the first place, losses that occur with relative frequency are predictable and are typically small losses that can be assumed by the business without too much financial difficulty; they are often budgeted as "normal" costs of doing business and thus are included in the prices paid by your clients. A common example is bad-debt losses. Second, where the probability of loss is high, a more effective method of managing or controlling the risk is to reduce it by adopting appropriate precautionary measures.

Always remember the overriding importance of the first rule of risk management: Do not risk more than you can afford to lose. Clearly, the probability of a fire, theft, or casualty loss is less important than the possible size of the loss should the casualty occur.

Insurance Planning

Insurance planning begins with a consideration of the insurable risks faced by your business. In general, the following risks can be covered by insurance:

1. Loss or damage of property—including merchandise, equipment, supplies, fixtures, and building
2. Loss of income resulting from interruption of business because of damage to the firm's operating assets
3. Personal injury to customers, employees, and the general public
4. Loss to the business from the death or disability of key employees or the owner

You should be aware that a standard fire insurance policy pays the policyholder only for losses that are directly due to fire. Other indirect losses, known as consequential losses, may be even more important to the small firm's welfare. You can protect yourself against these losses by obtaining business interruption insurance. Some of these consequential losses are:

1. Loss of use of your business premises
2. Continuing expenses after a fire—such as salaries, rents paid in advance, and interest obligations
3. Extra expenses of obtaining temporary quarters
4. If you are a landlord, loss of rental income on buildings damaged or destroyed by fire

Under common law as well as under workers' compensation laws an employer is liable for injury to employees at work caused by his or her failure to (1) provide safe tools and working conditions, (2) hire competent fellow employees, or (3) warn employees of an existing danger. In every state an employer must insure against potential workers' compensation claims; however, employee coverage and the extent of the employer's liability vary from state to state.

General liability is liability for any kind of bodily injury to nonemployees except that caused by automobiles and professional malpractice. In some cases this liability may even extend to trespassers. Also, a small business owner may be legally liable for bodily injuries sustained by customers, pedestrians, delivery people, trespassers, and other outsiders, even in cases where the owner exercised "reasonable care."

Cars and trucks are a serious source of liability. Most business firms own one or more vehicles. Even if they do not, under the doctrine of agency, they could be held vicariously liable for injuries and property damage caused by those employees who are operating their own or someone else's car in the course of their employment. Of course, your firm would have some coverage under the employee's own liability policy if he or she had one, but even under these circumstances, the limits of the employee's liability might be grossly inadequate. If you have many employees it would be impractical to check their individual liability coverages. If your employees will or may be operating their own vehicles while on company business, you would be well advised to acquire nonownership automobile liability insurance.

The best form of general liability insurance for the small business firm consists of a comprehensive general liability policy. This, combined with a comprehensive auto liability policy and a standard workers' compensation policy, represents the practical ideal.

Types of Coverage

Insurance can be purchased to cover almost any risk. Among business owners, the following types of coverage are most common:

1. Fire and general property insurance—covering fire losses, vandalism, hail and wind damage, floods, electrical, and lightning

2. Plate-glass insurance—covering window breakage

3. Consequential-loss insurance—covering loss of earnings or extra expenses in case of suspension of business due to fire or other catastrophe

4. Burglary insurance—covering forced entry and theft of merchandise and cash

5. Fidelity bond—covering theft by an employee

6. Fraud insurance—covering counterfeit money, bad checks, and larceny

7. Public liability insurance—covering injury to the public, such as customer or pedestrian falling on the property

8. Workers' compensation insurance—covering injury to employees at work

9. Life insurance—covering the life of the owner(s) or key employee(s)

10. Business interruption insurance

11. Product liability insurance

12. Malpractice insurance

After listing the insurable risks and the types of insurance available to cover them, you must then consider how much of a loss you can afford to bear yourself, the possible losses that you would prefer to transfer, and the insurance company's fee for assuming part of the risk. The cost of the various kinds of insurance must be weighed against the possible loss and your ability to bear the cost.

Some insurance companies handle specially written policies to cover advertising agency circumstances. Basically, the kind of coverage you want will be for protection against claims for copyright infringement, theft of ideas, libel, and defense in legal actions arising out of such kinds of claims.

In addition to this coverage, which involves liability for actions you take, you should have some kind of errors-and-omissions coverage (E and O). This protects you against a client claiming that you were negligent in performing your services. If a client is sued because of something you as the agent did not know or made a mistake about, the client will just as likely sue you. This is where errors-and-omissions coverage comes in.

Premiums for E and O coverage vary, but you should expect to pay 1 to 2 percent of your projected gross income. As a side issue, one of the more recent developments with respect to E and O insurance has been that some companies do not issue a policy to an ad agency that engages in comparison tests. This is another way of saying if you intend to "take the Pepsi Challenge," for example, you won't get E and O coverage from certain underwriters.

In today's highly competitive business atmosphere (and advertising is one of the most competitive businesses of all), it is wise to have errors-and-omissions coverage.

Buying Insurance

You should seek cost estimates from at least three reliable insurance agents representing solid insurance companies, and should carefully evaluate them before buying any coverage. The feasibility of "package" insurance policies at discounted rates should also be explored.

Look in your phone book under the heading "Insurance" to find companies that specialize in business insurance. If none is listed under that title, make several calls until you find one. Having the services of a company which specializes is most important if your business is unusual in any way. Companies will also be of assistance as your business grows.

Your insurance agent can arrange financing of your annual insurance costs. It is usually set up in this manner: one-quarter (25 percent) down payment, and the balance spread over 9 months of payments, starting within 30 days after you order the insurance.

12

Contracts
and Regulations

The purpose of this chapter is not to provide legal counsel. But rather provide you with some basic guidelines that will help form better relationships between agency and client, help minimize potential risks in creating ads and campaigns, and hopefully help you and your clients avoid costly and time-consuming litigation over advertising.

First, it will be of interest to know a little about how the agency-client relationship developed.

Evolvement of the Agency-Client Relationship

In the beginning, as they say, the agency acted solely as agent for media. The newspapers, magazines, and outdoor companies paid these agents commissions on the advertising they solicited and contracted for.

Over the years that followed, "boutique," "á la carte," and house agencies that more or less specialized in various types of advertising grew, and eventually many of these evolved into what we now call full-service agencies.

Today, though advertising agencies are still paid commissions by the media, they actually represent the client.

The term *agency* could be considered a misnomer, since many functions performed by advertising agencies are not controlled by the clients they represent and often involve the agency dealing with third parties. These third party dealings may be legally binding on the part of the client. The opposite may also hold true. In cases where the client is dealing with third parties in agency-related work, those dealings may be legally binding to the agency.

Start with a Good Attorney and a Good Agency-Client Agreement

The appointment of your firm as the "agency of record" for a client marks the beginning of your relationship with that client. The terms and conditions you set forth at the start will determine the quality of that relationship. Having a good attorney who understands both the terminology and the mechanics of advertising is the first matter of business you should take care of. As was mentioned earlier in this book, finding the right attorney is one of the most important tasks you will face as an aspiring businessperson. Your attorney should be willing to spend time with you on the phone or in person to discuss questions and possible problems that may arise. In forming a relationship with a new client, it is important for you to discuss with your attorney what your long-term objectives are for this client. And these objectives can be reflected in your client agreement.

You should always try to have the relationship with your new client on your terms if possible. For example, the agency-client agreement can spell out terms for payment of bills, ownership of work produced, functions you are to perform, whether or not you are the exclusive representative for the client or one of a number of agencies that represent other products or services of the client. The agreement should specify how you get paid and how much. What information you are obligated to provide the client concerning each job you do. Whether or not you will extend credit on behalf of the client, and under what terms. It should also have language concerning the agency acting solely as agent of the advertiser making the advertiser solely responsible for payment of contracts the agency made on behalf of the client. (It should be noted here that since the recession of 1991 with many advertisers and agencies going out of business, a large number of media companies are demanding dual responsibility for payment of contracts. In such a case, if you feel your client may not be in the best of financial condition, you might want to provide for advance payment on all contracts with media that call for dual responsibility.)

Having the agency-client relationship on your terms can also be helpful from a time-saving point of view. For instance, if you specify at the outset that there will be 2 client meetings per week, and those meetings will be held at your offices, you can better plan out your weekly time schedules with other clients and new business prospects.

The following is a sample agency-client agreement.

Krieff Advertising
3854 Sheridan Street
Hollywood, Florida 33021

Standard Agency Conditions

1. The Ad Shop, Inc., dba Krieff Advertising, is the Agency or Agent referred to in this agreement. _____ is the Advertiser referred to in this agreement.

2. Advertiser engages Agency to act as its Agent in connection with creation and production of advertising of the products, developments, or projects of the Advertiser, known as _____.

3. The Agency will carry out the advertising and merchandising programs of the Advertising of the products, developments, or projects above set forth. The Agency is authorized to enter into contracts in behalf of the Advertiser to carry out such purposes. It is understood and agreed that Agency is acting solely as the agent of the Advertiser in all such contracts, and the Advertiser shall be solely responsible under such contracts for all payments due thereunder. The Advertiser agrees to indemnify and hold the Agency harmless from liability under such contracts.

4. Agency shall act as Advertiser's exclusive representative for the above products, developments, or projects and shall perform, at the request of the Advertiser, any or all of the following services to the extent necessary to meet Advertiser's needs:

- Study and analyze the Advertiser's product, developments, or projects and familiarize itself with the market therefore. Develop advertising programs designed to meet the Advertiser's needs and budgetary limitations.
- Plan, create, write, and prepare layouts and the actual copy to be used in advertisements of all types and produce advertising in accordance with media to be used.
- Analyze all advertising media and recommend those which are most suitable for use by the Advertiser.
- Prepare and recommend media schedules and make contracts on behalf of the Advertiser with the advertising media for space or time and with others to effectuate the advertising program and obtain the most favorable terms and rates available.
- Check and follow up on all contracts with the various media for proper performance in the best interests of the Advertiser, including the appearance, accuracy, date, time, position, size, extent, site workmanship, and mechanical reproduction, as appropriate to the advertisements used.
- Negotiate, arrange, and contract for on behalf of the Advertiser any special talent required and for all photography, models, special effects, layouts, and artwork, and for all printing, including any required engravings, electrotypes, typography, and any other necessary technical material for use in the advertising program.

5. This agreement shall become effective on _____ and shall remain in force for a minimum period of _____. This Agreement shall be automatically renewed on a thirty (30) day basis thereafter unless either party shall terminate the agreement by a sixty (60) day written notice prior to the termination date of this contract sent by registered or certified mail to the address of the other party set forth above.

The obligations of the Agency and the Advertiser under this contract shall continue in force during the period of the notice, including the ordering and billing of advertising in media where closing dates fall within such period. Any uncancelable contracts remaining in existence upon the termination of the contract shall be carried to completion by the Agency and paid for by the Advertiser.

Upon termination of this agreement, and providing that all moneys owed by the Advertiser to the Agency or to anyone with whom the Agency has contracted in behalf of the Advertiser shall have been paid, the Agency will transfer all property and materials in its possession or control to or at the direction of the Advertiser. Until such time, the Agency shall retain a lien against all of such property and materials and shall retain the right of possession of them. All work shall remain the property of the Agency until paid for by the Client. In the event of default of moneys due Agency from Client, Client agrees to discontinue use of all materials produced by Agency until a court ruling.

In the event Advertiser has approved any copy of materials prepared by Agency which has not been used by the termination date of this agreement but which is used thereafter by the Advertiser, Agency will be paid an amount equal to the commissions on the advertising in which the copy or material is used.

6. Any rejected or unused advertising concepts and ideas formulated by Agency shall remain the property of the agent to be used as it sees fit, provided such use does not involve any confidential information concerning Advertiser's business or method of operation.

7. Agency will provide written estimates of costs and charges to the Advertiser for its prior approval and authorization. The prices quoted, unless clearly stated as agreed or upset, will be based on estimates made by Agency or submitted by suppliers and will be substantially adhered to insofar as possible. Such estimates will contain descriptions of proposed advertisements. Unless Advertiser objects to estimates within five (5) working days from their delivery, approval and authorization by the Advertiser will be deemed given; except that the period will be reduced to three (3) working days with regard to corrections on interim work proofs, artwork or other finished material. For the convenience of the Advertiser, oral orders, oral change orders, or oral alteration orders will be accepted by the Agency. However, such orders shall be deemed to have been done in accordance with the terms and conditions hereof.

8. The Advertiser shall pay the agent in advance for all costs to be incurred in its behalf as set forth in the estimates, including, but not limited to, media charges, production charges, out-of-pocket costs, including travel and sales tax.

In the event media or other charges increase or decrease after the submission of an estimate, either before or after payment by the Advertiser, the Advertiser shall pay for any increase or be given credit for any reduction, as the case may be.

In all events, Agency will bill Advertiser for time and space so that Agency will receive the money prior to the time that the obligation arises to the media for payment (known as closing dates). All payment discounts allowed by the media and earned by the Advertiser will be passed on to the Advertiser providing its account with the Agency is current. In the event that the Advertiser has any disagreements with or disputes any bill, invoice or charge made by Agency, it shall notify Agency in writing within fifteen (15) days of receipt of said bill, invoice, or charge of the nature of its disagreement or dispute, or said bill, invoice, or charge will be deemed correct.

9. In addition to the fee which has been paid to the Agency as a creative concept fee in the amount of \$_____, Agency will be entitled to be paid a minimum service fee of \$_____ per month, in advance commencing, _____, and on the first day of each month thereafter for the duration of this agreement. At the end of each month commissions on all media (15 percent of the gross or 17.65 percent of the net media costs on noncommissionable media insertions) shall be calculated, and to the extent that such commissions exceed \$_____, the service fee for that month shall be deemed to be increased to that extent and shall be paid by the Advertiser together with the minimum service fee for the ensuing month. Production and mechanical costs shall be paid by the Advertiser, whether or not the material is used.

10. It is the intent of the parties that no credit be extended by the Agency and that prior to the Agency incurring any obligation or involving itself in any expenditure on behalf of the Advertiser, the Advertiser will pay the Agency the proposed cost of such expenditures. In the event, however, moneys become due and payable to the Agency and are not paid within five (5) days after demand therefore, such moneys shall bear interest until paid at the highest rate permitted under the laws of the State of Florida. Advertiser shall indemnify and hold Agency harmless against any and all claims and demands whatsoever in regard to this agreement or in regard to any information or materials provided by or approved of by Advertiser. In the event Agency is subject to any legal action as a result of such materials or information, Advertiser agrees to pay any and all cost, including reasonable attorney's fees incurred in Agency's representation.

Advertiser has the right to examine any records relating to its account during normal office hours and upon reasonable notice.

The laws of the State of Florida shall generally govern the interpretation of this contract.

In the event Agency is obliged to employ the services of counsel to enforce its rights under this contract, Advertiser shall pay any reasonable attorney's fees incurred by the Agency in that connection.

In the event the Agency does extent credit to the Advertiser, it is agreed that all persons signing this contract in behalf of the Advertiser shall be personally and equally liable as maker and guarantor of this Agreement as one of the principals.

11. This agreement, which shall not be assignable by either party without express prior written consent, contains the entire agreement of the parties and shall not be altered except in writing.

ACCEPTED BY:

Client signature (Advertiser) _____ Witness _____

Print Corporate name in full _____

Krieff Advertising (Agency)

By:_____   Witness _____

Other Important Points to Consider in Your Agency-Client Agreement

- Specifics of agency appointment by client.
- Services agency will perform: study of product or services and competitive products and services; creation and planning of advertising and marketing; ad-

ditional compensation for services like research, media planning, analysis and placement, production for broadcast and collateral materials, tear sheet checking, billing, dealer meetings, talent contracts, securing music rights, and so on.

- Is your company the sole agency? Will you be handling additional products later?

- Agency compensation: 15 percent of gross (17.65 percent of net) on media placements; fees, production charges, or commissions on other services; annual or monthly fee or retainer in lieu of commissions; special work performed by agency.

- Contracts with outside vendors.

- Competitive bidding on outside purchases: How many bids? Should you disclose dealings with companies your agency may be affiliated with or controlled by? Problems that may arise out of sales taxes due.

- Termination of agreement: 60, 90, or more days notice; agency rights to compensation of media placed before termination date; assumption of agency's liabilities under terms of vendor and media contracts; protection of third party rights; ownership of advertising materials.

- Indemnity: client indemnifies agency against claims arising from trademark infringement, governmental actions, actions against product liability and comparative product claims.

- Liability to media and suppliers: dual liability problems; What if client fails to pay agency?

- Provisions for using outside "boutique" or "á la carte" services: Who owns advertising materials and creative elements such as slogans, photos, and characters? Who has control over purchases? If you use a media buying service and it fails to pay media invoices, who is liable? Possibly make provisions to use an escrow agent to hold funds for such cases.

- Safeguarding of property: Is agency responsible if media or suppliers do not return materials? Do you have responsibility for unauthorized use of a client's materials? Should client pay part of insurance coverage for loss of materials due to fire, theft, or other damage?

- Inspection of books: Do you want your books, contracts, correspondence, accounts, and sources relating to your clients' affairs available for inspection by the client or their authorized representative? Where does inspection take place?

- Provision for enforcing your rights under the contract: client shall pay reasonable attorney's fees; agency has right to charge interest on moneys past due.

Now that you have the basis for a strong agency-client agreement, all you have to worry about is becoming involved in litigation over advertising.

How Can You Protect Yourself?

There is no formula or set of rules to protect you from legal retribution. People who appear in a photo of a crowd scene, for example, can sue you for unauthorized use of their picture and a dozen other reasons they will manage to dream up. Something as simple as a secretary getting a paper cut from a collateral brochure you produced can get you into court. Failure to specify in a model release that you have the right to use a photo or likeness any way you want, can be a very costly mistake. (See Figure 12-1.)

You and your clients and probably all other parties connected with any such incident must defend themselves when a plaintiff goes after "deep pockets." Suing

---

CONSENT AND RELEASE

For Value Received I Hereby Give _____ **Krieff Advertising**
3854 Sheridan Street, Hollywood, Florida 33021

its successors and assigns, and any one acting under the authority or permission thereof (herein called licensee) the unqualified right to make and copyright photographs of me, and to use or distribute such photographs or any reproductions thereof, or my name, signature, or endorsement, together or separately, anywhere, in any manner at any time hereafter and as often as desired, for any commercial, public or private purpose. Photographs as used herein include any reproductions of my likeness made by any process, in black and white, or color, or any combination thereof, alone or in conjunctions or settings, under any historical, fictitious or other names, or based on or involving any stunt poses, distortion, optical illusion, additions, alterations, retouching, compositions with other reproductions of any kind, or any feature, however unusual. Further I waive all right of inspection or approval and irrevocably release the licensees and each of them from claims or demands which I may or can have on account of the use or publication of such photographs, by name, signature, or endorsement as herein authorized.

I hereby warrant that I am of full age and free to give this permission and release which I have read and understand. (Strike out the foregoing sentence where not applicable.)

Signed in the presence of:

_____

Address _____

I, the undersigned, parent or guardian of the above model, hereby consent to the foregoing:

Signed in the presence of:

_____

Address _____

Dated the _____ day of _____ 19 _____

Signature _____

Address _____

Dated the _____ day of _____ 19 _____

Signature _____

Address _____

Parent or Guardian _____

Fig. 12-1. Sample of a consent and release form.

companies, both large and small, has become an enjoyable pastime for many people, and their attorneys. So how can you minimize your risks? How can you be sure that all the claims you make in an ad are true? How can you protect yourself if a client's product is not properly labeled? Or if the client's product causes harm to a buyer?

Be Cautious—and Keep in Touch with Your Attorney

Most large agencies have lawyers on staff to advise on the substantiation of claims, implications of copy and visuals, governmental and broadcasting regulations, and other legalities of advertising. Since you will not have this luxury, the best advice you can take is to be both sensible and cautious about what you say and how you say it. When you can, run it by your attorney. But don't run into the mistake of letting your attorney write your ad. Because given the chance, attorneys would love it and you would end up with advertising that says very little, if anything at all.

It's okay to be aggressive and creative with your advertising rather than dull and bland. After all, that's what effective advertising is all about. Safe advertising that's ineffective will help you in avoiding losing lawsuits—but you may end up losing sales and clients.

The Bait and Switch

The bait-and-switch method of advertising occurs when the advertiser tries to switch consumers from buying the advertised merchandise in order to sell something else, usually at a higher price. The bait ad attracts just the target the advertiser is looking for. Once the customer is "hooked," the advertiser will try to discourage the sale of the less expensive merchandise, sometimes by actually berating it, or flatly refusing to sell the advertised merchandise, claiming it is sold out or not otherwise available any more. You run the risk of legal problems when you purposely use false statements in advertising copy or label and packaging information.

Ads That Use Comparatives

This very common type of advertising is used to compare the virtues of one product over those of the competition. As long as claims are substantiated and not deceptive or defamatory, this form of advertising will be considered within legal bounds.

Deceptive Advertising

You say in your ad that your client's product provides "relief" from pain. Is the relief permanent? It it's only partial or temporary relief you would be safer to say so rather than run the risk of someone misinterpreting or misunderstanding what the ad says. If an item is "repaired," don't claim that it is "rebuilt." If a product or service is not actually a one of a kind, don't say it's "unique." Never falsely state the make-up or ingredients of any product. Never state that a product will do something common sense tells you it can't do.

Defamation of Character

Defamation of character is a statement causing harm to a person's reputation, either by the spoken word (slander) or in writing (libel), and communicating it to a third party. The law says the third party must actually interpret the statement as defamatory. The more people the statement reaches, the more serious the consequences could be.

The person claiming slander must prove harm has been caused in some way. Proving slander is usually more difficult than proving a person has been libeled.

Copyrights

When the composition, wording, photographs, and illustrations of an advertisement are copyrighted, the rights of the owner are protected by law. If you, by chance, use a headline for a banking ad and that headline was copyrighted originally for a deodorant product, you might get by with a "fair use" defense, since the purpose and type of use in your case is different than the original intention of the headline, and the effect of the copyright owner's market may not be harmed.

Trademarks

Trademarks not used for a period of two years, without a specific reason for non-use, can be considered abandoned and cause the marks to fall into public domain and be adopted by another. This can cause a problem if, for instance, a company updates its old mark with a new one without exercising care. A competitor could adopt the old mark and benefit from the built-up goodwill that mark has attained.

Lottery

A game or promotion is considered a lottery, and is prohibited in use to assist in the sale of goods, if it includes three elements: prize, consideration, and chance. If any one of these elements is eliminated, it is no longer a lottery. The trickiest element is consideration. If a player has to pay to play, that is clearly consideration. But if a player has to mail in an entry or drive to a store to register to play, is the cost of postage and gasoline considered consideration?

Guarantees and Warranties

When an advertiser gives a formal assurance to do something specific if the product or service doesn't work, that assurance is considered a "guarantee." When the advertiser assures the buyer as to what the product or service will do, that assurance is considered a "warranty."

When your advertising involves disclosing warranties or guarantees, make sure that statements concerning product performance that may be relied upon by the purchaser are accurate and true. Always identify the guarantor in your ads, the duration, conditions, and the specifics of the guarantee.

Advertising Regulations
That Protect the Consumer

In addition to the responsibility for meeting the consumers' needs for product information, the advertising agency is also responsible for meeting regulatory requirements for its advertising content. Legal requirements cannot be separated from the interests of consumers because most regulation in this field is designed to provide protection for the consumer and maintain fair competition.

To meet legal responsibilities, the ad agency needs to know which are the regulatory agencies and what their areas of concern are.

Agencies Regulating Advertising

The regulation of advertising is a complex topic because many different agencies at federal, state, and local levels are involved. Agencies such as the Environmental Protection Agency (the EPA) both approve products and regulate what can and cannot be said about them. The Food and Drug Administration (the FDA) is another such agency. In matters concerning broadcast advertising, the Federal Communications Commission (the FCC) is the regulatory body. In addition, there are many regulatory bodies that have been established by various local and national business groups such as Better Business Bureaus. In some areas of the country, the local Department of Transportation may have the authority to allow or disallow outdoor billboards.

Of the several federal agencies concerned with the regulation of advertising, one of the most important would be the Federal Trade Commission (the FTC).

The Federal Trade Commission was established as an independent regulatory body by the Federal Trade Commission Act of 1914. Its original purpose was to prevent trade practices that would injure competition. Among the unfair trade practices attacked by the Commission was false and/or misleading advertising.

The Wheeler-Lea Act of 1938 strengthened the FTC and extended both its jurisdiction and the legal remedies available in cases concerning false advertising. False advertising was more specifically defined as advertising that misleads either through untrue assertions or through omission of material facts. Over the years, the scope of the FTC's authority and the meaning of unfair advertising have been broadened and more fully defined through precedents set in Commission and court cases.

The Commission staff monitors advertising for infractions and also acts on complaints received from companies and consumers. If the situation warrants, the Commission issues a complaint against the offending advertiser. These complaints may be settled by negotiation, sometimes resulting in issuance of a cease and desist order (an order to stop the unlawful practice) or a consent decree (an agreement to stop the practice in question without agreement as to its illegality). The decision of the Commission can be appealed by the advertiser through the federal court system—the Circuit Courts of Appeal and the U.S. Supreme Court. In some severe cases, charges can be brought against responsible individuals with fines and/or prison terms imposed.

Advertising Legally Speaking

The laws concerning advertising are complex. Making a simple mistake can be extremely hazardous to your business as well as your client's business simply because both of you can be held equally liable for that mistake. When in doubt about something, call an attorney. The cost of legal advice is inexpensive compared with the cost of defending yourself in a lawsuit.

Part 3 Action Checklist

- ✔ The first decision in establishing your agency is deciding on the type of business structure you want: sole proprietorship, partnership, limited partnership, or corporation.

- ✔ If you are forming a corporation or partnership arrangement that is not too complicated, you may not need an attorney. However, consulting with a competent attorney and accountant before establishing your business can ensure that the correct legal procedures in your state are followed.

- ✔ If you are running a business under a name different than yours (if you are a sole proprietor or a partnership) or different than your corporate name, check out the fictitious-name requirements in your state.

- ✔ Good banking relations are important not only for borrowing money when you need it, but also because your banker can be a big help to you with good advice and valuable credit references. Establish a relationship with the manager of the bank you select. Try to avoid moving your account from bank to bank. Don't be afraid to discuss business difficulties with your banker. He or she may know a lot more about how to solve a problem than you do.

- ✔ Be sure your business plan provides for borrowing money during growth or rough financial periods. It won't hurt to go over your business plan with your banker, since he or she may well be the source of your financing.

- ✔ If you are seeking outside investors, be prepared to give up a portion of your business.

- ✔ When selecting an attorney or accountant, look for professionals with a knowledge of your business. When selecting an accountant, make sure he or she is a CPA. Don't be shy to ask other agencies or businesspeople who they use for legal and accounting services. Your banker may also have a few suggestions. And after overcoming any shyness you may have had, don't be shy about negotiating the fees for these services.

- ✔ Should you hire a business consultant to help formulate your business plan? When you consider that you are starting a new venture with your own hard-earned savings, and you are probably so enthusiastic about it you can't see the forest for the trees, buying the knowledge of a business consultant could prove to be a worthwhile investment. Just be sure whomever you hire really has the expertise you need.

- ✔ Establishing a new business means you need various licenses and/or permits in order to comply with local regulations. These include your business license, sign permits, and zoning variances, if needed.

✓ As a business owner and employer, you will be responsible for collecting state and federal taxes and remitting these to the proper agencies. This means that you will need an employer ID number, which makes you responsible for withholding federal income tax and social security tax, as well as making payroll, corporate, sales, and use tax payments.

✓ Check with your accountant or state revenue department as to whether or not your state imposes a professional fee and/or advertising tax on production and media charges that originate in your state.

✓ When purchasing insurance coverage for your business, contact a few reliable companies for advice on the various types of specialized and general coverage you might need. Compare premiums and don't forget that insurance costs can be financed, eliminating the burden of laying out the entire annual premium up front.

✓ Types of coverage you should consider essential include: loss or damage of property; loss of income resulting from business interruption; personal injury to clients and the general public; workers' compensation; and loss of business due to death or the disability of key employees.

✓ An important element in establishing your business is establishing a good agency-client agreement, one that is on your terms, if possible. A well-planned agreement will determine what is expected of both parties, exclusive representation by your agency, the amount of your compensation and the terms of payment, termination procedures, indemnity and liability of both parties, and provisions for enforcing your rights under the agreement.

✓ In dealing with people, products, and procedures, protect your business as best you can. Get model releases before you use photographs. Be sure you have no liability when making claims on behalf of a client. Be knowledgeable about copyright and trademark laws, slander and libel, and advertising games, guarantees, and warranties.

✓ Keep your attorney's phone number handy—for advice, and help, should you need it.

Part 4

Record Keeping and Accounting

13

Records

Record Keeping

There are two main reasons to keep records of a business operation: They are required by law, and they are useful to you in your functions as a manager.

Records determine the tax liabilities of the individual or business. Regardless of the type of bookkeeping system employed, the records must be permanent, accurate, and complete, and must clearly establish income, deductions, credits, employee information, and anything else specified by federal, state, and local regulations. The law does not require any particular kind of records, only that they be complete and separate for each business.

When you start in business, the type and arrangement of books and records most suitable for your particular operation should be established, keeping in mind the taxes for which your business is liable and the times at which they are due. If this is not an area in which you are competent, outside professional help is called for. Setting up a system for good record keeping need be done only once; doing it efficiently makes things much easier later on.

Double-entry bookkeeping is usually the preferred method for keeping business records, making use of journals and ledgers. Transactions are entered first in a journal and then monthly totals of the transactions are posted to the appropriate ledger accounts. The ledger accounts include five categories: (1) income, (2) expense, (3) asset, (4) liability, and (5) net worth. Income and expense accounts are closed each year; asset, liability, and net worth accounts are maintained on a permanent and continuing basis.

Single-entry bookkeeping, although not as complete as the double-entry method, may be used effectively in the small business, especially during its early years. The single-entry system can be relatively simple, recording the flow of income and expense through a daily summary of cash receipts, a monthly summary of receipts, and a monthly disbursements journal (such as a checkbook). This system is entirely adequate for the tax purposes of a small business.

All business receipts should be deposited in a separate bank account, with a petty-cash fund established for small expenses. All business expenses paid by cash should be supported by documents that clearly show that the expenses were incurred for business purposes.

All disbursements should be made by check, if possible, so that business expenses can be well documented. If a cash payment is necessary, a receipt for the payment, or at least an explanation of it, should be included in the business records. All canceled checks, paid bills, duplicate deposit slips, and other documents that substantiate the entries in the business records should be filed in an orderly manner and stored in a safe place. Accounts should be classified in groups relating to income, expense, assets, liabilities, and net worth. Asset accounts should be classified as current or fixed and the dates of acquisition, cost, depreciation, and any other items affecting the accounts should be recorded in detail.

Record keeping and production in the advertising agency business are closely related. There is no one way to keep records, of course, but you can modify the guidelines presented in this book to suit your particular needs.

Business Papers

Carefully preserve all underlying business papers. All purchase invoices, receiving reports, copies of purchase orders, invoices sent to customers, canceled checks, and receipts for cash paid out must be meticulously retained. They are not only essential to maintaining good records but may be important if legal or tax involvement is ever incurred on any of these items.

When taking on projects, open what is called a job ticket or job jacket. This is an envelope with a form on which are written instructions to various people in the ad production process. In a small agency, there will be little need for a highly structured, departmentalized approach. Yet at every stage, particularly when you perform billable functions for your client, you will have to keep a record of your activity.

Record keeping is central to client-agency relationships because from well-kept, clear records come your fees. We will show you a way to keep records so that the fees you charge are easily billed to your client's account. What records are they? They consist of bills, purchase orders, checks, expense reports, receipts, and similar expenses as well as your record of creative services performed on behalf of your client.

Payroll Records

An employer—regardless of the number of employees—must maintain all records pertaining to payroll taxes (income tax withholding, social security, and federal unemployment tax) for at least four years after the tax becomes due or is paid, whichever is later.

There are many kinds of employment records that must be maintained just to satisfy federal requirements. These records are summarized below.

Income Tax Withholding Records

    1. Name, address, and social security number of each employee

2. Amount and date of each payment of compensation

3. Amount of wages subject to withholding in each payment

4. Amount of withholding tax collected from each payment

5. Reason that the taxable amount is less than the total payment

6. Statements relating to employees' nonresident alien status

7. Market value and date of noncash compensation

8. Information about payments made under sick-pay plans

9. Withholding exemption certificates

10. Agreements regarding the voluntary withholding of extra cash

11. Dates and payments to employees for nonbusiness services

12. Statements of tips received by employees

13. Requests for different computation of withholding taxes

Social Security (FICA) Tax Records

1. Amount of each payment subject to FICA tax

2. Amount and date of FICA tax collected from each payment

3. Explanation for the difference, if any

Federal Unemployment Tax (FUTA) Records

1. Total amount paid during calendar year

2. Amount subject to unemployment tax

3. Amount of contributions paid into the state unemployment fund

4. Any other information requested on the unemployment tax return

Other Records to Retain

Records supporting the items on a federal tax return should be kept until the statute of limitations expires. Records relating to depreciable property should be retained for as long as they are useful in determining the cost basis of the original or replacement property. Copies of federal income tax returns should be kept forever; they may even be helpful to the executor of your estate.

14

Bookkeeping

Daily Bookkeeping Is a Must

Picture this scene; lots of checks have arrived in the mail; your clients have been aggravating, to put it mildly; and your staff seems to be fresh out of award-winning ideas.

Time to close up shop and call it a day?

No way! It's time to enter the day's transactions into a general ledger.

Any small businesses, including advertising agencies, should keep detailed records on a daily basis and tie their books down at the end of every month. Otherwise, you could run into trouble at the end of the year.

Accounting Methods

If you are not an accountant, don't expect to understand accounting language. Though this chapter involves specific terminology used in the accounting field, we have tried, whenever possible, to explain things in layperson's language. In any event, it is a short chapter, which means if you read it quickly, it will be practically painless and you'll be finished with it in hardly any time at all.

Basically, there are two methods of accounting—the cash method and the accrual method.

Cash Method

The cash accounting method is probably the easiest to use, but it is the least informative. In simple terms, it is the method of recording transactions that concern cash that is received and cash that is paid out. If you invoice your client in April, but that invoice is not paid until May, you would record the sale in May. If the cost of the items invoiced in April were received from your vendor or supplier in May, but not paid until June, the transaction would be recorded in June.

When using the cash method, little or no attempt is made to relate the cost of billing to that specific billing and, therefore, there is no method of determining whether or not the agency is earning a profit on the items billed for.

However simple the cash method may be, it is often recommended as the system to use, since it enables the agency to control the amount of cash it has at the end of the year for tax reporting. Since in this method tax is assessed only on the actual amount of cash it has at year end, the agency can prepay bills to vendors and media, pay the rent in advance, pay for next year's insurance in advance, and so on, in order to reduce the cash-on-hand balance and, of course, pay tax on a lesser amount.

There is nothing wrong with closing your books at year end using the cash method. Though all taxpayers, including corporations and other types of businesses, should always pay their taxes as good taxpayers do, the cash method may in fact be the best way for small agencies to go, since it enables those firms that are cash poor to preserve what cash they do have, rather than pay a portion of it in taxes.

Those who advocate the cash method usually maintain that companies must use the same accounting method used for tax-reporting purposes throughout the entire year. Requirements for keeping books and tax reporting on different accounting basis, but all that should be left to your CPA, who is up on the latest tax changes that will affect your business.

Accrual Method

In the accrual method of accounting, all transactions are recorded as they occur. When a client is invoiced, the sale is recorded in the month in which the invoice is dated. When a purchase is made, the obligation is recorded at the time an invoice for that purchase is received from the supplier. In addition then to knowing the cash balance at any time, you also know who owes you and how much, and who you owe and how much. Most important, you have all the information necessary to relate the actual cost of billing to the specific invoices and thus determine actual gross profit by invoice, client, and agency. Further, you have the actual operating expenses incurred for the period being accounted for. Now it is possible to tell if your agency is making a profit. The time at which your agency collects money owed to it or the time when the agency pays money it owes is unrelated to profit accountability.

Keeping Records Up to Date

Here are the records you should post and reconcile weekly and monthly:

Weekly

- *Accounts receivable:*   Take action on slow payers.
- *Accounts payable:*   Take advantage of discounts.
- *Payroll:*   Records should include name and address of employee, social se-

curity number, number of exemptions, date ending the pay period, hours worked, rate of pay, total wages, deductions, net pay, check number.

- *Taxes and reports to state and federal governments:*   Sales tax and withholding tax.

Monthly

- All journal entries are classified according to like elements. These should be generally accepted and standardized for both income and expense and posted to the general ledger.

- Prepare a profit-and-loss statement usually 10 to 15 days after the close of the month. This shows the income for the business for the month, the expense incurred in obtaining the income, and the profit or loss resulting. From this, take action to eliminate losses.

- A balance sheet should accompany the profit-and-loss statement. This shows assets (what the business has), liabilities (what the business owes), and the investment of the principals.

- Reconcile the bank statement—that is, the firm's books—with the bank's record of the cash balance.

- Balance petty-cash account. The actual cash in the petty-cash box plus the total of the paid-out slips that have not been charged to expense should total the amount set aside as petty cash.

- Make all federal tax deposits and withhold federal and state income, FICA, and other taxes.

- Note all past-due accounts receivables.

Financial Formulas and Definitions You Should Know

Net profit. Gross profit. Hard dollar costs. Soft dollar costs. The language and formulas used to prepare an agency income statement can be very confusing. On the other hand, they can be very enlightening and useful in helping to improve profits when you understand what they are all about. Your accountant will be the one preparing your statements so you don't have to calculate the formulas or completely understand all the definitions of terms. The following definitions are designed to help shed some light on what some of the terms mean and how they relate to your agency's profit picture.

Gross profit—Same as gross income or revenue. Represents the dollar difference between the gross amount billed to a client and the actual dollar cost of that billing spent on media and production with outside sources.

Gross profit percent—The percent of gross profit earned on a client's billings. Can be calculated by job, client, and agency by dividing the dollars of gross profit by dollars billed. For example:

$30,000 gross profit divided by $200,000 billing = 15% or
$24,000 gross profit divided by $148,000 billing = 16% or
$17,000 gross profit divided by $70,000 billing = 24%

Operating profit—Same as operating income. The gross profit less every operating expense you have in running the agency (salaries, utilities, insurance, vendor costs, equipment, general administrative expenses, etc.).

Operating profit percentage—Divide the operating profit by gross profit. For example:

$40,000 operating profit divided by $200,000 gross profit = 20%

Direct expense—These are the expenses outlaid by the agency in order to complete a job for which the agency is not always reimbursed. Such expenses may include fax and telephone charges, shipping and courier costs, agency travel expenses, food and entertainment costs as well as other expenses you may not wish to bill a client for, or they may be expenses a client may refuse to pay for. These unbillable expenses actually are part of the production costs of a particular job. The agency can elect to absorb these charges if they will cause friction with the client, or if they are not too exorbitant, you may want to add them to other billable items that the client is expecting to pay for.

Indirect expenses—These are the operating costs spent to run the agency. These expenses are not generally related to the costs incurred in servicing clients. They include such expenses as salaries, rent, and general administrative costs.

Nonoperating income and expense—Of the many items that contribute to net operating before tax profit, nonoperating income/expense has the least to do with determining the success of the agency operation. Nonoperating income refers to income from invested funds, bank interest, and earned discounts. Nonoperating expenses would be costs like life insurance for officers and employees, bonuses, discounts allowed, contribution to profit sharing and pension fund plans as well as medical plans for employees.

Standard operating allowances—These are allowances that have been developed over the years and are based on surveys of agency operations by various trade associations. They include operating expenses as a percent of gross profit; for example, salaries held to 50 percent of gross profit; rent 5 percent of gross profit; auto expense 2 percent, and so forth. While the allowance for each expense may vary for each company, all agencies should try to hold operating expenses to 80 percent or less of gross profit, guaranteeing at least a 20 percent operating profit.

Billable hourly rates—This refers to the rates that each agency staff member is billed for on a particular job. This rate is determined by dividing the annual salary of each employee by 1600 (the average amount of hours an employee works in a year after deducting vacation time, holidays, illness, and personal time off) then multiplying that amount by three. This gives you one-third for employee salary, one-third for overhead, and one-third for agency profit. For example:

$40,000 per year salary divided by 1600 = $25.00

$25.00 multiplied by 3 = $75.00 (that is the employee's billable rate)

Capitalized billing—By treating all gross profits as though they represented 15% of everything billed for charges, an agency can determine its capitalized billing. The problem with this system is that it does not represent a fair comparison between agencies, since the gross profit percentage varies from agency to agency. Those agencies with fairly heavy media billing would generate mostly a 15 percent gross profit. But those with heavier production and collateral billing would produce a higher gross profit percentage, owing to hourly billing and mark-ups on outside costs higher than the usual 17.65 percent.

Next, let us look at the Chart of Accounts.

15

The Chart of Accounts

In the starting up of a new agency, some degree of control is needed to show a true picture of the company's growth. In this chapter you will see a typical agency chart of accounts (see Figure 15-1). Basically, it is a "table of contents," customized to the needs of an advertising agency. The key word here is customized. The primary purpose of a chart of accounts is to provide detailed information for the balance sheet and the income statement. The information taken from the chart of accounts may also be used to generate other financial statements (see Figure 15-2).

The Balance Sheet

The balance sheet items shown on the chart of accounts are fairly standard in most types of businesses, though there are differences in itemizations of both income and expenses that are more likely to be beneficial to an ad agency or other type of similar service company such as public relations firms and studios. Many smaller businesses list a one-line accounts payable item on their chart of accounts, and all moneys that the business owes are lumped together and carried in that category. But in the ad agency business, you will be dealing with many types of creditors: media, production, and administrative expenses. You will learn very quickly that the demands of each creditor are different, and these differences will require decisions concerning the outflow of payments. In times when the flow of cash is tight, management must decide who gets paid first, how much you pay, and when. If payables are broken down by type of creditor, it follows that the "aged accounts payable trial balance," prepared at the end of every accounting period, will also be broken down, thus making the

XYZ AGENCY

Chart of Accounts

Account	Type	Account description	Tax line #
101	A	Cash in Bank	
104	A	Certificate of Deposit in Bank #	
105	A	Money Market in Bank #	
106	A	Certificate of Deposit in Bank #	
107	A	Certificate of Deposit in Bank #	
108	A	Investment—ABC Company	
109	A	Investment—DEF Company	
115	A	Exchange	
119	A	Prepaid Sales Tax	
120	A	Federal Income Tax—Deposits	
154	A	Auto Equipment	
156	A	Machinery and Equipment	
158	A	Office Equipment	
160	A	Leasehold Improvements	
165	A	Accumulated Depreciation—Auto Equipment	
167	A	Accumulated Depreciation—Machinery and Equipment	
169	A	Accumulated Depreciation—Office Equipment	
170	A	Accumulated Depreciation—Leasehold Improvements	
191	A	Deposits—Security	
210	L	State Unemployment Tax Payable	
211	L	Federal Unemployment Tax Payable	
212	L	Payroll Tax Deposits	
213	L	Withholding Tax Payable	
214	L	FICA Payable	
218	L	Sales Tax Payable	
219	L	Sales Tax Exchange	
260	L	Loan Payable Stockholders	
291	L	Capital Stock	
295	L	Retained Earnings	
301	R	Media	
302	R	Production	
303	R	Retainers	
340	R	Commission Income	
345	R	Revenue	
402	E	Production Costs	
404	E	Media Costs	
419	E	Contract Labor	
420	E	Production Labor	
503	E	Auto Expense	
504	E	Auto Expense—Reimbursed	
509	E	Bank Charges	
517	E	Commissions	
519	E	Contributions	
520	E	Depreciation	

Fig. 15-1. A typical agency chart of accounts.

XYZ AGENCY

Chart of Accounts

Account	Type	Account description	Tax line #
525	E	Dues and Subscriptions	
529	E	Entertainment—Promotion	
537	E	Insurance—General	
538	E	Insurance—Group	
540	E	Interest	
545	E	Legal and Accounting	
547	E	Licenses and Taxes	
550	E	Medical Reimbursement	
552	E	Miscellaneous	
557	E	Office Supplies	
559	E	Payroll—Officers	
560	E	Payroll—Administrative	
562	E	Payroll—Other	
563	E	Payroll Taxes	
565	E	Profit-Sharing Expense	
566	E	Pension Plan Expense	
567	E	Penalties	
568	E	Postage and Delivery	
570	E	Professional Fees	
571	E	Rent	
573	E	Repairs and Maintenance	
585	E	Telephone	
587	E	Travel	
593	E	Utilities	
605	R	Sale of Auto	
608	R	Loss on Investment	
609	R	Gain on Investment	
610	R	Interest Income	
612	R	Miscellaneous Income	
615	R	Sales Tax Commission	
802	E	Federal Income Tax	
803	E	State Income Tax	

A = Asset; L = Liability; R = Revenue; E = Expense.

Fig. 15-1. (Continued)

XYZ AGENCY

Statements of Revenues Collected and Expenses Paid
Cash Basis for the Periods Indicated

	1 Month ended Mar. 31, 19XX	Percent of total revenue	10 Months ended Mar. 31, 19XX	Percent of total revenue
Total Revenues	$101,087	100.00	$967,947	100.00
Total Cost of Sales	23,335	23.08	411,223	42.48
Gross Margin	$ 77,752	76.92	$556,724	57.52
Operating Expenses				
Auto Expense	$ 680	0.67	$ 12,590	1.30
Contributions	25	0.02	85	0.01
Depreciation	1,530	1.51	15,300	1.58
Dues and Subscriptions	63	0.06	848	0.09
Entertainment—Promotion	1,494	1.48	16,040	1.66
Insurance—General	1,208	1.20	6,420	1.66
Insurance—Group	0	0.00	12,221	1.26
Legal and Accounting	375	0.37	3,465	0.36
Licenses and Taxes	70	0.07	3,774	0.39
Miscellaneous	32	0.03	1,449	0.15
Office Supplies	119	0.12	2,276	0.24
Payroll—Officers	17,033	16.85	149,712	15.47
Payroll—Administrative	4,625	4.58	40,070	4.14
Payroll—Other	3,366	3.33	43,949	4.54
Payroll Taxes	2,318	2.29	15,448	1.60
Profit-Sharing Expense	250	0.25	275	0.03
Pension Plan Expense	250	0.25	418	0.04
Postage and Delivery	3,581	3.54	11,030	1.14
Rent	8,706	8.61	43,485	4.49
Repairs and Maintenance	468	0.46	6,105	0.63
Telephone	1,691	1.67	10,868	1.12
Travel	0	0.00	(8)	0.00
Utilities	182	0.18	2,449	0.25
Total Operating Expenses	$ 48,066	47.55	$398,269	41.15
Income (Loss) after Operating Expenses	$ 29,686	29.37	$158,455	16.37
Other Income (Expenses)				
Interest Income	1,159	1.15	12,629	1.30
Sales Tax Commission	43	0.04	380	0.04
Federal Income Tax	0	0.00	(5,486)	(0.57)
State Income Tax	0	0.00	(2,000)	(0.21)
Total Other Income (Expense)	$ 1,202	1.19	$ 5,523	0.56
Net Income (Loss)	$ 30,888	30.56	$163,978	16.93

Fig. 15-2. A typical financial statement generated from information taken from the chart of accounts.

decision process a lot easier. However, most decisions on which outside services get paid during tight money periods will depend on which services you need the most at the time.

The Income Section

Often, income is shown in a breakdown that includes sales, cost of sales, and gross profit. This breakdown will not provide enough information for good control of agency growth. In the section of the chart of accounts shown, account numbers 101 through 345 and 605 through 615 are designed to show the source of income by media, production, fees, and agency services as well as miscellaneous income. By this method of itemization, you will know not only the total gross profit but also where those profits came from and how much.

Operating Expenses

The operating expenses of the agency are itemized by account numbers 402 through 593 and 802 through 803 on the chart of accounts.

Direct Expenses

Direct expenses must be separated from those needed to run the agency if you want to know the true cost of servicing your clients.

Nonoperating Income and Expenses

Nonoperating income and expenses are also itemized on the chart of accounts to help provide the information that will show a more accurate picture of the agency's operations. In summary, the chart of accounts shown may appear to provide more information than you actually need in a start-up situation. It is recommended that you install a full chart of accounts in your accounting procedures anyway and as the business progresses, expand or reduce the controls to meet your specific needs.

16

Billing Procedures

Billing the Client

Proper record-keeping and accounting procedures will help simplify your billing. Using and keeping time sheets, job orders, purchase orders, media orders, tear sheets, and so on, are absolutely essential not only for accurate billing, but also because these records are your back-up data that clients may insist on seeing, especially if you bill in advance for media or other purchases. By keeping a record of every expense and commitment you incur on behalf of a client, along with proof of publication and broadcast, and keying those records to each job for each client, you will have the billing support you will need to satisfy a client's request for back-up verification, as well as for your own use.

If your client-agency agreement calls for verification of charges and the keeping of backup records, original invoices, tear sheet files, and so on, it is recommended that you keep these records in audit condition with additional copies just in case the records you give the client are not returned. It would be best to include an "inspection of records" provision in the contract that the client or an authorized representative view these records in your office during ordinary business hours.

Billing the Agency Fee

Unless your client-agency agreement calls for quarterly or semiannual fee billing, the fixed retainer agency fees for services should be billed promptly at the first of every month for the services that are to be provided that month. The fee should be payable by the client by the tenth of the month.

Some client-agency agreements call for special fee arrangements. One such arrangement might be combining or applying fees with or against media commissions. Another might be combining or applying fees with or against production charges and markups. Whatever the arrangements are, if the agency fee is tied in with media and/or production, it should be billed at the same time you bill for those charges as it relates directly to them.

Note: In some states, professional fees can be exempt from the state sales tax if they are invoiced separately and worded properly so as to exclude taxable services such as production costs and labor costs. Consult with your accountant or tax attorney for proper wording and advice.

Billing for Production

The cost of production materials, services, and markups should be billed for upon the completion of each production job (usually at the end of each month)—or if cash discounts are earnable—upon receipt of supplier invoice. Invoices should be submitted in an itemized format. As mentioned above, if verification of costs is part of your agreement with the client, proof of charges billed to you by your suppliers of outside purchases should be attached to each invoice.

There may be times when production projects take longer than a month to complete. In such a case, you should send partial billing for those jobs each month until they are completed.

Invoicing the client in advance on certain production charges has become standard practice in agency billing procedures. Often when an agency is using a new supplier (one with which the agency has no credit history), that supplier will require some sort of advance payment as a show of good faith. It might be half up front and the balance on completion and delivery. Or in the case of agency commitments that involve large amounts of money, the supplier may require a payment schedule of one-third before the supplier starts production, one-third on delivery of a proof by the supplier, and the final one-third upon completion and delivery of the job. Television production companies and printers usually work this way. That same payment schedule should apply to the client.

When appropriate, use your resale tax number. When you do, you will not have to lay out the cash to your vendors. Instead, you will have to file the necessary forms with your state's sales-tax collection bureau on a monthly or quarterly basis, depending on state requirements.

Media Billing

When placing print and broadcast orders with most media companies, the advertising agency assumes responsibility for payment. In order for the agency to best protect itself against slow-pay or no-pay clients, it should request an advance payment on billing at the time of the insertion or start date of the schedule. When making such a request of your client, be sure to guarantee the client backup data when your invoices are received from the media. More and more agencies are billing media in advance and adjusting discrepancies when backup data is available. Your clients will realize that the agency cannot be placed in the position of financing their advertising programs and they should not object to advance billing.

If the client will not agree to advance billing, or you have reason to doubt the ability of the client to pay promptly, you should work out arrangements to have the media invoice the client directly or on a COD basis for the net cost of the media placement. Then the agency should invoice the client for the 15 percent (of gross amount) commission due the agency, assuming the client-agency compensation agreement is based on commissions.

If you are working on a fee-in-lieu-of-commissions basis with your clients, it will be to everyone's benefit to try to have all media bill the clients directly at *net*. All contracts would show your agency as the recognized agency of record, thereby justifying the 15 percent discount to the client. Such an arrangement is beneficial to the media because they may feel more secure in knowing they will be paid by the client rather than by the agency. It is beneficial to clients because when they pay media bills directly at net, they can be sure they are saving the 15 percent and they have direct-from-the-media verification of all costs. And the agency benefits by not risking its money on a doubtful client, and eliminating additional bookkeeping and bill-paying chores.

Having the media bill the client directly probably will not get the agency "off the hook" on responsibility for payment, since the agency still has to place the media order. And though your media insertion order may be very specific about the fact that you are "acting solely as agent for the client," many media companies now require the agency and client to sign a media contract that calls for dual responsibility for payment.

Whether your primary reason for advance billing is client concern or not, all media costs should be billed sufficiently in advance of your payment date to media to enable you to take advantage of all available cash discounts.

Billing Adjustments

All billing or rate adjustments should be credited or charged to the client on the first billing date after the agency has been invoiced by its supplier, or as soon afterward as is practical. Attach verification of these adjustments to your invoice.

Passing Discounts On to Clients

Cash discounts earned on agency purchases made on behalf of a client—including but not limited to media, art, printing, and mechanical work—should be passed on to the client, provided the client has complied with agency billing procedures and there is no overdue indebtedness to the agency at the time of billing.

Treat Your Invoices
as You Would Your Ads

Make sure your invoices are itemized in format and as descriptive as possible. Have them proofed for typos and accuracy. Be sure they are neat in appearance and easy to read. Address them to the proper person at the client's office who will okay your invoices for payment.

If you are charging for purchases ordered at the last minute by someone working for the client and you processed the order without a purchase order, identify the charge in your description along with the name of the individual who placed the order and the date it was placed.

Qualifying New Accounts Fiscally

Checking out the credit of new client prospects *before* they become clients will save you a lot of aggravation as well as possible legal and collection costs later.

Credit information on prospective or existing clients can be obtained from various sources, such as Dun & Bradstreet and TRW. You can become a subscriber to these services by paying a yearly fee, though membership is not always required to get the information you will need.

Calling the former advertising agency that serviced the account (if there was one) can be very helpful in giving you a good idea as to what you can expect from this client. Just make certain that you can rely on the word of a former agency and that it is not giving you misleading information to "get back" at a former account.

If you can find out which bank the prospect uses, your bank can inquire to verify average balances. If their average balance is below what you expect their billing to be, stay away or work strictly on a cash-in-advance basis.

Media reps and other suppliers that call on the advertiser can also provide you with important information regarding the prospective account's payment habits. Here, too, keep an open mind. If you get a negative report, it could mean the advertiser has dropped the supplier in favor of a competitive company, and the response you are getting could be based on "sour grapes."

The most meaningful information for you to find out is the advertiser's record of payment. A prompt payer is what you are looking for. If the account is slow or very slow, or has a history of lawsuits concerning payments, stay away or work out a cash-in-advance arrangement.

Interpreting Invoice Terms

Terms are usually anywhere from net 10 days to net 30 days. As with most businesses, agencies may apply interest to balances not paid by the due date. Provisions for interest should be spelled out in the client-agency agreement, and agreed to by both parties.

Net 10 days. Does this mean 10 days from the date on the invoice, 10 days from the date it was mailed, or 10 days from the date the invoice was received? Even with the fastest-paying accounts, getting invoices approved and processed and having checks cut and mailed could take 2 weeks. It is more likely you will be paid within 30 days of the invoice mailing date. This is normal and should not create a drain on your funds. But 30 days is the limit. After that, contact the client and ask for payment. And, by the way, don't procrastinate. The money belongs to you and you are liable for payments you must make against those funds.

Clients That Use Your Money for Their Business

Some clients slow-pay their agencies as long as they can in order to use those funds for their own purposes. If you allow them to do it, you in effect have become their banker, and you are "giving them" short-term loans at little or no interest.

Other clients are slow-pay because they are constantly short of funds. In this case, the ones who get paid first are usually the creditors who make the most noise most often.

Don't be embarrassed about making noise, either. This kind of account is probably into a last-ditch attempt to save itself with a strong ad campaign. Chances are it won't last very long as a client or as an entity in the field. So the quicker you get your money and concentrate on servicing your good-paying accounts, the better off you'll be.

Then there are the clients who come up with a myriad of reasons why they can't pay you right away. One is that they never received your invoice in the first place. Or it was mislaid and they never had a chance to call you to get a copy. Or it's somewhere in the office waiting to be approved and as soon as the person doing the approval gets back from Europe, he or she will put it through. Or you'll have to send another invoice with proper backup attached. Or one item seems to be priced incorrectly and as soon as that's straightened out the rest of the bill will be paid. Do yourself a big favor: Get tough and demand payment. The worst that can happen is that you'll anger the client and lose the account, which may turn out to be for the best.

Collection Procedures

In Chapter 26, "Agency Compensation," we go through the various collection procedures that your agency can use to collect delinquent funds. However, sometimes a normally good-paying account is slow making some payments because the paperwork did not go through the payment cycle as quickly as usual for one reason or another. If this occurs, try not to lose your cool and become a screaming creditor. A friendly call from your bookkeeper to the client's bookkeeper may be all that's needed to get your payment.

If the friendly call doesn't work, it will be necessary for agency management to get involved. Try using the tack that the client, who has always been a fast-paying account, has never been this late, and you are concerned that perhaps the agency invoice "has been lost or misplaced." This approach will probably produce positive results. If there is no payment forthcoming, call again and try to get a personal meeting with the client and a definite date for payment. If that doesn't work either, the next course of action should be your asking for a payment plan. If the client does not offer one, reply that all client schedules in progress or ordered are being canceled and you are turning this matter over to your attorney for proper legal action.

Each step in attempting to collect what is owed to you, up to the time you bring in your attorney, should be by direct conversation, either by phone or in person. Leave the letter writing to your attorney, whose first letter should offer the client 10 days to arrange for a payment schedule before litigation procedures start. If no payment schedule is offered by the client, start litigation immediately.

Being sued is costly, time-consuming, and embarrassing. And while some clients may act as though they actually welcome a lawsuit and go through it all the time, most do not and will probably offer to settle before the matter gets to court.

When you get to this stage, if you have not already resigned the account, assume that your agency will be dropped by the client. If you hear that another "lucky" agency has been selected to handle the advertising, you might want to put on your "good Samaritan" hat and alert the agency about their new client. If you'd rather not do that, consider "leaking" information concerning your legal action against the advertiser to the trade.

Depending on how much you are owed, and how long it may take to collect it (if ever) through normal legal channels, you may want to engage a collection agency or go through Small Claims Court yourself, rather than use an attorney. Most states allow claims up to $1500 and some even higher. It is a simple process to file a small claims action, and it costs relatively little compared with the fee your attorney will charge or the percentage of the total collected that a collection agency will charge. If the court rules in your favor, collection is still up to you. Should the debtor not pay in spite of the court ruling, you may get an attachment on the debtor's bank account or other tangible items, equal to the full amount owed plus court and filing costs.

Part 4 Action Checklist

- ✔ It is essential that you keep accurate, complete, and separate records for your business that clearly establish income, deductions, credits, employee information, and everything else required by federal, state, and local law.

- ✔ At the time you establish your business, establish which method of accounting (cash or accrual) you will use and how you will keep your books and records. Get professional advice if you are not knowledgeable in this area.

- ✔ Deposit business receipts in a separate bank account. Establish a petty-cash fund for minor expenses.

- ✔ Keep records of all business expenses. Make disbursements by check, if possible.

- ✔ By keeping job tickets, purchase orders, invoices, and delivery receipts, you will have a stage-by-stage record of billable elements of each job.

- ✔ Maintain employee payroll tax records for at least 4 years after the tax becomes due or is paid.

- ✔ The federal government requires specific information on employees pertaining to income tax withheld, social security tax records, and federal unemployment tax records. You should be familiar with the requirements.

- ✔ Know when the statutes of limitations expire on records you are keeping.

- ✔ Keep your accounts receivable, accounts payable, payroll records, tax payments, and reports up to date—if not daily, certainly weekly and monthly.

- ✔ Try to familiarize yourself with the language of financial formulas and definitions. It will help you understand your income statements better.

✓ Keep a chart of accounts. Not only will it give you a clear picture of how your business is doing on a month-to-month basis; it will also provide the information needed for your balance sheet and income statement and will detail your operating, direct, and nonoperating income and expenses.

✓ Bill for agency fees on the first of each month unless your client-agency agreement calls for another schedule.

✓ Invoice for all media costs sufficiently in advance of your payment date to media to permit prepayment of those media bills and/or so you can take advantage of all cash discounts allowed.

✓ Bill for production materials and services on completion of the production job (usually at the end of each month)—unless the job takes months to complete. In that case, send partial bills until it is completed.

✓ Whenever possible (if required by your client-agency agreement), attach proof of billed charges from agency suppliers to your client's invoice. That also includes media bills, media tear sheets, proof of broadcast affidavits, media insertion orders (if you are billing in advance), and agency purchase orders to suppliers.

✓ If the client is in good standing with the agency moneywise, pass along cash discounts on agency purchases made on behalf of the client.

✓ Credit or bill any rate or billing adjustments on the first billing date after the original invoicing.

✓ Be sure your invoices are self-explanatory, explicit in detail, and neatly presented in an itemized format. Have them proofread for typos and accuracy before they are sent.

✓ Don't procrastinate in pursuing collection of overage receivables. Be courteous, but relentless.

✓ Be on the lookout for regularly late payments and "payments on account," which suggest that the client doesn't have the money and is trying to have you finance its advertising. Make personal contact immediately for the balance of the money owed.

✓ Don't accept obvious stalls when a client goes in arrears. Be firm and demand a definite date for payment or a payout schedule.

✓ Don't hesitate to resign a chronically bad-paying client, cancel the advertiser's schedules immediately, and turn the matter over to your attorney for legal action, if all else fails.

Part 5

Personnel
Issues

17

No Employee Is Perfect

Embezzlement and Kickbacks

Besides making sure that what you say in your ads is legal, and worrying about clients paying their bills promptly, and keeping clients and employees happy all the time, try to find some time to watch over some in-house areas that could be tempting to unscrupulous employees: embezzlement, kickbacks, and "lost" supplies.

Because a small agency has relatively few people, there is a tendency to delegate certain functions to those individuals you trust. For example, you may select one person to be in charge of all financial matters. Or one person to be in charge of buying supplies and dealing with outside vendors. Hopefully, the people you entrust with these duties will do the job well and honestly—but the theft of agency funds and materials is more fact than it is fiction.

It All Starts with the Hiring Process

As the head of a new business with limited resources, you most probably will be limited to hiring employees from the local talent pool or local personnel placement services. Look through the classified ads in your newspaper for similar job offerings. Perhaps a salary range is indicated. If not, you might want to call one of the numbers and ask what the salary is.

Determine the skills needed for the job you have open, and the salary you can afford for someone with those skills. Try to be competitive in what you are offering. One well-paid person with proper motivation is often more productive than two or even three underpaid employees. "Beating" prospective employees down to a very low starting wage can be the inspiration they need to try to "steal" what they think they are worth.

Stay away from hiring relatives and friends. It is easier to set company and job policies and enforce those policies with strangers than it is with people you know well. It is also easier to dismiss someone who is not a relative or friend. And if you have to bring charges against someone for embezzlement or theft of agency money or property, you won't be bringing those charges against someone you may have to be in contact with again in the future.

Look out for and try to discourage office "romances." There have been times when confidential information was passed along to a "lover" by an unsuspecting person in the accounting department. Be sure to have all applicants fill out a detailed application form that includes at least three or four former job references as well as credit references. Check those references very carefully. Standard application forms are available from most stationery supply houses.

Interview the applicant personally and in depth with the application in front of you. If you pick up any differences or "get a feeling" about someone's intentions in a particular situation, try to check the applicant out further, if possible.

Always hire new employees for a specified trial period. Usually 3 months is more than enough time to get to know people well and whether or not they can handle the position. Make sure they understand that they are on a probationary basis. Do not hesitate to terminate someone you are not happy with.

See Chapters 19 and 20 for more detailed information on hiring copywriters and an art director, and Chapter 21 for information on what to look for when hiring a media buyer.

How to Help Prevent Temptation

The best approach is to have employees bonded if they are entrusted with the handling of money or supplies. This will insure you against any losses. If possible, have more than one person share the responsibilities of the job.

Have all mail sent unopened to a specified person, such as the office manager. The person who opens the mail should be responsible for distributing the mail and accounting for cash receipts for all checks received. You might want to have that person endorse all checks for deposit and post them to a deposit slip before passing them on to the accounting people for posting to the accounting records.

The approval for all check disbursements should be with someone outside the accounting department. Check disbursements should be attached to the invoices they are for. Check the amount to be paid and the name of the person or company they are being paid to.

Reconcile your bank account on a regular basis. Verify that all checks have been properly signed and recorded in the accounting records. Also, review expense and supply requests before approving them. Check previous requests and purchases to determine why certain supplies are needed so often.

Try to keep notes in an employee's file if he or she has applied for credit or if outsiders call for information. Keep an eye on the work habits of those in responsible positions. Why do they work overtime so much? Who covers for them when they are on vacation? Do they talk about company dealings to other employees or outsiders?

Have your CPA look over your vulnerability to embezzlement or theft and suggest ways of minimizing these risks.

Kickbacks and Paper Clips

Kickbacks by suppliers to agency employees is a widespread occurrence in the advertising business. If kickbacks are being made to one or more employees, it could mean you are not getting the best prices for the work you are giving out. Usually employees who are in the position of purchasing printing, specialty items, office and art supplies, outside creative services, and to a lesser extent media may be offered money as an inducement to get your business.

Possible kickbacks could come from:

- Printers
- Office and art suppliers
- Engravers, color separators, and paper supply houses
- Display fabricators and designers
- Photographers
- Actors, actresses, models, announcers, and musicians
- Free-lance artists, copywriters, and media buyers
- Commercial producers and jingle mills
- Travel agents, trade show producers, and convention managers

Kickbacks are not easy to detect. They are not always in the form of cash. A kickback could be a free weekend at a resort or free tickets to a show that are given to your media buyer by a radio station rep.

Try to discourage vendors from giving holiday gifts to your employees. You might want to make it a company policy not to accept or give any gifts for any reason.

To help discourage the practice of kickbacks, try to deal with more than one vendor for particular services. Always get at least three competitive bids on every order you are giving out, whether it be a purchase for a client or one for the agency. Keep an eye out for employees who become "chummy" with vendors. Try to change vendors on a fairly consistent basis. Go over all vendor bills carefully. Sometimes you may spot a notation that would indicate that someone in your office is on "the take."

When it comes to employees walking off with office supplies, keep in mind that most employees do not consider taking a pen or paper clips or transparent tape a crime, especially if it's off their own desk. Still, the cost of replacing these items can be substantial when you multiply the number of items taken by the frequency and number of people doing the taking.

Periodically go over your bills for in-office supplies to see if there are any purchases that are showing up more often than they should be. It should be a matter of company policy to explain to all new employees that every dollar spent replacing a lost or "acquired" office item is a dollar less that the agency has to spend on raises, bonuses, better working conditions, and other benefits to employees.

Employee Relations

The foundation of good employee relations is a sound personnel policy which commits a corporation to providing regular work, good working conditions, fair compensation, opportunity for advancement, recognition of accomplishment, good supervision, opportunity for self-expression, and desirable benefits to employees.

An employee relations program cannot gain the goodwill and understanding of employees of a corporation which underpays, overworks, plays favorites, and disregards the welfare of its employees. Close coordination between the employees and management is essential in effective employee communication.

Employees are interested in information about the company—its background and present organization, how products are made and used, policies which affect them, information about changes in methods, chances for advancement, the outlook for the business and the prospects for steady work, the company's income and its profits and losses, and the possibilities of layoffs.

Communication with employees must function as a two-way system from management to workers and from employees to management. Written memos should be used to minimize the distortions of meaning that sometimes occur in oral communication.

Communicating Policies and Practices to Employees

To ensure that employees understand its philosophy, policies, and practices, a corporation must carry on communication procedures to inform employees and give them a way to express their views about company affairs.

Employees should be given information about company practices in which they have a personal interest: employment, working conditions, fringe benefits, sales, new techniques and methods, research and development, corporate finances, wage negotiations, expansion, payroll, personnel, promotions, and other matters affecting their work.

Failure to inform employees about corporate policy and developments affecting their interests leads to misunderstanding, false rumors, and criticism. If employees are not informed about matters that concern them, they make their own assumptions (which are often false) or they listen to outside sources that provide inaccurate information.

Part 5 Action Checklist

- ✔ When going through the hiring process, determine the skills needed for the position and the compensation you can afford for someone with those skills.
- ✔ Check out the classified to see what similar jobs are going for. Try to stay competitive with your offer.

- ✔ Avoid hiring friends and relatives. It is easier to enforce company policies or dismiss people if you do not know them well.
- ✔ Check references carefully. Find out why the person left his or her last position.
- ✔ Interview the applicant personally with the application in front of you.
- ✔ Hire all new employees on a trial basis—usually 3 months. Make sure they understand it is a trial period.
- ✔ If possible, have employees bonded if they are entrusted with financial matters.
- ✔ Have one person responsible for handling mail and opening correspondence to your company.
- ✔ Have someone outside the accounting department approve check disbursements. Each check should be attached to the invoice it is for.
- ✔ Reconcile your bank account regularly. Review expense and supply requests.
- ✔ To help discourage kickbacks to employees, use more than one vendor for a particular service. Get at least three competitive bids on every job given out.
- ✔ Periodically check your office supply bills for purchases that show up more often than they should.
- ✔ Keep employees informed about what is going on in the company, fringe benefits, new techniques, promotions, and other matters that affect their jobs. Written memos help avoid distortions of meaning.
- ✔ Employees who are not informed about matters that concern them may make false assumptions about what is happening with the company.

Part 6

Agency Departments and Their Functions

18

The Traffic Department

Just What Is a Traffic Department?

In a sense, the traffic department is the heart and lifeblood of the agency. The main function of this department is to ensure that from the moment a new job is opened to the time it is completed and delivered, all the elements and materials involved with that job flow through the agency in an orderly manner, on time, and within the approved budget.

The traffic department's functions actually encompass the coordinating and administering of many phases of many projects. Personnel in this department should have the ability to keep overall goals and priorities in focus. They should have a good working knowledge of production materials and techniques involved in the creation process, and the time elements involved in order to complete the many different tasks included in the production of advertisements and collateral pieces.

The traffic function requires the balancing of client needs, creative and production capabilities, and conflicting priorities elsewhere within the agency. It is therefore important that traffic report to those in agency management with the authority to resolve conflicts in priorities that may occur within several departments.

The account executive working with the client is responsible for coordinating agency capabilities with client needs. It is also the responsibility of the account executive to establish creative objectives, budgets, special requirements (such as legal requirements and copy), and deadline dates for every job, and to secure approvals for both creative and production costs on each job.

Starting a Job

The initial input of information that goes into every new job must be complete in content and understandable. The account executive gives the traffic department all the input for the job, which is opened by the traffic department with an assigned job number. Traffic will then check all specifications for production materials required, verifying input information, making up schedules (including allowing time for client approval and deadlines), and finally distributing actual materials to the pertinent creative personnel and copies of job work orders to media, production, accounting, and account executives.

Following Up on Each Job

Each job work order should include deadlines and other timing requirements provided by the traffic department. One of the main reasons that agencies lose clients is missed deadlines. The traffic follow-up to make sure the various production elements are on time can help solve this problem. In many agencies, the traffic department circulates a list of timing recommendations and requirements on various production tasks, thereby helping eliminate or at least minimize the danger of getting off the time schedule.

By providing the creative personnel with copies of the traffic and production due dates at least 2 days prior to each job's due date, the creative department can give traffic advance notice if the schedules cannot be met. Traffic can then reschedule or reassign that job. But it comes down to the people in all departments working in harmony, so that all jobs flowing through the shop can be expedited in the most creative, efficient, and timely manner.

At the time when layout and copy are received by traffic from creative, these materials should have already been shown to the account executive to make sure that they conform to the needs and desires of the client.

After traffic receives the layout and copy, they are sent to those employees involved in job estimating. When an estimate is completed, traffic turns the estimate, layout, and copy over to the account executive for presentation to the client. When outside charges are involved, such as printing or television production, the traffic department should get at least three estimates of cost for the client. Some agencies require as many as six estimates before they give out any outside work.

The account executive is responsible for securing client approvals on original and revised estimates.

The creative and production departments have the responsibility to cooperate with traffic to set time schedules and cost estimates and to notify traffic about anything that will significantly alter either. It is also their responsibility to assist traffic in the preparation of a regular job status report.

Creative and production should never perform work outside the agency traffic system. It is also dangerous for them to give out unauthorized time or cost estimates directly to the account executive until they have been verified by estimating. It is also their responsibility to use purchase orders for all outside purchases and to notify traffic if approved estimate amounts will be exceeded. If that is the case, the account executive must notify the client that the original estimates were below what the actual cost will be. It is then up to the client to approve or disapprove the additional costs. Sometimes, because of agency error or for reasons beyond the agency's or suppliers' control, estimated costs may go up while a job is in production. If, for instance, a print job was originally estimated on a certain type of paper, but that paper is no longer available, a substitute material may be more costly. Traffic should immediately notify the account executive, who should in turn advise the client and make a decision on how to proceed.

Prepare and Update Initial Job Orders

The initial job order with information from the account executive should be considered a "first draft" that may have to be updated dozens of times before the job is complete.

Traffic coordinates with creative and production to establish scheduled due dates for all work. To do so, traffic must be aware of, and consider, existing workloads, timing requirements of new work, timing requirements to secure client approvals, publication and broadcast deadlines, and due dates required by the client (e.g., for printed matter).

As a matter of agency policy, final estimates should be prepared for all jobs and approved by the client *before* any substantial financial commitments are made or before production work sent to outside sources has begun. It is traffic's responsibility to coordinate with creative and production to prepare the estimate as quickly and accurately as possible on each job.

Traffic is responsible for follow-up to ensure that approvals have been secured at every stage of the job: copy, layout, legalities, media schedule, insertion dates, and so on. Most important, the traffic department must follow up with the account executive to be sure that the final estimate has been approved.

Traffic must know the status of each job in all its stages, and should prepare and circulate a regular production status report for all departments involved. That report becomes the focus of the weekly production status meeting attended by creative, production, and administration, at which time all concerned will attempt to develop solutions for any problems that might have come up.

Basic Traffic Forms Used

Sometimes called the active client book, the *job log* shows the work order number assigned to that job, a brief description of the job, the date it was opened, the expected completion date, and the date the job was completed and closed out. Some agencies also include the dates that estimates are approved in their logs.

Sometimes called the job starter or traffic sheet, the *job work order* includes the initial input of information provided by the account executive. It identifies and describes the job in detail, specifying exact sizes, colors, mechanical requirements of the publication or other medium, and critical due dates for copy, layout, finished production, and delivery to the final destination. The work order can also be used as a basis to establish the final budget for the job (see Figure 18-1).

The *time allowance schedule* lists various production functions and the general time it takes to complete them. With this list as a basis, it is possible to estimate

WORK ORDER

DATE JOB OPENED _____

JOB NO. _____

CLIENT: _____

DESCRIPTION OF JOB:

_____

_____

_____

_____

Newsp. Ad _____
Magazine Ad _____
Radio _____
TV _____
Billboard _____
Site Signage _____
Collateral _____
Sales Office_Exhib. _____
Other _____

OUTSIDE VENDORS: (Name, Address, Type of Service) Estimated Cost:

_____ Vendors Number _____

_____ Vendors Number _____

_____ Vendors Number _____

_____ Vendors Number _____

Copy Due	Layout Due	Mechan. Due	Del. to Public.		Order Space	Order Veloxes	Engravings by	Est. Prod. Cost

PUBLICATION	ISSUE	CLOSING	SPACE	SCREEN	DIMENSIONS

KRIEFF ADVERTISING

Fig. 18-1. Example of a job starter or job work order.

the time it will take to complete a particular job. This schedule should be updated periodically, taking into account new production methods that may be instrumental in cutting production time.

Since client approvals are normally required at various stages of a job and each client has different requirements, levels of approval, and turnaround time, the account executive should make known any specifics that apply to the job on *client information sheets*. These might include the names of client personnel authorized to approve estimates, copy, and layouts. The information can be attached to the job work order or written directly on the work order if space permits.

Estimate forms show the amount of money that the agency is estimating it will cost to complete the job or various phases of the job. One job might require a dozen or more estimates before the agency can estimate the total cost. For instance, in the production of a four-color brochure, there will be estimates on the layout, copy, mechanical production, photography, art illustrations, model and talent fees, color separations, printing, shipping, phone calls, fax and courier charges, and more. Agencies may use many kinds of estimate forms. Most all use print estimates. There are also forms for television production and radio production, for original music, for photography sessions, and more. Whatever the nature of the estimate form, it will spell out all pertinent information concerning the job and its costs. It lets the agency know what has to be spent, and gives the agency the information it needs to negotiate purchases. If all departments in the agency stay within client-approved estimates, budgets will not be exceeded and the agency will avoid the leading cause of agency-client split-ups: lack of cost-consciousness. There is no excuse for omitting an estimate from agency procedures, even though the particular kind of job may be done often (see Figure 18-2).

The *purchase order* is one of the agency's key controls for making certain that the right costs are assigned to the right job. Also, the purchase order serves as a backup when invoicing a client without the actual bill from the supplier (see Figure 18-3).

The *job status report* lists all open and in-progress jobs, shows where they stand in relation to scheduled due dates, and indicates any problems that require agency or client management action.

Summary of Procedures, Responsibilities, and Interrelationships Between Traffic and Other Departments

The following outline of traffic procedures is designed to provide all departments in an agency with an overview of the responsibilities of and interrelationships between traffic and other departments. It should assist all departments in increasing their rate of efficiency and production and, therefore, will increase the efficiency and production of the agency as a whole.

1. Initiating a Job
   a. The account executive opens the job with basic input information, including directives, reference materials, mandatories, budgets, target dates, and media (whether tentative or definite). In the case of new ads, ad campaigns, or new collateral, preliminary signed client approval should accompany job starters.
   b. The traffic department processes the job starter by assigning a job number, checking all specifications for production materials required, verifying the account executive's input information, making up schedules, and finally distrib-

PRINT
Estimate

Krieff Advertising

3854 Sheridan Street, Hollywood, Florida 33021 • Tel: (305) 987-9973 (Dade) 940-9973

PRINTING SPECIFICATIONS   Date_____

CLIENT:_____JOB NUMBER:_____

IDENTIFICATION OF PIECE:_____.

DATE DUE:_____

QUANTITY:_____

NUMBER OF PAGES:_____ COVER:_____ SELF-COVER:_____

TYPE OF STOCK:_____COATED: UNCOATED:

SIZE OPEN:_____No.FOLDS_____SIZE FOLDED:_____

SPECIAL FOLDS:_____

DIE CUT(S):_____ SCORING:_____

No. OF COLORS (1st SIDE):_____ 2nd SIDE:_____

No. OF HALFTONES:_____ SIZES:_____

No. COLOR SEPS:_____ SIZES:_____

TYPE OF COLOR ART - TRANSPARANCIES:_____ REFLECTIVE:_____

SPECIAL SCREENS/ DUO-TONES,etc.: _____

BLEED:_____ STITCHING (Type):_____

SPECIAL PACKING INSTRUCTIONS:_____

DELIVER TO: _____

PRICE:_____   PRICE FOR REPRINTS:_____

NOTES:

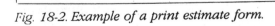

Fig. 18-2. Example of a print estimate form.

PURCHASE ORDER

To _____

_____

_____

Purchase Order No.

Date _____

Krieff CA **Advertising**

3854 Sheridan Street, Hollywood, Florida 33021 • Tel: (305) 987-9973 (Dade) 940-9973

CLIENT:

Delivery Date _____   Job Number _____

Terms _____

Ship Via _____

Advise immediately on receipt of this order if delivery date cannot be met. Krieff Advertising will not be liable for materials delivered late unless otherwise approved for extension in writing by both parties.

DESCRIPTION:

The above is approved and authorized by _____   Date: _____

Client-Authorized Agent

Note: Please invoice separately for each job in duplicate. Itemize all charges on invoice. All materials supplied or purchased by Krieff Advertising or its clients will remain the property of the Firm and must be returned or replaced. Acceptance of order denotes acceptance of the terms & conditions of this purchase order.

Fig. 18-3. Example of a purchase order form.

uting actual materials to the pertinent creative personnel and copies of job starters to media, production, accounting, account servicing, and management.

2. Job Follow-Up

   a. Traffic provides creative personnel with a copy of daily traffic and production schedule due dates 2 days in advance of due dates. If dates cannot be met, traffic should be notified immediately so that rescheduling or reassignment can be made.

   b. At the time when layout and copy is received by traffic from creative, materials will have already been seen and approved by the account executive. All parties up to that point should have initialed the work to verify who was involved.

   c. When approval of above materials by agency personnel is secured by traffic, layout and copy are then given to the production or estimating department for estimation of costs. Estimates are prepared as soon as possible, according to the nature of the materials. When an estimate is completed, traffic turns the estimate, layout, and copy over to the account executive for presentation to the client. Before estimates are presented to the client, traffic and production should verify bottom-line figures before markup.

3. Production of Materials

   a. After the account executive has secured client approval, he or she will supply traffic with any additional or new information concerning the job, along with a definite media schedule for print advertising, and whether collateral, definite delivery date, and instructions for shipping are required. A client-signed approval must accompany all information and materials at this time—before any production can begin. If for one reason or another the client approval is not available, authorization by the account executive or agency management is needed so that a credit limit to the client can be established. (*Note:* If materials are rejected and need to be revised or redesigned, steps a, b, and c of item 2 are to be repeated.)

   b. Traffic processes materials to pertinent creative personnel for specification of typography, photography sessions, illustrations, and so on. At this point, the schedule for mechanical is established, so creative can give materials to the art studio for completion of the mechanical stage of the job. When copy is set in house or sent out to be typeset, galleys are turned in to traffic by either the art studio or the production department for stamping and approval by the copywriter and art director before the actual pasteup is completed.

   c. When the mechanical is completed, the art studio turns it over to traffic, which gets approval from the copywriter, art director, and account executive. The account executive then secures approval of the mechanical from the client.

   d. When the mechanical is approved by the client, the account executive turns it back to traffic for production of necessary materials for print advertising or, if it is collateral, for release to the printer or outside supplier involved in the project. (*Note:* If revisions are required at this time, steps a, b, and c of item 3 are to be repeated.)

   e. At the time when materials such as progressives and proofs are received by traffic from production, traffic secures approval from the art director and the copywriter. After such materials have been approved, traffic instructs production to proceed and forward whenever possible. In the case of blue lines from a printer, approval is also secured from the account executive, who then gets approval from the client. With client approval achieved, traffic instructs production to complete and ship the project. (*Note:* If there are blue-line changes, steps a, b, c, and d of item 3 are to be repeated.)

   f. When production completes all materials, the job jacket and samples are given to traffic for final completion of the project.

4. Completion of Job

   a. When the job jacket and samples are received by traffic from production, the work order (also sometimes called the job opener or traffic sheet) is pulled and marked completed in the job log. This copy goes to accounting with sample of produced material for final billing. Accounting returns the work order to traffic after completion of posting.

Traffic and Production Tips That Can Save Your Agency Money

- When ordering production negatives or color separations from your color house or printer, order several extra copies. Duplicates are fairly inexpensive if they are ordered at the same time as an original. If your client decides to run a particular ad months later in different magazines with the same mechanical requirements, it is simple to go the the file and pull out a ready-made negative or color separation of the ad.

- If the same ad runs in the same publication over a period of time, it is not necessary to send new negatives or seps each time the ad runs. Just send in your insertion order to the publication and make a note on it to reuse the materials from the previous time it ran. Your art will be on file and the publication will reproduce your ad as your insertion order directs. The cost of running the ad will be the same, but your production costs will be eliminated.

- Most publications keep advertising art for a period of 12 months, whether an ad is repeated or not. Suppose a client runs an ad in a magazine in July, then wishes to run it again in October. It is a simple matter for the advertising agency to send an insertion order without any accompanying art, but with a notation that the magazine already has the art on file.

- Suppose you create a great ad for a client and run it in various publications. Then suppose you lose the account and the advertiser decides to rerun the ad on its own. The publication will charge the advertiser full retail price for the space, since the client does not qualify for the 15 percent agency discount. Even though your agency does not place the ad, the publication is obligated to pay you commissions on the space each time the ad is rerun by the client at full noncommissionable rates.

Computerized Traffic

An agency's traffic procedures can be very detailed. There are many software systems designed for advertising agencies that can easily handle the normal clerical procedures associated with traffic. If your agency is at the beginning stages of computerization, an inexpensive computer with a word processing program can be helpful. A word processor gives you the means to set up and maintain the job status reports and is helpful for setting up and revising estimates, timing guidelines, and client profiles. A word processor or computer can also assist you in keeping track of hundreds, maybe thousands of pieces of artwork, copy, and other materials for your clients. These systems are covered along with other computer advantages in later chapters.

19

The Copywriting Department

Nothing is more frail or more delicate than an idea. Add something to it and it's out of balance. Take something away from it and you may take away its effectiveness. Make even a slight change and the whole meaning can be changed.

Coming up with a good idea, one that will attract an audience is part of what writing copy is all about. Putting that idea into just the right words that will make the audience take action is what good copywriting is all about.

The Copywriter

Have you ever wondered how writers get most of the important information about a product or service into the first paragraph of copy? Or how some people can write a headline that stops readers dead in their tracks? Or how someone can condense pages and pages of descriptive verbiage into 50 words of elegant, clever, flowing copy?

These are some of the challenges facing the copywriter, the person who writes the copy for the advertisements your agency will produce. Whether it be copy for the medical field, insurance and financial services, used cars, fast food, or industrial machinery, a good copywriter is expected to be an expert in every field, and effective with every word.

A copywriter is also expected to write for broadcast as well as for print. He or she should know proper grammar and style, and should be as effective with the words used for a catalog or collateral piece as with the words used for a billboard that drivers pass at 50 miles per hour.

Will Your Copy Department
Be In House or Free Lance?

It's a fact that many new ad agency owners are creative people themselves. Some are veterans of big agencies. This is a help when starting your own business, since creativity is the essence of effective advertising.

If you are an idea person, or a copywriter in particular, you may be able to handle this function yourself, providing you don't get bogged down in other essential administrative and account contact areas.

However, if you feel that as the owner of the business you should involve yourself primarily in the sales end of building up of your new agency, you will need to hire a copywriter or creative director who can write copy. Or you can elect to hire a free-lance writer for those times you will need creative writing.

Since you are in the process of building your agency, it is important, especially in the beginning, that you have the agency's creative talent available at all times. An investment in creative staff personnel is essential in establishing the creative capabilities of your new company in the community, as well as in setting up the proper internal procedures for running an efficient operation. If you decide to go the free-lance route, the best advice is to go with a highly experienced person.

Advertising for an Advertising Copywriter

In filling the copywriter position, keep in mind that what you are looking for is a good idea person. An idea person could have a background in art or writing or both. In this case, you are interested in someone who is primarily a writer and who can work with an artist to develop the right mix of words and graphics that will effectively sell your client's products.

As the head of a start-up agency hoping to get off the ground quickly, you can't afford to run a training camp for inexperienced writers—or anyone, for that matter. Trying to save money on someone just out of school can be a very costly mistake. This is not to say that a young, inexperienced copywriter can't be a great one—or that you should not give someone inexperienced, but with great ideas, a chance to break into the business. However, someone with maturity and experience will not only be able to serve your clients' needs but also, through his or her experience, will add to your ability to get new business.

The salary for a good writer with at least 5 years of agency experience is a negotiable item. By watching the classified ads and calling personnel agencies or other ad agencies, you can get a pretty good idea of what the going range is in your area.

Since many of the more experienced creative people are long-time subscribers to or readers of advertising trade publications, this is a good place to start advertising for your copywriter. Other outlets such as the classified "professional help wanted" sections of local and regional newspapers and local city magazines, as well as the Department of Labor Relations, might be excellent places to find the right person or people for your agency.

Sometimes, high-priced creative people register with aggressive headhunters. This is a good, but costly way to find talented people, since you will probably be required to pay a fee or repay the employees you hire, if they are paying the fee.

The following are two examples of "creative" help-wanted ads:

**WE'RE AT
A LOSS FOR
WORDS**

We're an aggressive, new ad agency in need of a good copywriter/creative director. If you're as good with words as you are with concepts, if you have at least 5 years' agency copy experience, if you can handle collateral as well as ads, we want to talk to you. But first, please send your résumé to Allan Krieff at Krieff Advertising, 3854 Sheridan St., Hollywood, FL 33021, or call 987-9973

**WE NEED
A GOOD
RIGHTER**

The very best. And we'll make that writer very happy. With great accounts, challenging work, and an excellent place to live. If you're good, and this sounds more refreshing than your 9–5 job, talk to me, Allan Krieff, about joining us at Krieff Advertising in Hollywood, Florida. Don't wait, call me today at 305/987-9973

If your background is not in the creative end, you will need to know something about copywriting and how it fits in with all the other agency services. The following "crash course" in the subject will help you understand the complexities of the job and the talents necessary to fill the position of copywriter properly. It will also help you understand the "language" of the business.

Copywriting and the Print Ad

Every print advertisement is made up of several elements. Most ads use them all. They include:

- The headline or display line
- The illustration
- The body copy or text
- The slogan, trade character, seal, and other marks
- The logotype or signature

Headlines

The headline or display line that appears in most advertisements serves several functions. Along with the illustration, it is an attention-getting device. It also selects an audience by targeting the message directly to a specific group, as this line does:

"What a Man Should Know When He Buys a Hathaway Shirt." Finally, it is the key factor in getting people to read the body copy. Unfortunately, only a small percentage of those who see most advertisements read them completely. Thus the headline, because it is the part most likely to be read, is especially important, and every care must be taken to make sure that it does the job.

Illustrations

In addition to headlines, most advertisements contain illustrations. The illustration, like the headline, attracts attention, targets the audience, and stimulates interest in body copy. What is more, the illustration can be invaluable in showing the product or product use and explaining graphically certain ideas or situations that are much too cumbersome to put into words. The old saying that "one picture is worth a 1000 words" has much merit in it.

The term *illustration* as it is used in describing an ad can actually be an illustration—a drawing, painting, design, graphic, or other kind of artwork—or it can refer to a photograph.

Body Copy

Let's begin with an explanation of the word *copy*. Sometimes copy is used to refer to all the reading matter in the advertisement, including headlines, subheads, captions, and text. At other times copy refers to the completed artwork for the engraver. Everything depends on the context in which the word is being used. Frequently, the terms *body copy* and *text* are used to refer only to the copy, usually set in smaller type, in the body of the advertisement—that portion of the advertisement excluding the headline, illustrations, and logotype. Some advertisements use no body copy, but most use some, with the amount differing considerably from advertisement to advertisement. The job of body copy is to stimulate interest in the product or service or idea being advertised, create desire for it, and urge action. This is a big task and calls for the right words. Although headlines and illustrations clear the way, it is body copy that must carry the burden of the selling job.

Slogans, Trade Characters, Seals, and Other Marks

A number of different marks and devices may appear in an advertisement, including slogans, trade characters, and seals. Generally, when an advertiser uses one or more of these devices, they appear automatically in all its advertisements. For example, the Golden Arch is always included in McDonald's Restaurant advertisements. The automatic use of these elements in the advertisement does not diminish their importance. In fact, as marks and trade characters become known around the world, often the mark or character shown by itself without any reference to the name of the company is enough to get positive recognition. Disney's Mickey Mouse ears and the arm and hammer of Arm & Hammer Baking Soda are examples.

Slogans.   The use of slogans is cyclical. There was a time when advertising people believed that a "snappy" slogan was at the heart of a good advertisement. But the advertising business has since become more sophisticated and has learned that it takes more than a well-turned, easy-to-remember phrase to turn prospects into customers. This is not to say that a slogan cannot be of value.

Once established (this may take considerable time), the slogan may become an easy and quick way for the consumer to remember a brand and salient brand features. Most people have little difficulty identifying brands with slogans. Today the slogan has become more of a "war cry." It is that phrase or those words that sum up the campaign, fight the competition, and, internally, give the advertiser's personnel and salespeople something to live up to—for example, "You're in good hands with Allstate." The slogan is the memorable encapsulation of the campaign theme, and hence it is tremendously important to continuity. Slogans become "logo" lines for print advertisements, "supers" for television commercials, and "tag lines" for radio. Slogans may be purposely designed, but often they come out of successful headlines.

Trade Characters.   A trade character is best described as a characterization developed from a human being, an animal, or an inanimate object made animate. Examples are the Pillsbury Doughboy, Morris the Cat, the Jolly Green Giant, and Chiquita Banana, to mention but a few. The idea behind the use of trade characters is to encourage greater identification and to provide a vehicle around which to build a promotional program. Even when an advertisement does not feature the trade character, the character often is included somewhere in the advertisement.

In addition to being used for print advertisements, trade characters have been most effectively used in television, where they can deliver animated advertising messages. They also lend themselves to good use in other promotional efforts. For example, the Michelin Tire Character has given store demonstrations, and Ronald McDonald makes personal appearances at functions and on television shows.

Like a product itself, the trade character must frequently be updated. As people's attitudes and tastes change, so do trade characters. Generally, trade characters like Charlie the StarKist Tuna reflect an image of humor and warmth. They also may be used to add credibility and authoritativeness, like Betty Crocker, who has been considered a serious adviser in home economics as well as an emotionally appealing character.

Seals.   Seals are offered by some organizations to companies whose products meet the standards established by these organizations. They are valuable to the advertiser as an endorsement by a recognized authority and give the advertiser added prestige.

Popular seals like the Good Housekeeping Seal of Approval and the Parents' Institute Seal as well as seals depicting environmentally friendly products are coveted by many advertisers. When an advertiser has obtained permission to use one or more of these seals, they generally will be included in all its advertisements. Their value is obvious. They provide an independent endorsement of the product being advertised. Unfortunately, from time to time, seals and awards of questionable integrity have been featured in advertisements. These have weakened the value of seals that are valid.

Other Marks.   Trademarks are automatically included in most advertisements. In addition, certain advertisers have other marks and devices that are put in all their advertisements, including notice of patents, copyrights, and guarantees.

Logotypes

Logotypes (logos), or signature cuts, are special designs of the name of the advertiser or product and are used repeatedly in that product's advertising. Examples of some well-known logos are Sony, MasterCard, AT&T, and *People* magazine. Most advertisers have such designs, which frequently are the same as the trademarks on the products themselves. A well-designed logotype will give the product individuality and provide for quick identification at the point of purchase. As in the case of trade characters, logos are constantly in need of updating to keep the company image up to date.

Kinds of Copy

Different advertisements are designed to overcome different problems in reaching their ultimate objective of maximizing the profits of the advertiser. There are various kinds of copy that adapt themselves to these problems:

1. In straight-line copy, the body text begins immediately to develop the headline and/or illustration idea in direct selling of the product, using its sales points in the order of their importance.
2. Narrative copy may be of two kinds:
    a. The establishment of a story or specific situation which, by its nature, will logically lead into a discussion of a product's selling points
    b. The so-called institutional type of advertising, in which the copy sells an idea, organization, service, or product, instead of presenting the selling features
3. In dialogue and monologue copy, the characters illustrated in the advertisement do the selling in their own words (testimonials, pseudo-testimonials, comic strips, and continuity panels).
4. In picture and caption copy, the advertiser's story is told by a series of illustrations or photographs and captions rather than by use of a copy block alone.
5. Gimmick copy consists of unclassified effects in which the selling power depends upon humor, poetry, foreign words, great exaggeration, gags, and other trick devices.

A single advertisement may contain more than one of these kinds of copy. An analysis of the advertising objectives usually will suggest which ones to use. As might be expected, straight-line copy is most often used, for it is applicable to most situations. A copywriter cannot afford to specialize in one type of copy, however, for he or she may be called upon to write any kind of copy and should be prepared to do so.

Friendly Persuasion

While editorial, technical, publicity, and other kinds of writing may have a variety of purposes, the main purpose of copywriting is persuasion.

There is a logical order to persuasive advertising that carries the audience to the point of favorable action. Various authorities on the art of persuasion have advanced numerous formulas for this process, but they are all fundamentally variations on a relatively simple theory: AIDA.

The AIDA theory suggests that in order to persuade, an advertisement must first attract *attention,* then create *interest,* next stimulate *desire,* and finally get *action.* There has been some criticism of the AIDA principle on the grounds that it is too academic and assumes that the reader of advertisements always responds rationally. Undoubtedly, the sophisticated copywriter recognizes that writing advertisements is not always so simple; still, this process is basic to the art of persuasion. Only after learning it can the copywriter go beyond it.

Attention

To begin with, if the copywriter is going to persuade someone to buy any product or service, he or she must first grab the attention of the person reading the newspaper or magazine, listening to the radio, watching television, or passing a billboard on the road. The best advertisements are useless if nobody notices them.

In general, there are two types of attention-getting devices. One includes external factors, such as the position of the ad in a publication, over which the copywriter has little or no control; the other involves internal factors, such as headline and illustration, which are to a large degree directly under the copywriter's control.

One important external factor is the medium in which the advertisement appears. For example, the readers of some magazines regard advertising as editorial matter. A *Cosmopolitan* magazine reader is interested in the fashions the various advertisers are showing. When advertising is closely related to editorial content, considerable attention is likely to be paid to it. On the other hand, in general-editorial magazines, in which there is little relation between the advertisements and the editorial content, advertisements elicit little spontaneous interest from readers and there is need for stronger attention-getting devices.

Size is another external factor influencing attention. Obviously, the larger the advertisement, the more likely the reader will be to notice it. Likewise, position affects attention. An advertisement appearing on the fourth (back) cover of a magazine will attract greater attention than that same advertisement appearing in an ROP (run of paper) position.

Techniques to Get Attention

News	Personal conflict
Curiosity	History
Conflict	Shock
Analogy	

A word of caution about attention-getting devices. Attention is a means of attracting readers to read the whole advertisement. Therefore, these devices should be related to the rest of the advertisement. The reader whose attention is attracted by a headline, only to find that it has little or no relation to the rest of the advertisement, is apt to be resentful. Using an illustration of a scantily clad woman in an advertisement for office furniture will disappoint the reader—who may lose interest in the copy or think it is in bad taste—and that becomes a negative reflection on the advertiser.

Because few people read advertisements in their entirety, attention-getting devices should try to include as many of the other AIDA factors as possible. If a headline, in addition to gaining attention, can also promise some benefit to the consumer and identify the advertiser, it is likely that more people seeing the advertisement will get the message. For example: "Wesson Oil is 100% pure vegetable oil," or "If you really want to lock in freshness, you really want Tupperware." In addition, the illustration can be used to call attention to the product and the package.

Interest

Ideally, attention-getting devices should lead the reader to the body copy and hold his or her interest. There is no better way of stimulating interest than by appealing to the reader's self-interest. All too often, the copywriter writes for the advertiser rather than for the consumer. The approach needed is what is referred to as the "you" attitude. Consumers are not necessarily interested in how wonderful the company is; they want to know what the product will do for them.

Some appeals to the emotions of the audience that offer the promise of reward and that are effective in sustaining interest are:

- Appeals to basic needs—food, drink, sleep, physical health, and comfort
- Appeals to emotion, feelings, and attitude
- Appeals to social motives

Desire

Having stimulated interest, the copywriter's next task is to stimulate the reader's desire for the product. The easiest way to stimulate desire is to show that the product will benefit the reader—and prove it. Again, the emphasis should be on consumer self-interest. Claims may be met with skepticism, so it is necessary to convince the reader that the advertisement's claims are valid. Not only should they be substantiated; they must also be believable.

Action

No advertisement is complete unless it "asks for the order," some kind of action on the part of those experiencing the advertisement. This may be a general call to action like: "Try it soon and see" or "Get some soon." In some cases the urge to action is explicitly stated. It can be urgent: "The sale ends tomorrow, get here today!" The copy can ask you to respond to an 800 telephone number or mail in a coupon. It can suggest that you tell or bring a friend. Using a "fear" theme, it can be an effective motivator in getting people to respond to a public service type of message, such as "Any woman can do a breast self-examination in the privacy of her home."

Length of Copy

How much copy should a copywriter write? There is little question that he or she has to capture and hold the target audience; and the longer that audience has to be held, the more likely the copywriter is going to lose it. Yet the rule "The shorter the copy the better" is not necessarily sound. There are advertisements that contain very lengthy copy and still get high readership. Perhaps a sounder rule is that copy should be as long as is necessary to tell your story but without unnecessary verbiage.

Possibly the most crucial step in the creative process is developing the campaign theme or idea. It is the heart of all the advertisements in the campaign. A good theme gives direction for developing the individual advertisements in the series. Once the theme is established, new advertisements in the campaign become variations on that theme and generally are relatively easy to develop.

In most instances the task of the copywriter is to work with other agency personnel and the advertiser to establish campaign objectives. From this set of objectives the copy platform can be developed and the copywriter can concentrate on the creation of individual advertisements.

When you consider the vast amount of money expended for advertising, and the incredible influence that advertising has had on the lives of nearly everyone in the world, you can appreciate that clearness, conciseness, and force are great considerations in writing advertisements. Words, sentences, and paragraphs, whole compositions—even punctuation marks—have concrete values in real dollars and cents. Any mistake in the proper selection of words in advertising can entail severe penalties.

Take the headline. The importance of the few words that make up the headline cannot be overestimated. Upon them often falls the task of capturing the attention of the audience and providing the stimulation for the audience to learn more. The gist of the appeal is usually contained in those four or five words, and the effectiveness of the entire advertisement may depend on how well those words are chosen.

Writing the Headline

Experts have indicated that the headline is the single most important element of the advertisement. Certainly it is an essential element in getting attention.

Types of Headlines

A headline that tells readers something they want to know about the product is known as a *news headline*. Wanting to keep up with the latest developments in any field is a very common human trait. The news headline plays upon this desire by telling the audience what is new with the product advertised. Such news should be pertinent to the product advertised and of real interest to the audience. In other words, it should show how the product will benefit the user. Here are some examples of news headlines:

"World's Only Dog Food That Makes Its Own Gravy"

"Dry Sack On-the-Rocks Changed Men's Minds About Sherry"

"New no-drip, no-break bottle"

The *advice and promise headline* advises the audience to use the advertised product and promises gratifying results if they do. It is essential, of course, that the product fulfill the promise. Examples include:

"You Get a Lot to Like With a Marlboro"

"Compare cleansers: Comet removes both food stains and pot marks better than any other leading cleanser"

A headline that deliberately conceals what the advertisement is all about is called a *curiosity headline*. The object is to get the audience to want to know more. However, if the audience is not challenged to read or listen to the copy, it is likely that the advertisement will be completely wasted, for the headline does no selling. Curiosity headlines may be divided into two categories: provocative and dramatic story.

Provocative headlines challenge the reader to read on. An example is:

"How to send your child to college for only $5000"

The dramatic story headline appeals to the rather universal interest in a good story. Examples are:

"Where did life begin?"

"Few things in life work as well as a Volkswagen"

If the objective is to single out a particular audience for the advertiser, the copywriter may use a *selective headline*. Such headlines may select the audience through the nature of the subject discussed or by addressing the particular audience. Examples of selection through the nature of the subject include:

"Feet Hurt, Burn?"

"Relieve Hemorrhoid Problems"

Headline-Writing Hints

It is rare for the copywriter to come up with the final headline on the first try. A good technique is to put all ideas down on paper. Then the copywriter can rework, combine, and refine the copy. In some instances, one headline will serve as a theme for a number of advertisements in a campaign with little or no change.

Copywriters disagree as to how long the ideal headline should be. To be sure, a short headline can be grasped more quickly as a person turns the pages of a magazine or newspaper. However, brevity can sacrifice effective statement of an idea. Subheads are additional display lines that provide the transition between the headline and the body copy. They usually amplify the main headline, and because they are generally set in smaller type, they may be considerably longer. The same kind of care must be taken in writing subheads as in writing the major headline. The importance of the headline cannot be overstated. If the headline does not do the job it should, the advertisement may be a total waste because the attention and interest of the audience will be lost.

Writing the Body Copy

In most cases the headline is written first; then the copywriter turns full attention to the body copy. Although many critics of advertising claim that copy is dashed off by copywriters with machinelike ease, this is hardly the case. Good copy requires careful and painstaking thought and knowledge.

Get the Facts, Folks

Good copy is not written in a vacuum; it happens only after the copywriter has thoroughly digested all the facts about the product, the marketing objectives, and the nature of the targeted consumer. The copywriter should become familiar with the product, use it, make comparisons with competitive products, determine the product's merits, and believe in the product.

On the other side, the copywriter must learn all he or she can about the consumer. Who are the consumers for this product? What are their attitudes? What are their buying habits? With a knowledge of the product and the consumer and an understanding of the marketing objectives, the copywriter can begin to identify what appeals can be used most effectively to persuade the consumer to buy. It is during this stage of getting the facts that the copywriter can use marketing research to find some of the answers. Good writers never assume they are typical consumers, for by the nature of their role, theirs is a very biased and distorted point of view.

Think Like a Consumer

A well-written advertisement will seem to readers to have been written for them alone. Again, this effect depends upon what is frequently referred to as the "you" attitude. The copywriter should never refer to "they" and should avoid "I" or "we."

Consumers are rather self-centered and are most concerned with their own problems. The copywriter can communicate better when writing in the language of consumers, since they can appreciate best those situations and circumstances that are similar to their own.

Basic Copywriting Guidelines

1. The first step in the creation of advertising is one that involves the intake of communication rather than the output of communication.
2. The first responsibility of the advertising writer is to:
   a. Gather the facts about the product or service to be advertised.
   b. Gather the facts about the people who buy or use it.
3. Analyze and evaluate the facts.
4. Determine which are the most important at this time and in relation to the specific objective of this particular ad.
5. The copywriter's job divides into two coequal and commingling parties:
   a. A search for ideas—the "what to say" in an advertisement that provides the brilliant solution to an advertising problem and,
   b. A search for new and different ways to express those ideas—the "how to say it" and "how to show it" techniques of preparing an advertisement that provide the brilliant execution of the ideas and copywriter wants to convey.
6. The copywriter employs three separate techniques:

    a. Copythinking
    b. Copy structure
    c. Copystyle

Copythinking

In this stage of preparing copy for an individual advertiser or a continuing campaign, the copywriter must give a great deal of thought to the product or service to be advertised, the people who will buy it, and the media in which it will be presented. The facts to be considered must be complete and true, and the evaluation of those facts must be accurate. Incorrect evaluation in the copythinking stage is a primary cause of ineffective advertising.

One of the important considerations the copywriter has to know is what the product will and will not do for the people who buy it. But first, he or she must get the facts about the people who are the buyers. Are they men or women or children or the general public as a whole? Are the women part of the work force? Which sex accounts for a larger share of the market? What age dominates? Is income a critical factor in making the purchase? Does occupation affect the purchase? Who influences the purchase? With inexpensive products like soft drinks and candy, one person usually decides. Larger purchases such as cars, TVs, and travel may involve the decisions of two or more buyers. Are the best prospects in the upper-, middle-, lower-income bracket? Is the advertising to be directed to a specific ethnic or inner city market? How do prospective customers buy this product—seasonally, frequently, on impulse, or only after considerable thought and planning?

The next step in the copythinking process is to gather all the facts about the product.

- *What is it made of?*   Even a service like an insurance company or an airline has ingredients; for example, Japan Air Lines uses the cultivated background of the hostesses in their ads.

- *How well is the product made?*   Maytag washers and dryers use a copy theme emphasizing the repairperson who never gets to service any machines Maytag makes.

- *What makes the product superior?*   All football teams have 11 men—some become Super Bowl Champs? The reason may be skilled players and skilled coaches.

- *What does the product or service do?*   A copywriter's task is to determine the primary satisfaction or need the product fills and not allow lesser ones to obscure it. For example, a new dishwasher design may look great in the kitchen, but the primary reason of purchase is to make a recurrent household chore easier for the homeowner.

- *How does the product or service compare with that of the competition?*   The copywriter must determine which of the advantages this product offers against the competition are most important to the particular segment of the market toward which the advertising is aimed.

- *How can the product or service be identified?*   It is the copywriter's responsibility to tell the reader how the product can be identified, where to buy it, and if it is a product that could be in more than one department in a store, where in the store it can be found.

- *How much does it cost?*   The copywriter should know the recommended retail price of the advertised product and of competitive products as well. If the product costs more than competitive ones, determine the reason why people should pay more for it.

The copythinking process is also an analytical process in which the copywriter must balance the selling points and the benefits of the product. A *selling point* is a characteristic of the product itself which can contribute to the satisfaction of a need or desire of the buyer. A *benefit* is satisfaction received from the purchase or use of the product. In presenting the selling points and benefits, the copywriter, in order to explain what the product will do for the buyer, must consider the following.

- Will the product make the purchaser feel more important, happier, more comfortable, or give the buyer greater security?
- Will the product make the work easier for the purchaser?
- Will it make the purchaser more attractive, distinctive, or better liked?
- Will the product improve, protect, or maintain the purchaser's health?
- Will the product appeal to the purchaser as a bargain?

The copywriter must analyze the selling points and the benefits they support and focus the message around the one or two that are the strongest in order to provide a central selling idea for the ad. Some copywriters gear their ads to sex appeal, getting ahead, and health, since these are important human desires; therefore products like soap, toothpaste, clothing, and eye glasses can be geared to sex appeal in their marketing approach. This is okay, but be sure and select the one that is most logical and believable. An idea must be related to reality to solve a problem. A creative copywriter can combine intuitive understanding with a sense of perception thereby relating previously unrelated things and creating innovative new ideas.

Copythinking also involves the media in which the ad or campaign will be presented. The copywriter's copy can be set in type for printed media such as magazines, newspapers, and direct-mail pieces, or it could be spoken by announcers on radio and television. The copywriter must visualize how the copy will be presented in any particular medium (the print layout, radio script, or TV storyboard).

Few ads rely on words alone. Print ads make an impression through words and pictures which support each other. Print ad layouts deal with the arrangement of these elements plus such others as headlines, subheads, captions, borders, trademarks, and product name, in addition to the main text or body copy. The copywriter's visualizations of print ads are sometimes referred to as "rough-roughs," or thought sketches, and can be used to help convey ideas for graphics to the artist or layout person.

Radio scripts must consider music and sound effects. Copy for television storyboards must also include music, sound, illustrative material, action, and camera cues. In print and TV advertising, the viewer sees a combination of verbal and graphic signs or symbols which must work together to present the theme or central selling idea of the advertising message.

Copy Structure

From the facts gathered, the copywriter is now ready to get to the job of being a "wordsmith." Starting with visualization, he or she will now develop a concept for a headline idea and then go on to the body copy or text. Words and illustrations will be modified, revised, refined, and polished before the copy is completed. But the basic idea is to get the readers' attention, inform, and motivate them to buy.

The AIDA (attention, interest, desire, action) formula, explained earlier in this chapter as a plan for creating a personal selling effort, may also be used to structure the advertising message.

Many professional copywriters organize copy structure for an advertisement through these four elements:

- The headline idea—this is the "grabber."

- The headline extension—the bridge that relates, or extends, the original reader interest idea to the product.

- The presentation and support of product claims. Most effective advertisements use a combination of emotional, reason-why, or rational copy that may appeal to the newsworthy aspects of the product, the benefits purchasers will realize after buying the product, or something as simple as plain old curiosity.

- The closing must get the reader to act, either directly (by a call) or mailing in a coupon.

Copystyle

Copystyle can be defined simply as a distinctive mode of constructing, presenting, and executing an advertisement for a product or service.

Style is basically how it is said, or the choice of words and their arrangement. Every word should be believable, readable, and to the point. A copywriter has written good copy when it contains a unique idea and is simple and recognizable in its format, interesting and dominating in content, and convincing in its message. Copywriting is not an end in itself, just a means toward an end—the acceptance of an advertiser's message by a consumer. The copywriter should never forget that copywriting is a form of communication that goes only one way. And the copywriter should always be concerned with every element that will appear in the message, whether that message be in newspapers, in a brochure or mailer, or on radio, television, or outdoor billboards.

A Few Thoughts About Negative Advertising

Basically, an advertising appeal is a promise made to consumers concerning the benefits to be derived from using the advertiser's product or service. These benefits can be expressed either positively or negatively.

A negative copy approach might be one that says "Low-quality materials are never used to build our homes." The positive way of saying the same thing is "Only high-quality materials are used to build our homes."

If the copywriter has the choice between a positive approach and a negative approach, which should be used? Over the years, advertisers have expressed some prejudice against the use of negative appeals, maintaining that it is better to present positive, optimistic, and cheerful ideas about their product. However, research evidence does not always support this intuitive feeling. In recent years there have been a number of successful negative ad campaigns such as: MCI inviting callers to hang up on AT&T, a Tums ad giving Rolaids heartburn; and Coors asking beer drinkers to can Budweiser.

In general, while negative copy approaches may be more distinctive and sometimes successful, the choice between a positive and negative approach in an ad or campaign should depend on the product, the situation, and the competition.

Any copy—negative or positive—needs a frame, of course. That is where art and the rest of the media team come in.

20

The Art and Production Departments

If you think the above ad for an art director is asking too much of any one person, think again. Art directors literally control the fate of every campaign produced by every advertising agency. If they are hot, what they do on the layout pad can make a good campaign great. If they are cold, or only lukewarm, they can make the greatest campaign ideas look sad.

Moreover, how the campaign will attract depends to a large extent on their layout skill. The first think an advertisement has to do is flag attention and stop the people you want to sell. And it is the art director's responsibility to design an ad that will stop them.

Just ask any copywriter. When writers come up with the finished copy, they may make a little rough layout of the way they visualize it being handled. The art director regards this tolerantly. There might be something usable in it. And if there isn't, the art director can stand firm and pay no attention at all to it.

After copywriters and art directors talk over the campaign and get all the details straight, the copywriters go back to their desks—with the uncomfortable feeling that the fate of their brainchild is in other hands. In this they are entirely correct.

A good art director is a many-sided individual—an artist who gets greater satisfaction in planning work than in carrying it through to finished form. But the art director must think only of what pleases other people. Therefore, it follows that he or she must have sure judgment of popular taste.

Good art directors will put aside their personal tastes for those with greater audience appeal. Through all their work they must combine artistry with salesmanship. An art director who is a capable designer can go far. But an art director who is also a competent advertising person can go much farther.

Art directors function best when they are part of the whole advertising scheme. Thus they meet with the other departments of the agency as members of the team, and they become familiar with all sides of the client's problems and with all the reasoning behind agency recommendations. They are encouraged to think in terms of the account as a whole rather than as an assembly-line worker.

The best art directors generally have a good instinct for writing, just as good writers have a flair for picture ideas. And there may be times in your agency operation when an art director gives the copywriter a good run for the money and, on occasion, noses the copywriter out. By the same token, the copywriter, on occasion, can come up with better layout and picture ideas. Of course, that isn't generally the way it works out—but when it does, it should be welcomed. Neither department stands on its prerogatives. If an idea makes for better advertising, nobody cares where it comes from.

This "sense of working together," of being part of a team or family, is one of the things that makes an agency great—both for its clients and for the people who work there.

When staffing up for your new agency, try to hire an experienced art director who will not mind doing much of the nitty-gritty mechanical preparation work. Second choice should be a good production artist who can handle layouts with direction from the account executive and copywriter. As with the other top personnel you will hire, salaries in this area are negotiable.

Where Does the Art Department Begin?

The artist begins with rough layouts. A layout is a diagrammatic scheme or plan which shows how all the elements of the advertisement will be arranged and how the illustrations will be handled.

Kinds of Layouts

There are several different kinds of layouts, and each serves a particular purpose; any one advertisement may use all of them or only some of them. They are thumbnail sketches, rough layouts, finished layouts, comprehensive layouts, and working layouts. They may be executed in several ways but are most frequently done with drawing pencils or felt-tip pens. They are generally drawn either on tracing paper or on bond paper. These layouts are used as guides in the various stages of advertisement development by those working on the advertisements and by those who must approve them.

Thumbnail Sketches

Thumbnail sketches are miniature sketches that are used by some art directors to convey the basic layout style and treatment without spelling out small details. They offer a quick and convenient method for putting alternative layout ideas on paper. They are drawn in proportion to the actual space, but much smaller—usually only a few inches high. The art director may draw only a few or a great many, until he or she finds one or more that seems worthy of being worked up more completely (see Figure 20-1).

Rough Layouts

Rough layouts, or visuals, are prepared for almost all advertisements. They are the same size as the finished advertisement—except for outdoor posters, which are smaller, but drawn to scale. Some layout artists prefer to start with rough layouts instead of thumbnail sketches, whereas others develop rough layouts from thumbnail sketches.

Finished Layouts

The next stage is the preparation of the finished layout, which is worked more carefully than the rough layout. Finished layouts suggest in considerable detail the style of the illustration and the headlines, and therefore serve as a guide to artist and typographer. Generally, finished layouts are the ones submitted to clients for approval. TV storyboards are finished layouts for TV commercials (see Figure 20-2). While some agencies charge for layouts as part of their creative fees, other advertising agencies generally absorb the cost of finished layouts in the commissions they receive from media.

Comprehensive Layouts

Occasionally a client is unable to judge the effect of the finished advertisement by looking at a finished layout. In such circumstances, a comprehensive layout is prepared. These layouts come very close to resembling the finished advertisement. The illustrations (in color, if the ad is a color ad) are carefully drawn. When a photograph is used, a rough proof of the actual photograph to appear in the ad may be pasted into position. Headlines are carefully hand-lettered to resemble the actual typeface,

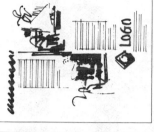

CENTER AXIS.
the units run horizontally
flush on alternate sides
of an implied axis

LETTERING
ILLUSTRATIVE
heading or logotype or
part of either made
illustrative of an implied
axis

ILLUSTRATION RIGHT OR LEFT
illustration to left or right

COMMON FORMS
ad appears as a
newspaper page.
cartoon strip or
magazine article

CIRCLE
normal pattern with
illustration in circle

OVER, DOWN, ACROSS
heading runs over to the
right. copy or illustration
down and logotype
across of an implied axis

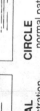

FULL ILLUSTRATION
illustration covers whole
area of ad with copy

HEADING NORMAL
heading first, illustration,
then copy and logotype

OBLIQUE AXIS
layout tips either to right
or left

Fig. 20-1. Examples of different types of layouts.

CLIENT: SEALY
TITLE: "BIG SEALY SALE" :30 SEC.
TAPE NO. TV-8925 No.3

1) Once again, E brings you the ...

2. It's our Big Sealy Sale.

3. Wide selection to choose from Twin, full, queen, king.

4. Firm, extra firm, super firm.

5. Luxurious damasks,...

9. All reduced below our regular low STORE NAME prices.

10. Save $100.00 to $500.00 during this special sale.

11. Order your new Sealy mattress now at STORE NAME...

12. ...and beat the high cost of sleep. Sale ends Saturday.

uality and comfort Sealy.

Fig. 20-2. Example of a storyboard (visual) for a television commercial.

or set in the typeface that has been decided on (these may also be in color if the finished ad calls for it). And the body copy is sometimes actually set into type and is pasted into position. Comprehensive layouts are obviously very expensive. Frequently, they are prepared for the agency by a free-lance artist or an art studio, and the client is usually billed for the additional expense.

Working Layouts

A working layout is not really a layout, but a sort of "blueprint" for production, indicating the exact position of the various elements and appropriate instructions for the typographer and engraver. Working layouts are also known as mechanicals; in work prepared for offset lithography, they are called keylines or pasteups.

Pointers About Layouts

The various elements of an advertisement have an infinite number of arrangements. However, regardless of the arrangement of the elements, certain sound principles should be followed. These include balance, movement, unity, clarity and simplicity, and emphasis.

Balance

Balance, of considerable importance in a layout, involves artistically combining the various sizes and shapes that make up an advertisement. Essentially, there are two forms of balance—formal, or symmetrical, and informal, or asymmetrical. Both are good, if well executed. However, informal balance is probably more frequently used in advertising because it creates more interest and excitement.

The artist achieves balance in a layout by so combining elements that they are in scale in terms of size and weight. (*Weight,* in layout terms, refers to the lightness or darkness of an element.) The concept of balance can be visualized by drawing an analogy to a seesaw. In formal balance, equal weight must be placed on both sides of the center of an advertisement in the same positions. In informal balance, different weights may be used, but they must be so positioned as to keep the seesaw level. Whereas the seesaw principle provides balance between right and left, optical center is the key to balance between top and bottom of an advertisement. The optical center of an advertisement is a point halfway between the right and left of the advertisement, approximately three-fifths of the way up from the bottom—the point to which the eye is naturally attracted. Formal or informal balance is achieved by the way the elements are positioned above and below this point, in much the same manner as described for balance between right and left.

Movement

If a print advertisement is to get the reader's eye to "move" through it, the layout should provide for gaze motion, or structural motion. *Gaze motion* involves placing the people or animals in the illustration so that they are looking toward the next important element—such as the headline or body copy. The tendency is for the reader to follow the gaze of the individual in the illustration. *Structural motion* is designed to achieve the same results, but more subtly. Here the reader's eyes are carried from place to place in the advertisement in a manner desired by the advertiser by the structure of the layout itself. Shapes, arrangement of elements, lines, and so forth are all designed to "move" the reader through the advertisement.

Unity

Unity in layout refers to keeping the elements of the advertisement together so that the advertisement does not "fall apart." The injudicious use of white space between elements of the advertisement, for example, can result in the advertisement's appearing to be several separate ads on the page.

Clarity and Simplicity

Although it is important to make a layout interesting, care must be taken to see that it remains simple enough so as not to lose its clarity. The more elements added to an advertisement, or the more unconventional the arrangement of the elements, the more confusing it becomes. The result is lack of emphasis on the more important elements, lack of interest, and general confusion, all of which cause the reader to lose interest and abandon the advertisement and its message.

There is a noticeable exception to this rule, however. Certain advertisements announcing bargains and sales may appear unclear and complex, with a crowded layout that looks as if it was just thrown together. These layouts are referred to as "borax" advertisements. This type of advertising has an appeal to certain customers who are looking for low-priced merchandise. Frequently, considerably more care is involved in making them than the reader would suppose.

Emphasis

A good layout should make the advertisement, as a whole, prominent, and also emphasize certain more important elements. One of the techniques for creating emphasis is repetition. A headline, an illustration, or a trademark, for example, may gain added emphasis if it is repeated several times. Another technique is contrast of size, color, or style. A small boy at the end of a row of six men, all six feet tall, will attract attention to himself. If you color just one element in a black-and-white advertisement, that element will be emphasized. In an illustration of a group of live models, include one mannequin and it will receive the emphasis. A third technique for achieving emphasis involves the use of white space. It must be used carefully if unity is to be achieved, but it can be used effectively for emphasis. Place a small pill in the optical center of an advertisement and surround it by lots of white space. It is as if a spotlight were on it!

Remember

- Keep the layout clean and simple. Keep the number of elements to a minimum and arrange the pictures and words so that there is a logical place to begin and a logical itinerary from beginning to end. Avoid gadgetry, clutter, and patchwork effects.

- Whenever possible use human interest pictures—pictures of people or things which all of us are interested in and which relate to the copy or theme of the ad. Use familiar forms of art, photographs or realistic paintings, and drawings or cartoons. Try to keep the advertisement warm and attractive. Distortion, obscure symbolism, and bizarre designs detract from the effectiveness of any ad.

- Try for instant comprehension of the headline. If a headline is not too long, it is possible to place it in such a way that the reader comprehends it without being aware of any conscious reading effort. This calls for a compact arrangement of legible type or lettering. It rules out eccentric lettering which combines several different kinds of type (often used in an effort to get several degrees of emphasis).

- It is best to avoid ragged margins and line widths that are too narrow or too wide. (Too narrow means lots of hyphenated words and badly spaced lines, too wide makes it hard for readers to keep their place.) Proper line width is about the only thing in the design of an ad for which there are hard-and-fast rules. And yet every issue of every magazine and newspaper carries ads which suffer because somebody didn't know the rules or broke them for the sake of design.

- Make long copy inviting to a reader by breaking it up into paragraphs of varying lengths and by using proper space between lines and paragraphs as well as by using italics or boldface type, subheads, and spot illustrations judiciously.

- Make ads look fresh, new, and different each time by constantly being on the lookout for material which may inspire advertising design. Trade publications in the advertising field, such as magazines for art directors, are full of new and different layout ideas and graphic approaches. Many agencies build up vast reference files for layout, art, and copy ideas. These are sometimes known fondly as "swipe files," and more commonly as "idea" and "reference files."

Mechanics of Layout

Layout artists follow certain general rules in the mechanics of their production to achieve as nearly as possible the effect of the finished advertisement. One of these rules involves measuring out the space for the advertisement. If the image area (space) for an ad in a magazine measures 7 inches by 10 inches, the layout can use all the space contained within these dimensions. The margin of white space around the advertisement that appears in the actual publication is added to this size by the publisher. No rule should be drawn around the layout space unless it is purposely desired as a border. The proper technique is to define the outer limits of the space by drawing small, light blue guidelines away from the four corners.

By paying a premium charge, the advertiser may use the white margin around the advertising space. A page with no margin is called a *bleed page* because the ink "bleeds" off the edges of the paper into the *trim space* of the page—that is, the part of the paper which is trimmed off in the binding process. The technique of handling guidelines mentioned above is applicable here.

In illustrations which are to have tonal values, such as photographs and wash drawings, the tonal values should be indicated by shading the drawing on the layout. Merely outlining the objects in the illustration fails to show the proper weight.

Headlines, subheads, and logotypes are lettered in on the layout to indicate the general type classification to be used and the weight of the type, which must be in keeping with the mood of the layout. Light guidelines should be used to keep lines straight. Hairline outlines of letters will not do, as they do not suggest the proper weight or the necessary amount of space for the type. The lettering should be careful enough to suggest the general type style that will be used.

Body copy, unless it is very large, is not lettered on the layout. Instead, it is indicated by drawing a series of parallel lines of appropriate thickness and darkness to indicate the weight of the type. A finished layout to be submitted to a client for approval should contain no extraneous marks, such as mechanical instructions for typography and engraving, as these tend to distract from the appearance of the layout.

Creating the Finished Art

Once the okayed layouts are back from the client along with okayed copy, the finished artwork can be produced.

Illustrations in advertising usually are referred to as art. Most, though not all, advertisements contain artwork, for art serves many important purposes. The decision to use artwork in an advertisement will depend on whether art will serve any of a number of purposes, such as:

- To attract attention to the advertisement
- To demonstrate the product or its effect
- To emphasize certain features of the product
- To clarify or illustrate headline and copy ideas
- To transmit a visual image of the product, package, or brand name to the mind of the consumer
- To arouse interest in the advertising message or the product being featured
- To stimulate desire for the product

Perhaps the first purpose of the major illustration in an advertisement is to gain attention. Beyond that, however, it should help to create interest—in the product advertised and in the advertisement. Thus the artwork must be appropriate to the sales objective of the advertisement, and not an end in itself.

Art can create interest in many ways. One is through depicting action. Because so much of our daily lives consists of action and observing action, we are very much aware of action, including that in the illustration of an advertisement. Another way art can be used to develop interest is through a story or plot illustration, which invites the reader to find out more. Art can use realism for interest; we tend to respond more easily to what we recognize. A wonderfully human quality possessed by every-one in some degree is sentiment. Who can turn the page of a magazine without stop-ping to look at an advertisement showing a baby or a kitten?

Despite critical condemnation, sex remains a much-used art technique for ap-pealing to consumer interest. Provided that it is appropriately related to the selling situation, it is a powerful tool. Adventure also provides a useful theme for illustration. Its interest lies in escape and excitement, and it can take many forms, from pictures of far-off places to sports shots. Another form of illustration used to create interest is the unusual, which excites our curiosity, such as an illustration of how we may be living 100 years from now. And, of course, there is humor. Everyone enjoys an amus-ing situation and a good laugh. These appeals to interest through art are not mutually exclusive, and any advertisement may combine several of them.

Sometimes artwork works better than photographs to dramatize certain features of points about the product that you want to emphasize. In furniture ads, for instance, even with the best of photography, it would be difficult to set up, light, and shoot a roomful of furniture with emphasis on one particular piece. An illustration, however, can use "artistic license" to distort the view and dramatically emphasize that one piece.

Kinds of Artwork

Once the art director (working with the copywriter) has determined the nature of the art, the next step is to determine the art medium. A host of art media are available for producing the illustration, and each has its own peculiar qualities that make it desir-able, depending upon what is to be illustrated. The choice will be tempered some-what, however, by production (technical) limitations, cost, and the time factor. Indi-vidual advertisements may use a number of illustrations involving several different art media. Furthermore, individual illustrations may combine several of these tech-niques. Among the more frequently used art forms, alone or in combination, are (1) photography, (2) wash drawings, (3) line drawings, (4) scratchboard, and (5) pencil, crayon, and charcoal. In fact, there is no limit to the media that can be used in ad-vertising art. Any device capable of producing an illustration can be used, and occa-sionally an advertisement will even feature fingerpainting or collage.

Photography

As used in advertising, photography is generally considered a kind of artwork. Over the years it has grown in popularity as an art form in advertising. Photography sees things much in the same way the eye sees them and has as its greatest attribute, realism. Photography can show the pores in skin, the grain in wood, or the texture in cloth in a way few drawings can. It can bring an illustration to life. Furthermore, it tends to make the subject more believable. Photography can create a feeling of im-mediacy, giving the receiver a sense of being there. It also can stimulate emotional involvement, because people in a photograph are real. Commercial photography is by no means inexpensive, but in many cases it can be more economical than draw-ings. Photography is not always "practical"; it can, though, be of such great beauty that it rivals other art forms.

Commercial photography has become quite sophisticated and increasingly flexible, so that many special effects are now possible. Photographs can now be scanned directly into computers for laser enhancement, distortion, duplication, recoloring, or just about any special effect you can think of. Both the Scitex and the Crossfield processes can fill in a brown patch of lawn with a "piece" of green lawn taken from another part of the picture. Sky and water can be extended without detection. Before the age of electronic "repairs," the need for removal of imperfections and the need for corrections were handled in part by the photographer in developing negatives and making prints, and in part by retouchers who work with paintbrush and airbrush to improve the photograph.

An interesting legal aspect of electronic enhancement of photographs (or artwork) is ownership: Who has the rights to the new product? Suppose a photographer takes a dramatic photograph of a person on a camel far in the distance in the desert, with the pyramids of Egypt way off in the background. By feeding the picture into a computer, a technician can "move" the pyramids into the foreground and make it look like the photographer shot from behind a pyramid with the person on camelback in the background. The angles of the shadows cast by the sun can be changed. The color of the person's clothing can be changed. An oasis with sparkling blue water can be added smack in the middle of a hot sand desert. Two or three other people on camelback can be added. All without any cut marks or indication that the original was tampered with. It is no longer the same photograph. Or is it? Who owns the rights to the new picture?

Whereas drawings sometimes require models and props, photographs always do. That is, there must be something physical to photograph. Sometimes photographers work "on location" to use natural settings, but more often they work in studios.

The artist must decide whether to use photography or drawings, depending upon the nature of the illustration. Suppose the artist wants to illustrate a cake. Obviously, no drawing can capture the texture and composition as well as a photograph. Here a good photograph (especially in color) can make a picture so realistic that it activates the salivary glands. There must be just the right props—an appropriate cake plate, cake knife, and other accessories. If it is necessary to depict a small boy devouring a piece of that cake, a model must be hired. There are modeling and talent agencies for such purposes, but occasionally the art director or photographer will look for nonprofessional models if greater realism is wanted. Perhaps in this case a red-haired, freckle-faced boy with a missing front tooth is called for. A model agency may be unable to come up with such a model, and the "kid down the street" might do just fine.

Using Stock Photography. If time and budget do not permit the taking of original photography for advertisements, there are excellent creative sources for stock photography. Using stock photography means existing photography, usually shot by outstanding photographers from around the world, who place their photographs (color and black and white), into a "library" offered for lease by a stock photography house. The images cover nearly every subject and situation imaginable, including futuristic subjects.

By contacting a stock photo house and going through their catalogs, you are sure to find an existing shot that comes close to, or is more creative than, the one you wanted to take yourself. You can even describe the kind of shot you want, and with a computer search of its files, the stock house will come up with a wide selection of just what you need—or something pretty close to it—and will send you the actual pictures for inspection.

The charges for the use of the pictures, which are usually in 35mm or transparency form, are based on how and where the pictures are being used, the length of use, the size of the audience viewing the pictures, the size they are to be reproduced in, and sometimes the number of collateral pieces using the pictures that are to be printed.

Once you decide on how many pictures you want to "lease" and tell your source how they are to be used, a price will be determined and a contract for use prepared. All pictures selected come with a release for use.

If a picture is to be used full-page size in a national magazine reaching millions of readers, its cost will naturally be more than if it is one of a dozen other pictures in a locally distributed brochure with a print run of 5000.

Stock Illustrations and Stock Film or Video Footage.   Many stock photo houses also offer a wide selection of stock illustrations covering as many subjects and situations as photography. These illustrations are available in many different styles, some from the archives of museums with famous illustrations from the eighteenth and nineteenth centuries. Existing film and videotape on many subjects are also available from stock houses and other sources such as television network libraries. Both illustrations and film or video charges are based on many of the same usage factors as are stock photos.

Wash Drawings

Though we live in an age when astronauts landing on the moon can be photographed and detailed color shots of the inside of the stomach can be made, not all subjects to be illustrated can be photographed. For instance, it is impossible to photograph dinosaurs in action, or Columbus discovering the New World, or what life will look like in the year 2500. When realism of the type that a photograph ordinarily captures is not possible photographically, a wash drawing comes close to it and overcomes the limitations of the camera.

Wash drawings are made with brush and India ink or lamp black diluted with varying amounts of water to give the desired tonal effect. There are two general types of treatment of wash drawings—tight and loose. A tight drawing is one that is detailed and tends more toward realism. People cannot always distinguish a tight wash drawing from a photograph in an advertisement. A loose wash drawing tends to be more impressionistic. This technique is used most frequently for fashion illustration, in which a sense of the fashion is desired rather than a realistic rendering of a specific item. Loose wash drawings omit much of the detail and may exaggerate—for example, the fashion figure might be quite elongated to stress the "slinkiness" of an outfit.

Line Drawings

Line drawings are sometimes referred to as pen-and-ink drawings and line art. They do not contain tonal values. An exception is when a benday screen is used; this is a photoengraving process in which continual tonal values are added to specific areas of line drawings to give body to the art. Except in these cases, however, line drawings tend to be simple and leave much to the imagination. Line drawings are typically less expensive than wash drawings or photographs and ideally suited to situations in which production limitations preclude good reproduction of tone and detail. Line drawings are often used for small supplemental illustrations. Cartoons are generally drawn in this manner.

Scratchboard

Scratchboard drawings are made by using a stylus to scratch an illustration or other design through a surface of black that is applied on a white piece of drawing paper or board. This results in a special quality of finished artwork of white lines on a black background that gives the impression of fine workmanship similar to the quality found in old woodcuts. Scratchboard drawings should not be confused with reverse plate art, which is a photographic process that reverses values (making what is positive, negative).

Pencil, Crayon, and Charcoal

Pencil, crayon, and charcoal are used in advertising art less frequently than wash or line drawings. Therefore, they offer the advantage of novelty. These drawings tend to be informal and are therefore usually rendered in the form of a sketch.

Color

Over the years the amount of color in print advertising has increased substantially, largely because improved technology has resulted in better color at lower cost. Because color advertisements cost more than black-and-white advertisements, they must offer benefits to warrant the additional expense over black and white. Some of these benefits are:

- Attracting attention to an advertisement
- Representing objects, scenes, and people with complete fidelity
- Emphasizing some special part of the message or of the product
- Suggesting abstract qualities appropriate to the selling appeal
- Creating a pleasant first impression for the advertisement
- Creating prestige for the product, service, or advertiser
- Fastening visual impressions in memory (partly because of the performance of other functions listed above, and partly because of the inherent power to stimulate interest)

Whether color can achieve these ends better than black and white depends upon the nature of the product, the visualization, and the advertising objective. Illustrations of food, for example, do particularly well in color because color adds realism and appetite appeal and attracts greater attention. On the other hand, in most cases an advertisement for life insurance would probably do as well in black and white.

The advertiser using color has two general choices. One is to use black and one or more additional colors at the advertiser's option (sometimes black and two or three colors, or two or three colors and no black). Color used in this manner serves primarily to capture attention or to emphasize some particular element of the advertisement. The other option is to use the four-color process, which reproduces the full range of colors. When full color is used, color not only serves the purposes just mentioned but also creates great realism.

Almost all the art techniques mentioned earlier can be used with color. Color usage has advanced in technique to a considerable degree since the introduction of color computers and laser color printouts. The color counterpart of the wash drawing is the watercolor painting. In addition, oil painting is sometimes used for illustration art. Line drawings, pencil, and crayon can be worked in color. It should be noted that line illustration art or the other techniques drawn in black can be printed in color.

If the layout calls for an art illustration, either your own artist must do it or an outside artist must be hired for this specific job. Art studios and free-lancers (as well as stock photo and illustration houses) have different specialties. Put out a call for artists capable of doing the illustration you need. Look at their samples and let them put quotes in writing stating what they would charge you for the job. Once you select the artist you want, make out a purchase order for the amount of payment agreed upon. The price charged should not be your only reason for selecting a particular free-lance artist or studio. Ability and talent, dependability, and experience in a particular area should also be considered.

Should the illustration called for in the layout be a photograph, the same criteria should be used in selecting a photographer.

As stated above, the layout is the "guiding light" that helps define the finished advertisement. While it is an irreplaceable medium for conveying the idea and the impression you are striving for, the layout cannot possibly convey the way an illustration or photograph will reproduce in a newspaper, magazine, or printed piece. So before preparing the art, seek out samples of similar art printed in the type of medium that your ad will appear.

In general, original art is classified as line copy (such as type or pen-and-ink drawings); or as continuous-tone copy (such as photographs or artists' shaded illustrations); or often a combination of both. Continuous-tone art must be reproduced by the "halftone" method. If an illustration is to contain important line detail, you may want the line and tone components prepared on separate surfaces, to avoid screening the lines, or so that each can be printed in different colors. Original illustrations for color reproduction may be in the form of reflective art (paintings, color photoprints) or color film transparencies. In either case, the color originals must be copied in the process of color separation—the first by reflected light, and the second by transmitted light.

Typography and Typesetting

The next step in producing the ad is selecting a typeface and setting the approved copy in type. If you don't have your own typesetting equipment, the artist can specify the typeface selected for the particular advertisement. Specifications should also be made for the size of type and the manner in which the type is to be set. It should follow the layout. Type can be purchased from a typesetting house or engraver. If you send a copy of the layout along with the ad copy, the typesetter will follow the layout as closely as possible and return the set type in galleys to your production department for pasteup on the mechanical.

Typography is both art (design) and technology. It is that part of the graphic arts dealing with the selection and arrangement of type. Letters can be composed in metal (manually or by machine.) Or they may be composed electronically on photographically or photosensitive paper or film. Preparation of virtually all advertisements must include typographic considerations because of headlines and body copy. In some instances, because a special effect is desired that is unattainable through metal or phototypography, the art director will have the headline hand-lettered. But even hand lettering (calligraphy) usually follows the principles applicable to good typography. To the layperson, type is type. Readers do not generally take conscious notice of the fact that there are a great many kinds of letter styles. This is as it should be, because good typography does not draw attention to the type itself. But even though it is not consciously noticed, type is one more means of making an advertisement as effective as possible. Deciding which typeface is right for a particular advertisement is a complex task. Beyond this, the designer faces the problem of using type correctly, for there are many factors to consider in getting the type to work for you.

Legibility

Perhaps the single most important principle of typography is that type should be legible. Certain typefaces tend to be more legible than others, and type groups with which people are most familiar are generally most legible to them. Legibility, or in a wider sense readability, is also achieved through care in using the type. Generally, lower-case type (small letters) is easier to read then upper-case type (capital letters). Proper spacing between words and letters increases not only the aesthetic qualities of type but also its readability. Likewise, spacing between lines of type (called leading, to rhyme with "heading") can increase the legibility of the copy. For obvious reasons, the size of type will affect legibility as well.

Legibility also depends upon the length of the type line and where it is broken. The eye is capable of spanning a certain number of words on the printed page at one time. If the line of type is too long, quick scanning of the line becomes more difficult. Readers are slowed down and perhaps lose their place, and, most important, they may not get the message or may give up trying to read the advertisement. The correct line length will be determined, in part, by the type size. In body copy it is not usually possible to complete a sentence in one line, so it is necessary to break the sentence and paragraph into a number of lines. Sometimes it will be necessary to split a word at the end of the line, but hyphenation should be kept to a minimum for highest legibility. Obviously, a brand name should never be hyphenated in the copy. Sometimes it may be necessary to break a line in a headline, but because the length of headlines can be varied, it should never be necessary to break a word. When headlines are broken into more than one line, the primary consideration is to break for meaning. The following headline, broken into two lines, loses much of its meaning:

ARE YOU GETTING ENOUGH
MILEAGE OUT OF YOUR MONEY?

It is much improved when presented in either of the following ways:

ARE YOU GETTING ENOUGH MILEAGE OUT OF YOUR MONEY?

ARE YOU GETTING
ENOUGH MILEAGE
OUT OF YOUR MONEY?

Aesthetic Appeal

Aside from enhancing legibility, good use of type will improve the "looks" of an advertisement, making it more effective. Type should be harmonious with the product advertised, the spirit of the advertisement, and the illustration. Different typefaces suggest different feelings and moods. Some types suggest masculinity, others femininity. Some suggest the old, some the new. Some suggest delicacy, others strength. Some suggest formality, some informality.

Contrasting type can be used for emphasis. One method is to use more than one type style, but caution should be taken so that contrast is not achieved by mixing too many different typefaces, the result of which is a lack of unity. More subtly, contrast can be achieved by using variations on a single type family.

Type Groups

Some typefaces are similar enough in design to be regarded as a group. Authorities differ as to how many groups there are, but many agree on the following basic classifications: roman, sans-serif, square-serif, script and cursive, blackletter, and miscellaneous.

Roman.   The most popular type group is roman. This group may be distinguished by the common characteristics of a combination of thick and thin strokes finished by serifs, or short crosslines at the ends of unconnected strokes. Roman faces may be subdivided into two broad classifications—old style and modern—with a transitional group between these two. Both classifications were developed centuries ago, but the distinction is still apt. The old style roman faces tend to be less severe and less formal than the modern faces. The modern roman faces have greater formality and cleanness of line, reflected primarily in the serifs, which tend to be straight and thin.

Sans-serif.   Sans-serif types are the second most popular group of faces. They are also known as block (a term mainly used in Great Britain) or Gothic, but this term suggests Gothic architecture, the design of which is the very antithesis of block design. The sans-serif group is characterized for the most part by its lack of serifs and the uniform (or relatively uniform) thickness of its strokes. Although the sans-serif group is used for both display lines and body copy, it appears more frequently in the display lines, with roman for the body copy.

Square-serif.   Square-serif letters usually have the same uniform (or nearly uniform) stroke thickness as sans-serif styles. However, they are designed with rather pronounced, heavy square or slab serifs. Square-serif types are almost exclusively used for display matter.

Script and Cursive.   The script and cursive group is characterized by its similarity to handwriting. Script letters appear to be connected, whereas cursives stand as individual letters. Because they are not very legible when set in quantity and in small sizes, these faces are used almost completely in headlines.

Blackletter.   Blackletter (or text) is the oldest of all typefaces, having been used by Gutenberg, the inventor of metal typecasting. Its design, with heavy angular strokes and great ornamentation, makes it so illegible that its use in advertising is limited to brief special effects when a suggestion of great antiquity is desired.

Miscellaneous.   A sizable number of typefaces do not fit into any of the other categories. Their designs differ considerably. They provide for novelty, and because of the special effects they can achieve in advertisements, they are frequently used for headlines. With the use of computers and scanning devices, it is possible to have a calligrapher hand-letter a complete alphabet (including numbers and punctuation marks) in a unique face. The letters can then be scanned into a computer graphics program to create a unique new alphabet of letters (such as a "child's writing") in every size and style (heavy, light, open, slanted, or shaded), and use it exclusively for a particular client or for a particular type of ad.

Overlapping Type Styles.   It must also be noted that there are many type styles which, in their design, overlap two of the broad groups outlined here—for example, sans-serif styles with the typical letterforms of a roman face.

Type Families

Within the broad type groups, there are design families of related faces identified by names such as Caslon, Bodoni, Avant Garde, Cairo, and Futura. The design remains the same within a family, but there are variations in the weight, width, and angle of the characters. This provides contrast and emphasis without changing typefaces.

The most common variations within a type family include bold, extra bold, condensed, extended, and italic type. Not every family will contain all the possible variations. Italics were at one time a separate type group, but today they are designed as a slant version of the other faces and have therefore become part of those families. In some block faces, italic is called oblique. There are also some other variations in type families, which usually have a novelty appeal. Letters may be open (outlined), or shaded (shadow effect), for example.

Type Measurement

The graphic arts have their own system of measurement, which is generally used in advertising in place of the usual American system of measurement. Type size (height) is measured in *points*. (There are 72 points to the inch.) The most common point sizes of type are 6, 7, 8, 9, 10, 12, 14, 18, 24, 30, 36, 42, 48, 60, 72, 84, 96, and 120. A unit of 12 points is known as a *pica*. (Thus 6 picas equal 1 inch.) The pica is the most frequently used measure of width in typography.

Another printer's measure is the *em*. The em measures in two directions at one time—height and width. Thus it is square measure. The size of an em depends upon the point size of the type. An 8-point em is 8 points high and 8 points wide; a 12-point em is 12 points high and 12 points wide, and is generally referred to as a pica em.

The *agate line* is used as a measure in newspaper advertising. There are 14 agate lines to the column inch.

Phototypography: Display Composition

Phototypography encompasses the process of exposing letters of the alphabet (display or text) onto film or photosensitive paper, and the arrangement and makeup or stripping of such material. Photographic composition is used most frequently in advertising typography because of its economics, its sharpness, its aesthetic advantages (especially with regard to interletter and word spacing), its compatibility with the photoplatemaking processes, and its wide selection of available letter styles.

Things You Should Know About Type

As you steer each job into typesetters' territory, you may think your route is pretty well mapped out. With the type family, and probably the face, already indicated on the layout, you have some solid signposts to point you in the right direction.

But when it comes right down to it, type speccing is an an area in which you can easily go astray. One false step and you may fall into the type trap, with type that is uninviting to the eye and uncomfortable or even difficult to read. And after all, if the message doesn't get read, you've defeated the entire purpose of the job.

In speccing the type for a printed piece, always begin by considering the compatibility of the typeface and the stock you've selected. Will the type size and style reproduce well on that particular paper? Obviously, for example, you'll get poor legibility if you try printing a small face with delicate serifs on a rough-surfaced stock that has a tendency to absorb ink!

Make it a habit to pay special attention to any type you plan to reverse or to print in color. Will your type size and style remain clean and effective when reversed in your color background, your illustration, or your photograph? The surface texture of your stock can make a different here, too. Then, will your typeface and weight be legible if printed in the color you want?

If you're working with color stock, take extra care in creating the total "look" of the type mass. Will the type seem to be dense enough? Too dense? Color stock can present different requirements for type from those of white stock.

Above all, evaluate your type tactics every inch of the way. A minor oversight in speccing may emerge as a glaring readability problem when the piece is printed. And then it's too late to make that one, perhaps subtle, change which could have avoided the problem in the first place.

Mechanical Production

Someone, somewhere, somehow named the preparation phase of creating advertisements mechanical production. To be sure, it directs "production," but the "mechanical" portion is to a degree not true, since few, if any, machines or tools are used.

The name originated, perhaps, because the work is directly concerned with all the mechanics of advertising printing, so let's continue to call it mechanical production as has been done for many years.

The work concerns large-scale mechanical reproduction of the advertising message, or "multiplied salesmanship." Through the use of typography, engravings, film, paper, ink, and high-speed printing presses, it is possible to multiply over and over again the advertiser's sales message.

For instance, a single press in a modern newspaper or printing plant can produce tens of thousands of copies per hour of the most complicated, colorful, and detailed publications and brochures—and they come off the press dried, folded, collated, stapled (stitched), with or without inserts and tip-ins, and wrapped for shipment. There are presses that do nearly everything, including "reading and criticizing" what they print.

What Is the Mechanical Production Department?

Mechanical production purchases and supervises the preparation of necessary printing materials for magazines, newspapers, trade-paper advertising and collateral material such as point-of-sale pieces, salesperson's portfolios, catalog sheets, and posters. In a small agency this department will also handle preparation of materials for television graphics, outdoor media, specialty and sales promotional items. It is responsible for the specification and client acceptance of the necessary engravings, typography, film, and the like, all of which can be obtained from outside graphic arts suppliers. If these materials are produced in house, this department is also responsible for overseeing production.

The mechanical production department takes up the process of advertising preparation after the creative work has been completed and approved by clients. It directs the conversion of copy, layout, and art to the final product, which is used by printers in making the necessary number of duplicates the advertiser requires.

Traffic and Production.   The traffic department is a main point of contact with production. Traffic furnishes production with client-approved copy, mechanical layout, and finished artwork. It also provides production with a list of publications in which any one individual advertisement or group of advertisements will appear, dates of issue, and other pertinent information. The production department needs traffic's cooperation in getting materials promptly to allow normal lengths of time for the preparation of advertising in final proof form so that (1) high-quality materials may be purchased and the final printed reproduction will not be sacrificed, (2) premium overtime costs can be avoided, and (3) materials can be purchased at prices consistent with the client's budget and the standards of the agency.

Art and Production.   The art department may well be the most important point of contact with production since the people in production work constantly and closely with all its members. Consultations are held with the layout person and type specifier to prevent unnecessary expenditures of money and time after production is under way. Production and art strive to achieve the best possible results in typography, engraving and printing production. Production also seeks the cooperation of the art buyers in having finished art prepared so that (1) a high degree of fidelity may be obtained from it in printed results and (2) it will also meet mechanical requirements of any particular publisher, type of publication, or printing process for which such art is intended.

Copy and Production.   The production department works with copy so that all typography may be carefully checked for accuracy with the original manuscript and for correctness from a grammatical standpoint, and to secure the copywriter's approval of the general appearance of the advertisement in final proof form before submission to clients.

Media and Production.   Production advises media of poor printing of any advertisement so that adjustments can be made with the supplier.

Accounting, Account Executive, and Production.   Production furnishes accounting and account executive with cost estimates for the preparation of advertising materials so that these costs can be incorporated into the overall budgets given to clients for final approval. Accounting and production also work closely in checking invoices received from suppliers covering materials purchased before rendering invoices to clients.

The Ad Preparation Procedure

You're now entering the homestretch of your production journey. With the layout as your map, and the type and artwork firmly in hand, you can finally introduce each component of your piece to every other. It's a "meeting of the materials," so to speak.

The mechanical pasteup brings the materials together in the form of an accurate, camera-ready guide for the publication or printer. It brings all the art and copy elements into a single unit for photomechanical reproduction. The only graphic element that may not be included on the keyline or pasteup is separate art, which must undergo additional production steps, such as resizing and color separation, before it goes into position.

As you prepare the pasteup, you may assemble both line and tone elements in the same unit. However, because the printer uses different techniques to photograph different kinds of artwork, you may have to separate some elements from others. Often this is accomplished by pasting each kind of copy on separate surfaces—one group of elements on the base keyline board and the others on one or more overlays.

It's impossible to describe all the pasteup procedures here. Preferences vary from shop to shop, from publication to printer, and even from job to job. The best approach is to consult the mechanical requirements section of your *Standard Rates and Data Book*, or the rate card of the publication. If the job is to be a printed piece, "your printer knows best." Simply by virtue of being a printer, the shop will be able to tell you the best way to prepare the art for the individual printing requirements of each job. And just think, you may learn some shortcuts in the bargain.

Remember. In preparing the mechanical pasteup, you're essentially plotting a course to follow. Your ability to negotiate that course with unerring precision will contribute to—or detract from—the ultimate appearance of your advertisement. Here are some production checkpoints:

- Inspection (proofreading) for accuracy—spelling, grammar, punctuation, paragraphing, upper case versus lower case, italics, boldface, numerals, telephone, and address information, and so on. Retype the manuscript, if extensively revised, in order to minimize errors in typesetting. Revisions after composition are costly and rob you of precious time.

- Mark everything for type specifications—the typeface, size, line lead, paragraph lead, flush or ragged left and right, indentions, italics, boldface, small caps, numerals, special characters, ligatures, and so on. Leave nothing to chance or misinterpretation, and do it all clearly in typesetter's language. Keep a copy of your instructions. You will pay extra for any revisions in the composition which are not errors on the typesetter's part.

- Final adjustment of the layout for transmittal to the finished art department: Resolve all assumptions and "gray areas" that may have been part of the plan until now (even the finally approved layout is often tentative in many respects). Face all of the hard facts on layout paper before anyone has to face them in hard-to-change forms. All of the graphic elements must fit the plan, or else you will be making new plans right up until press time.

- Communicate clearly every aspect of the plan to each of the people who will become involved in its execution—typesetters, illustrators, photographers, film and print processors, retouchers, keyline artists, paster-uppers, mat-room and clerical personnel. Leave nothing to chance or assumptions on anybody's part. If advisable, go where the action is, and directly supervise it. Hard work on your part is almost always less costly than rework by somebody else.

- Final inspection of the finished art before transmittal to the printer or engraver: Look deliberately at every type character, every illustrative detail, every mask or overlay, every line-up, margin, bleed, fold, and trim detail, and all mark-ups for stock and ink specs, screens, drop-outs, reverses, combinations, enlargements or reductions for stripping-in, etc. Remember, the printed results will be only as accurate and as beautiful as your finished art—never better! The least costly corrections are those made in the original art before it goes to the printer.

- Go over everything, item by item, before the art leaves your shop.

This is a brief and very general guide to checkpoints in production. It is important to expand it to include specific quality-control measures suitable to operations in your agency.

Making the Engraving or Film

Once the final mechanical is done to the exact size of the ad or printed piece to be produced, it is sent to the engraver or printer to be shot for publication purposes. It is wise to request "proofs" or samples of the mechanical after it has been shot with the necessary screens and stripping that may have been added. This proof is your final checkpoint of all the elements before the engravings or negatives are released for publication. It is wise to have the client okay the proof.

Your long, hard effort is now ready to become a media product.

21

The Media Department

Media is the plural of *medium,* which in the simplest definition means "that which carries something." It is a familiar term. In art, it means the solvent for pigments; in spiritism, the person through whom the spirits speak; and in money, the currency of exchange. Used in advertising, media are those means of communication which are commonly employed among human beings; those avenues to the mind, specifically through the senses, by which we receive information, entertainment, and education.

Advertising makes use of communications media to carry its sales messages: through the eye, by means of newspapers, magazines, posters, and car cards; through the ear, by radio; and through both the eye and ear, by television.

One of the most important problems facing the advertiser is the proper selection and use of these media to reach the public eye and ear with a sales message. In fact, media selection is one of the essential steps in the advertising process, as necessary to good advertising as good copy or wise market planning. The materials of advertising—copy, art, commercial announcement, engravings, films, whatever they may be—are not really advertising until they have been published, until they have reached the eyes and ears of people. Media selection is the bridge which spans the gulf between what is created and what is seen or heard.

For advertising to be effective, this bridge must be a good one, logically and soundly constructed, carrying produced advertising over into publications that will reach the right people, in the right way, with the greatest economy. Building it is not a simple task. There is such an abundance and variety of media from which to select, that the proper choice requires expert knowledge, judgment, and experience, as well as imagination and courage. For example, there are five major advertising media—magazines, newspapers, outdoor, radio, and television—each with its many units, its particular audience, and its persuasive claims for preference. In addition, there are a number of minor media, such as match covers, theater films, skywriting, and direct mail. All have values worthy of consideration.

Much of media planning is judgment—informed judgment based on knowledge of the mechanics of each medium and some empirical evidence of how consumers react to media—but, nevertheless, judgment. Many of the decisions made on how to spend millions of advertising dollars are predicated more on convictions than on provable facts. Many critical questions remain unanswered. Experience and good marketing and advertising judgment fill in the gaps.

We do not know, for example, how often a consumer must see an advertising message for Product X before the consumer buys Product X. And yet, the rate of exposure to advertising is one of the most important factors in devising a media plan. Exposure rate, or frequency, determines to a great extent which specific media are best, and how much money is necessary to do an effective job.

Despite a lack of crucial data, media decisions must be and are made. To guide the media planner in making correct decisions (more appropriately, practical and logical decisions which are agreed to by the advertiser), a structure is sought. This structure is called a media plan.

Types of Media

Direct Media

All forms of printed advertising delivered directly to the reader are known as direct media. They include:

- Advertising handed over the counter
- Advertising distributed door to door
- Advertising delivered by messengers
- Advertising passed out by people on the street
- Advertising sent through the mail

Direct-media advertising can be delivered to selected groups of prospects who are difficult to reach economically through other mass communications media, thereby making it possible for both geographical and qualitative selectivity. Direct media advertising is flexible in format, size, color, etc., therefore enabling costs to be regulated.

There are, however, disadvantages to direct media. First, this method of advertising does not enjoy mass reader acceptance. It is also relatively high in cost per reader (postage, printing, addressing, handling).

In the case of direct-mail advertising, quantity and quality are determined by the advertiser's mailing list. The list should only include people in a position to use or influence use of product or service. The list should be accurate in spelling of names and titles, and updated (cleaned) periodically to include new addresses and other pertinent information. Lists may be purchased or compiled and used as a database. If a reply is desired, make it easy and inexpensive for the respondent by using an 800 telephone number, or a postage-paid reply card.

Print Media

An advertiser's message can be delivered to measurable groups of readers in a printed package consisting of other advertisements combined with news, entertainment, and similar noncommercial content. The message is usually invited into the home by the reader. The main types of print media include newspapers and magazines.

Newspapers.   Newspapers are usually a localized advertising medium that are selective in their audience geographically rather than qualitatively. The life of a newspaper advertisement is relatively short. The deadlines for inserting ads into newspapers are usually close to publication, giving the advertiser more flexibility with ad content.

Local newspapers provide broad coverage within a particular community. National newspapers deliver a qualitatively selective circulation which is national or regional in its scope. These include papers ranging from *USA TODAY* to *The Wall Street Journal.*

Newspapers use two formats or page sizes: standard (usually 6 columns wide by 21 inches deep), and tabloid (usually 5 columns wide by 13 to 16 inches deep).

Most newspapers publish on a daily basis (morning and evening publications) or on a weekly basis.

Many newspapers carry supplements which they publish themselves or purchase from a syndicate.

The various departments of a newspaper concerned with advertising include:

- Classified
- Display retail
- Display classified (also the special features sections)

Newspapers publish their various rates on a rate card. Sometimes newspapers charge national firms (which often include wholesale, automotive, financial, and transportation-related firms) a higher rate than they charge local firms. Supplement charges are based on color and position.

In comparing newspaper advertising rates, consider:

- Milliline Rate—Cost of delivering one line of advertising to one million people. (Line Rate × 1,000,000/Circulation = Milliline Rate)
- CPM—cost per thousand: cost of delivering 1000 lines or a full-page ad to 1000 subscribers

Both local and national newspapers can be bought by zoned editions.

Newspapers have many services that are available to advertisers, usually at nominal or no cost. They include:

- Sponsorship of research studies of subscription-buying habits and other subjects of interest to advertisers

- Merchandising or sales promotion assistance

- Creative services, including art and type composition, color separations, private printing of collateral (private printing is usually charged for at rates below what commercial printing firms will charge)

- Area demographics and marketing data

Magazines.   Magazines are basically periodicals containing a collection of articles, stories, or other features of interest to a selectively qualitative audience and sometimes also a geographic audience (city magazines).

The life of a magazine advertisement is relatively long. Magazines offer finer ad reproduction. However, deadlines may range from 2 weeks to 3 months prior to publication. Magazines are usually published monthly and their rates are based on guaranteed circulation that includes both subscription and newsstand sales. Rates are quoted in terms of pages or parts thereof, and can be compared by using the CPM basis. Regional and zoned coverage is possible through localization of issues of national magazines.

Magazines are printed in various formats:

- Large, usually trade magazines such as *Advertising Age*

- Flat, such as *Time* and *Newsweek*

- Standard, such as *National Geographic*

- Small (pocket), such as *Reader's Digest*

From the standpoint of editorial appeal, consider the following types of magazines:

- Consumer publications offering both general and special editorial appeal

- Business publications or trade magazines that appeal to a particular type of occupation or a reader's position in that occupation

- Farm publications

Like newspapers, magazines also offer a variety of services to advertisers:

- Conduct various types of marketing and research studies

- Provide limited promotional assistance

- Will help with merchandising

- Can provide reprints at a nominal cost

Broadcast Media

Radio and TV stations rely upon the air and ground around us to carry their messages. The broadcaster can control the direction in which the signal is beamed but has no assurance that it will be received.

Radio stations fall into two types: AM (amplitude modulation) and FM (frequency modulation). Local radio stations have a broadcast range of about 100 miles, while regional stations can cover an entire region or average size state. There are national radio networks such as ABC, NBC, CBS, and Mutual Broadcasting which are made up of company-owned stations and affiliate stations into a network. These networks furnish programs and news services to their affiliates, much the same way as newspaper and magazine syndicators do to publications.

There are various types of television broadcasting systems, including:

- Very high frequency (VHF)—Channels 2–13
- Ultra high frequency (UHF)—Channels 14–83 +
- CATV (Cable TV)—formerly used only in geographically isolated areas which cannot, under normal circumstances, receive television signals. Today, most neighborhoods are wired for cable reception.
- Pay TV—Similar to CATV but with the ability to generate programming
- The Networks—ABC, CBS, NBC, which furnish programs and news services to their affiliates and company owned stations.

Local radio and television stations offer various types of programming aimed at tapping a segment of their coverage area. These include entertainment programs, news, weather, traffic reports, and sports shows. Literacy is not a requirement in broadcast media as it is in printed media.

Advertising rates in both radio and TV are usually based on 10-second, 20-second, 30-second, 60-second, and larger time segments. Most broadcast stations offer package and discount rates. Network rates are based on time of day, type of program, and other considerations.

Audience circulation or coverage is based on the average number of actual listeners or viewers in any given time period. Various independent rating services provide this information.

The Federal Communications Commission licenses both radio and TV stations, regulates the amount of time that stations can devote to advertising, and ensures that signals will not interfere with each other. This agency also controls the growth and development of radio and TV and oversees the quality of advertising with an eye toward preventing obscene, profane, fraudulent, and deceptive advertising.

The types of broadcast advertising fall into two general categories: program sponsorship and spot announcements.

The types of programs available for sponsorship include:

- Entertainment
- Religious

- Agricultural
- Educational
- News
- Sports
- Talk
- Weather reports
- Traffic reports

Sponsorship of programs tends to lend increased prestige to the advertiser's image in the consumer's eye. Often, the program can be customized to a specific sponsor's needs (like Nike sponsoring a sports show). Sponsorship of a program also means guaranteed repetition of the sponsor's message.

Programs like the ones mentioned above can be filmed or videotaped, live, or remote pickups. They can originate from local stations, networks, or outside packagers.

Spot (nonnetwork) announcements (commercials) are usually aired during and between regularly sponsored shows, or on shows without regular sponsors. They represent a highly flexible method of advertising and are best suited for short messages. Spot commercials are substantially less expensive than program sponsorship.

Broadcast commercials run after program, billboard, and station breaks (the 42 seconds between half hour programs when a station must identify itself with call letters and location).

Traffic or Position Media

In this type of advertising, people or "traffic" must pass the location or position of the medium and the advertiser has the opportunity to choose the location and timing best suited for their message. Outdoor advertising includes:

- 24-sheet poster printed on paper, may be illuminated
- Painted display, can be illuminated
- Multivision (trivision) sign
- Electric spectacular
- Bus benches

In purchasing posters, quantity is determined by "100 showing" or how many posters are needed for 100 percent of the buying public to see a message in a 30-day period. Campaigns can be sold on a 30-day, 3-month, 6-month, or yearly basis.

The message used on outdoor media must:

- Attract attention through use of color, illustrations, and striking artwork
- Be brief and register immediately

There have been many attacks on outdoor advertising and attempts to restrict its use from environmental beautification committees and safety sources.

Other types of nonstandardized outdoor signs include:

- Roadside—These are often placed carelessly, are poorly maintained, and lack uniform design
- On premises—These signs can be fabricated in plastic and neon or they may be painted displays. They are sometimes referred to as reader boards.

Transportation Advertising

This type of medium depends on consumer usage of commercial transportation facilities and includes such types as:

- Car cards inside—audience is captive
- Traveling displays outside moving vehicle
- Terminal posters and displays

Point-of-Purchase and Other Media

Point-of-purchase (POP) advertising utilizes promotional materials situated in, on, or immediately adjacent to retail distribution points and is designed to build traffic for the retailer as well as sell merchandise. The types of point-of-purchase tools are:

- Signs—which furnish a bridge between external advertising and efforts exerted internally to consummate a sale.
- Window displays—important for shopping goods and impulse sales
- Wall displays
- Display cards
- In-store video
- In-store coupon machines
- Merchandise racks and cases
- The actual product package

Point-of-purchase advertising helps to establish and maintain the manufacturer's brand superiority at the point of sale, and encourages impulse buying.

Some of the problems in POP advertising are that the displays must be designed realistically, keeping in mind the true value of the product to the retailer. Their placement must be to the retailer's advantage to use the materials, and the costs of producing POP displays are usually high. Other disadvantages include short-term use and misuse, and an adverse selection of cooperating outlets.

Exhibitions and Traveling Exhibits

This type of medium is mainly used industrially, for professional advertising, for educational or informative purposes, or for demonstrations. The message delivered is usually more comprehensive; therefore design problems are more complicated.

Advertising Specialties (Remembrance Advertising)

These include:

- Calendars and novelties—where appropriateness is most important. The items should be closely related to the advertiser's business, and be novel to the locality.

- Executive gifts—here the cost factor is increased and the advertising becomes minimal and may even be eliminated. There is a risk of nonuse of expensive items which becomes a greater cost consideration.

Advertising on Film/Slides/Video

This medium is sometimes called "trailer" advertising where the message is shown before and between features at movies in certain areas. This type of advertising is most effective in areas where TV is not widespread. The message is similar in format and style to TV. Sometimes audiences resent these messages since they paid admission.

Directory Advertising

Allows the advertiser to call attention to product or service at a time when prospective customer is searching for that product or service. The extent of expenditures is such that directories should be related to the role which the telephone can or does play in the specific business.

Donation Advertising

Except in a negative sense, the advertising value is nil and, as such, these expenditures should be considered charitable donations or public relations.

Selecting Advertising Media

The basic problem of media selection is choosing media which reach markets or market segments you are trying to sell. Accomplishing this involves, broadly speaking, three steps or decisions. First, the general type or types of media must be decided upon. That is, should the advertiser use newspapers, magazines, television, and so forth, or a combination of these? Second, a decision must be made as to the class of media within a particular medium type. For example, if the advertiser decides upon magazines, should women's/men's magazines or home magazines be used? If television is decided upon, should network or local spots be used? If the advertiser sponsors a radio or television program should it be news, sports, drama, variety, music, or traffic reports? Third, a decision must be made concerning the particular medium. In the case of women's/men's magazines, shall it be *Cosmopolitan, Gentlemen's Quarterly,* the *Ladies Home Journal, Sports Illustrated,* or some combination of these?

Planning the Media

Although the advertiser has an obvious stake in the media plan and must ultimately approve, modify, or reject it, the bulk of media work is done by the advertising agency and the media. In the advertising agency, the media planning and buying function is delegated to the media department. In the media, the selling of space and time is delegated to the medium's advertising department and its sales force.

The Agency Media Department/Media Buyer

In the smaller advertising agency, the media department functions primarily in the capacity of media buyer, with the account executive largely responsible for media direction and general planning. However, in the large agency, planning and buying are the responsibility of the media department. Such a department typically is headed by a director of media with a number of associate directors (or supervisors) and media buyers. The associate directors in a large agency are responsible for the media plan. Generally, each is assigned to one or more accounts; if the agency uses the account group organization, the associate directors are the media department members of the account groups. In order to develop media plans adequately, they must be well versed not only in media, but in marketing and the creative aspects of advertising as well.

Qualifications of an Experienced Small Agency Media Buyer

WANTED:
AN AGENCY
MEDIA PRO!!

Must be experienced in strategic planning & buying for ALL media. Must be tough negotiator and know how to map tactics, target the right audience, set appropriate objectives, measure performance. Position requires proficiency with personal computers and excellent mathematic and analytic capabilities. Person must have great deal of patience when meeting with and hearing the pitches of media reps. Must also make neat appearance as a representative of agency.

If you were looking for a good media buyer for your new agency, look for the qualities and experience mentioned in the "ad" above.

Media buyers are specialists, their degree of specialization depending upon the size of the agency. There may be space buyers for newspapers and magazines and outdoor media, and time buyers for radio and television. Each is responsible for being an expert in his or her own media area. They interview media representatives, negotiate for space and time, and issue contracts on behalf of clients.

The Independent Media Buying Service

Boutique or independent media buying services have assumed some degree of importance. There are essentially two varieties of the service. A few provide complete media planning and buying services which are used by small advertising agencies that do not have adequate media departments of their own. Most, however, are hired by advertisers to buy the media which are in the plans developed by the advertising agency. They deal primarily with broadcast media, where advertising rates are generally negotiated. However, they can and do buy all media for their clients. Their usefulness, of course, lies primarily in their ability to get better buys. Usually they are compensated by getting a percentage of the difference between the dollars originally budgeted and the actual cost of the media they have purchased.

Media Representatives

Media advertising departments are actually sales departments created for the selling of advertising space and time. They prepare sales presentations, conduct research projects on their audiences and effectiveness, and structure advertising rates. Their salespeople are known as media representatives (reps). A medium may have its own salesperson or may use the services of agent sales representatives if they find it economically impractical to maintain their own representatives in various key cities where the majority of advertising agency business is located. These agents will represent a group of noncompetitive newspapers or television stations, for example. Not only do they offer a distinct service to the media, but together with media's own salespeople, they have much to offer to media buyers as well. A good portion of the media representative's time is spent making sales presentations. A good representative has a comprehensive knowledge of the market and medium and can save the buyer's time by providing this information.

The Media Buyer/Planning a Buy

Planning a media buy is the result of a great deal of basic knowledge and its application to a particular advertising problem. The selection of media is a custom-tailoring procedure, and every plan for every advertiser must be dealt with separately, specifically, and in terms of the individual problem presented. No formulas can be automatically applied. Every assignment is defined, information is analyzed and collated, and a custom-tailored recommendation is made. Such an approach means that the buyer works with the client or account executive to discover the advertiser's particular situation and its advertising needs. To work out a media selection, the buyer must know and consider a number of things:

1. *The Client Problem*—What is the advertiser's present situation? How much money is there to spend? What does the client need to do to secure profitable sales?

2. *The Product's Market*—Who buys the product? Why is it bought? What are the limits of its market?

3. *Media Facilities*—What are the natures and values of all the various media? What can be bought most profitably for this particular account?

4. *Media Information*—Within a given medium, what are the relative values of the different publications, or stations, or networks? What are the characteristics of their audiences? What are their rates? What are their editorial and entertainment appeals?

5. *Media Research*—How do the various media compare in audience size, in advertising effectiveness, in usefulness to a particular client for a particular product?

With this information in hand, the buyer works up and presents to the account executive or client a selection of media which will do the job needed within the budget available.

Buyers must exercise their most astute judgment, document their recommendations with all necessary reasoning and statistics, and present it convincingly.

After a media selection has been approved, the next steps are to put it into operation—that is, to do the actual buying. First, schedules are worked out, and having been approved by the client, the purchase of the media is made, contracts are issued, and insertion orders are authorized.

At this point, the buying job is far from done. The buyer continues to watch the progress of the campaign, keeps track of the way in which the media fulfill their contracts, and registers complaints and makes adjustments as to position in publications or the handling of radio and television announcements.

Finally, for all the agency accounts, the media buyer keeps up to date as to changes in conditions, watching rates, coordinating discounts, evaluating the shifting situations which arise, so that at all times the buyer is in position to advise the client and the agency contact person on dangers, new opportunities, and the directions in which media are moving.

It is obvious that, in these terms, the media buyer is not simply a buyer of time and space, not even simply a selector of media. In addition, and perhaps primarily, they act as a consultant to client and agency on all matters having to do with media problems. As such, he or she keeps every client informed of changes in the media picture, answers specific questions, and makes reports on special problems, prepares annual plans, and justifies every recommendation in client memos.

It is inevitable that the buyer should likewise be an agency contact with the client. The buyer should be called into client meetings when media subjects are under discussion, for the purpose of answering client questions directly, and presenting agency media proposals to clients when new campaign recommendations are made. Frequently also, the buyer is called upon to address client sales organizations and explain the logic and values of advertising programs to large client meetings. In this way, the media buyer plays an important part in the acceptance which the agency enjoys on accounts and the confidence which the agency's clients have in their guidance.

The media buyer's contacts go beyond the agency and client. There are the many different media from whom information must be secured and whose sales claims he or she must hear. The result is that the media department becomes an "open house" for all media representatives. A large part of a buyer's day is taken up with one office visit after another, and the buyer must always be interested and alert to give proper audience to every medium which demands their attention.

There is no question that the members of the media department have many more contacts with the outside than do those of any other branch of the agency. For this reason, they represent the agency to the advertising public, more consistently than do any other group.

Basis of Media Selection

For a buyer, the first step in planning a media program is the selection of the medium or types of media to be used. Two principal considerations govern this selection:

1. The purpose to be served by the advertising
2. The relative values of the various media in terms of this purpose

As for the first consideration, the purposes to be served are many. Among them (and by no means all which could be listed) are:

- Continuation of a successful consumer program
- A change in strategy to counteract a declining sales situation
- Readjustment to a change in market or competition
- Introduction of a new or improved product
- Concentration locally to meet a special regional or competitive challenge
- Promotion of a sales deal or premium offer
- Announcement of new packaging or pricing
- Cultivation of a dealer or professional group intimately concerned with sale and use of the product
- Seasonal promotion arising from buying habits or seasonal use
- Institutional promotion of company or product line
- Testing of market acceptance of a new product
- Testing of new creative approach

On many accounts more than one purpose prevails in any year's campaign. For example, a major tea company employs radio, television, magazines, newspapers (food sections), and coupons to reach the entire consuming public every month of the year, but uses 24-sheet posters from May to August to emphasize iced tea, runs a premium offer in June (supported by magazines and broadcast spots), concentrates on the summer market in the South through farm publications, fights competition in the New England and Middle Atlantic states with sales deals, and introduces its new tea bag in selected areas.

Each purpose dictates a certain media choice. The choices are governed by:

- The nature of the market
- The expenditure available
- The copy approach
- The timing necessary
- The geography of the effort
- The media facilities, especially locally

No single medium is categorically best in all these terms. As requirements vary with the purpose at hand, so do the values of media vary in meeting these requirements. If, for example, a food product is best presented by a tantalizing four-color illustration, magazines, television, and posters might be preferred. If demonstration of the article's operation is important, perhaps the choice is only television. If the market is local or regional, then national magazines and network broadcast are ruled out, but consideration is given to spots, newspapers, and Sunday supplements. A low-cost family commodity, like a soap powder, with prospects in every household and a large budget, is justified in buying any number of media for the sake of circulation tonnage alone. A high-cost item such as a home or an automobile with a limited expenditure must be carefully selective to secure those media most productive in reaching consumers able and willing to buy.

In any event—and this can not be emphasized too strongly—the buyer's selections must do the job required as of a particular situation and a particular time. In making this selection, the buyer has two responsibilities: first, to choose the media for the purpose; and then, to determine within those media the particular units most suitable to that purpose which magazines, if publications are the choice; which stations and time spots, if broadcast is indicated; and so on, according to the money the buyer has to spend, the product being advertised, and the market being exploited.

Media Information Sources

Obviously, media planning requires a great deal of information. Information relative to the brand, the marketing problem, and creative strategy is obtained from other parts of the marketing plan. Information relative to media strategy and techniques must be obtained and assembled by the media department. The material which follows is a brief description of the kinds of information which are available.

Reports by Media

The various media are a source of considerable information. They provide rate cards, information on coverage, and studies concerning their markets. Even though such information is very valuable, caution must be exercised in evaluating its worth—not because such studies are dishonest, but because each medium presents the information that puts it in the most favorable light.

Reports by Media Associations

The various classes of media—newspapers, magazines, television, and so forth—have associations such as the Bureau of Advertising of the American Newspaper Publishers Association, the Magazine Publishers Association and the Television Bureau of Advertising. These groups, among other activities, conduct research and prepare reports on the nature and merits of their own media. Publishers Information Bureau, a part of the Magazine Publishers Association, provides data on the volume of advertising lineage carried by magazines.

Standard Rate and Data Service

This firm provides directories of rates, circulation, mechanical requirements, issuance and closing dates, and other information for most major media types. It provides a quick source of basic information regarding media but generally must be supplemented with more detailed information from other sources. (See Figures 21-1 to 21-3.)

Audit Bureaus

The Audit Bureau of Circulations, the Business Publications Audit of Circulation, and the Traffic Audit Bureau are three of the major auditing bureaus which measure, check, and verify the circulation of many newspapers, magazines, business publications, and outdoor advertising.

Advertising Research Foundation

This organization provides a series of continuing studies on readership of newspapers, farm publications, weekly newspapers, business papers, and transportation advertising.

Independent Media Information Services

There are a large number of independent firms that conduct media research and studies, provide data on media audience demographics and product usage, and supply figures on the volume of advertising lineage carried by newspapers, tabulated by product classification. Others provide similar information for magazines, farm publications, and nationally distributed newspaper supplements as well as business publications. One large firm provides advertising readership studies of a number of newspapers, magazines, and business papers. For broadcast media The Pulse, Inc., and A. C. Nielsen Company, among others, provide a variety of media research data.

To these sources the buyer adds his or her own experience, daily observations, acquaintance with publishers and broadcast officials, and the information and promotional material coming from salespeople and through the mail.

Characteristics of Media

Although there is no formula for selecting among media, there are certain accepted characteristics each of which serves as a guide to the buyer in distinguishing between them as to their suitability for use in a given situation. Briefly they may be compared as follows.

Market Coverage

Magazines are, with a few exceptions, published for national distribution, and an advertiser can reach all sections of the country with the use of a single magazine. Circulation will not be heavy but evenly spread according to population, and a number of magazines are required to secure a large audience. Any of the other media can be bought on a national scale, but since they are local in origin—radio and TV stations, newspapers, outdoor billboard companies—they must be organized into networks or combinations in order to cover the country geographically. They concentrate heavily in their immediate areas and are most effective for localized efforts. In its prime, network radio was truly national and able to carry the same sales message simultaneously throughout the country. Network television now has national stature and even international stature with satellite transmission, but because of clearance difficulties and time zone differences, varies considerably from region to region.

Cost

Magazines are least expensive for a national campaign because minimum representation can be purchased in a single publication. The other media are substantially more costly, since purchase is by combinations of local units, expenditure for a schedule depending upon the number of units and markets involved. On the basis of delivered circulation—cost per thousand—outdoor is least expensive, followed by radio, newspapers, and television in that order.

Selective Coverage of Prospects

Magazines have the greatest selectivity, since most of them are edited for specific groups. Television and radio are selective to the extent that the programs carrying advertising have different entertainment appeals and attract different types of audiences according to age, sex, and personal interest. Newspapers vary in editorial policies, but in many markets there is only one paper and therefore no reader choice.

Fig. 21-1. Sample page from Newspaper Rates and Data. *(Reprinted with permission from Standard Rate and Data Service's* Newspaper Rates and Data, *issued July 1991.)*

Outdoor is least selective because it is visible to the entire population without any selection by the viewer.

Frequency of Advertising Impact

Outdoor has 24-hour exposure and can convey an advertising message any time of day or night, as often as there is a passerby to view it. Spots on radio and television can be scheduled as frequently as affordable throughout the broadcasting day. News-

Fig. 21-2. Sample page from Business Publication Rates and Data. *(Reprinted with permission from Standard Rate and Data Service's* Business Publication Rates and Data, *issued August 1991.)*

papers offer daily opportunities. Magazines are most limited because of their weekly, monthly, or quarterly issue.

Year-Round Effectiveness

Magazines publish throughout the year with little variation in circulation or effectiveness from season to season. Outdoor is somewhat limited by weather conditions in different sections of the country, while newspapers, radio, and television tend

Fig. 21-3. Sample page from Print Media Production Data—Business Publications. *(Reprinted with permission from Standard Rate and Data Service's* Print Media Production Data—Business Publications, *issued August 1991.)*

to lose circulation during the summer months. Living habits vary by seasons, so that these media come in conflict with other interests of their audiences, especially during vacation and warm weather periods.

Life of Advertisement

Outdoor advertising, with 30 to 365 consecutive days of exposure for each poster, has the longest life. Magazines, retained in the home for a relatively long period of time and in many cases passed on to other people, are only a little less long-lived. A newspaper is generally good only until the appearance of the next day's issue, whereas radio and television commercials, of a few seconds or minute duration, once delivered live only in memory and depend for their effect upon how deeply they have momentarily penetrated, since there is no possibility of further actual exposure, unless the viewer videotapes the commercials.

Flexibility

Newspapers are most flexible as to budget control because of their short cancellation notice. Spot radio and television can be canceled on a few days notice (of course, network broadcast does not have the same flexibility); magazines have closings of from 2 to 12 weeks, and outdoor, because of production and posting requirements, is still less flexible. As to copy, radio and television (except for film) operate on shortest notice and are most flexible and timely.

Presentation of Appearance of Product

Magazines with their fine facilities for printing reproduction are unquestionably best suited for presenting a product's appearance in mass printed form. Outdoor is likewise pictorially effective. Newspaper printing is variable in quality and limited in fine detail, though many papers around the country now use state-of-the-art color presses and computerized color separation methods for crisp, clear reproduction. Unfortunately, most newspapers print on highly absorbent newsprint stock which has a tendency to blur edges and run colors together. Radio has no means of showing the product; however, television shows products off in fine detail and color, as well as in use.

Presentation of Features of Product

The chance that television gives for complete demonstration with a well-prepared commercial makes it the one medium in which the full story of a product's features and operation can be dramatized. Magazines and newspapers must rely upon printed copy, which can go into considerable detail but without television's advantage of demonstration. Outdoor can give only a flash impression, and radio is limited by lack of visual reference.

Other values are often necessarily considered, especially when the choice among media must be refined to specific applications. Among these are the prestige a medium can bring to a product, the attitude of the trade, consumer confidence and acceptance, and the adaptability of the medium to special copy requirements. These values change with varying situations and must be judged by each advertising situation. The responsibility of the buyer is to make judgments in the best advertising interests of the client, and to the most effective use of the media as his or her knowledge and experience dictate.

Media Scheduling and Related Matters

Once the media plan has been approved and the media decided upon, the job of scheduling must be undertaken. The media department must determine the size of advertisements, their position in the media, and what mechanical possibilities to consider, such as color, bleed pages, inserts, or gatefolds. Then negotiation with media must be undertaken, space and time schedules prepared, contracts written, and finally, insertion orders issued.

Size, Position, and Mechanical Possibilities

Size

Size is a factor in print advertising, just as length is in broadcast advertising. These are important considerations in media selection and scheduling because they will directly affect the advertising budget. But they are also a problem of creativity and marketing management. It is not possible to generalize about size, except to say that the advertisement should be as big as is necessary to accomplish the objectives of the advertising strategy. Creative factors influencing size include the length of copy, the nature of the illustration, and the visualization technique. Marketing management factors include the nature of the product, its competition, and the marketing objectives. Media considerations affecting size include not only the budget but also the effective audience potential of the medium, requirements of the media (some media specify minimum advertising space or time units), and readership habits of a print medium's audience (a hobby magazine may have extremely high readership, so that even the smallest advertisement will not be overlooked).

Proponents of large and small size ads are continually arguing the merits of their respective cases. In the final analysis, size must be related to cost: size must be large enough and cost low enough to produce the most sales at the least expense.

Positioning

The position of the advertisement or commercial plays an important role in determining its effectiveness. Advertising rates of media generally are based upon run of paper (ROP)—that is, position to be determined by the medium. Certain positions, like the back cover of a magazine, are particularly desirable and command premium rates. In broadcast media, "position" is determined by time periods, with better periods, those commanding larger audiences, getting higher rates.

Although most advertisers place print advertising on an ROP basis, some feel that preferred positions are worth the additional cost. Special position may be especially desirable because of the physical layout of the advertisement (e.g., one laid out for a right-hand page), or because it is appropriate for an advertisement to be close to specific editorial matter. For example, a food product advertisement may appear in the cooking section of a women's magazine. It is obvious that station break spot announcements following television programs with extremely high ratings are much sought after. But although position is important, it is relative to the quality of the medium. In an age when videotaping of programs for playback later is as common as going to the kitchen during a commercial, the importance of television positioning has been diminished only slightly. In newspapers, even though you buy on an ROP basis, there is some opportunity for position choice, for the advertising agency will express preferences and usually will be accommodated by the medium as much as possible. Of course, long-term contracts help advertisers to earn franchise positions.

Mechanical Opportunities

Some media offer certain mechanical possibilities, at additional cost, to improve the effectiveness of advertisements. For instance, many publications offer color, which may be of value to the advertiser in securing greater attention or making the illustration more realistic, as in food advertising. Bleed pages, offered by certain media, permit the advertisement to run off the edges of the page, which may give it stronger impact than it would have on a normal page.

Certain media offer gatefolds and wrap-arounds for oversize advertisements, inserts permitting the use of special papers and printing processes, coupon inserts, tip-ins, consecutive numbering of coupons, and so forth. These, plus the reproduction limitations of the media, must be taken into account, usually both by media buyers and creative personnel, who also must take into account the relationship of cost to impact.

Space and Time Buying

The media buyer still has the problem of actually purchasing space and time. To do so he or she needs negotiating skill and a comprehensive knowledge of rate structures. Today, broadcast purchasing is almost totally based on negotiation, with rate cards serving as only a starting point in accomplishing a buy. Print purchasing, on the other hand, still is done mostly from rate cards, although print packages at negotiated prices are becoming more and more fashionable. When negotiations are completed, contracts will be written by the media department on behalf of the client and the media. Finally, after the schedule has been decided upon, insertion orders will be written to designate the particular date, space, and position for each advertisement within the terms of the contract (see Figure 21-4).

Scheduling

Before the insertion orders can be issued, a schedule must be drawn up stating when the advertisements are to appear. This schedule is not determined haphazardly, but is designed to assure that advertisements are timed for maximum effectiveness.

There are several patterns of scheduling generally in use. One might be described as the regular or even schedule. Uniform time and space are used at regular intervals—every day, every week, every month.

In contrast, advertisers are increasingly making use of flights or waves of advertising. In flighting, the schedule is concentrated in short periods broken by time periods without advertising. This is especially valuable when the advertiser has a limited budget and would lose much of the impact of advertising if it were spread evenly over time. Thus, the advertising is bunched in high concentration flights to assure impact.

Another pattern is the skip schedule, in which advertisements are scheduled every other day, week, or month. In some instances the advertiser may alternate media—for example, *Cosmopolitan* one month, the *Ladies Home Journal* the next,

Krieff Advertising

MEDIA ORDER

☒ INSERTION ORDER
☒ REPEAT

ORDER NO. 1206
DATE

PUBLISHER	FT LAUDERDALE NEWS
	CHRIS D'AMICO 623-0299
ADDRESS	3333 S CONGRESS AVE
	DELRAY BCH FLA 33445
	FAX 407-243-6546
ADVERTISER	CENTURY VILLAGE @ PEMBROKE PINES CVP 1574
PRODUCT	

NO. of Columns / Depth	Times	Dates of Insertions
6 col x 10"	1X	Saturday, Nov. 23, 199

POSITION REAL ESTATE SECTION - right hand page - far forward please

COPY CUTS "Senior Prom"

ADDITIONAL INSTRUCTIONS
PLEASE RETURN ALL ORIGINAL ART, VELOXES OR ENGRAVINGS TO AGENCY.
6 col = 13"
45" contract exp: 3/31/92
CRA deadline: Wed. pm
cc#1119713
COD check to be picked-up @ Century Village

RATE	PREMIUM	COLOR	
$45.00		COMMISSION %	
GROSS $2,700.00			

ART RETURNED
CLIENT INVOICED
TEAR SHEETS REQUESTED XX

$0.00 | NET $2,700.00
$0.00
$0.00

Subject to standard conditions on back hereof

KRIEFF ADVERTISING

By Lana R Bowen

THE AD SHOP, INC. DBA KRIEFF ADVERTISING
AUTHORIZED AGENT FOR ABOVE NAMED ADVERTISER

CONDITIONS OF THIS CONTRACT

- The Agency represents that space is contracted for hereunder in accordance with a specific authorization signed and given to the Agency by the Advertiser, reading as follows:

  "We hereby authorize you, as our agent, to purchase for our account the space and/or time shown below. It is understood that the authorized signature below constitutes our approval of these insertions and we assume final responsibility to the respective vendors, including liability for non-cancellable contracts, incidental charges and so-called short-rates. We also understand that rates shown below are current published rates, subject to change prior to vendor's acceptance of your order. Please prepare advertisements for the media listed below, subject to our approval of matter."

- The Advertiser having accepted full liability, the Agency is hereby relieved of personal liability for space, engraving, composition and/or other items ordered under the Advertiser's authorization, in consideration of which the Agency shall, however, exercise the same diligence and good faith in collecting and forwarding moneys due the vendor as though it were personally liable.

- In the absence of written acceptance of this contract, insertion of an advertisement scheduled hereunder shall be construed as an acceptance. (Immediate written acceptance, however, is requested.)

- The Publisher (vendor) shall carefully inspect mats, plates, etc., on arrival and shall use same only if found in perfect condition. The Agency shall be notified at once as to imperfections and the given insertion or insertions suspended pending receipt of the Agency's further instructions.

- In case of mat shrinkage, the given advertisement shall be run in space mat occupies rather than space called for by insertion order.

- Omissions or incorrect insertions shall not be made good except upon specific instructions from the Agency.

- Each bill rendered to the Agency on the Advertiser's account shall state the cash discount date if previous to the 20th of the given month.

IMPORTANT:

It is understood, and made a condition of this contract, that all art work, engravings, electros or any other materials paid for by this agency or the client will be returned to the agency or client immediately upon completion of the schedule. The Publisher (vendor) assumes full responsibility for any such materials not returned.

Fig. 21-4. Sample of a computer-generated print insertion order (front and back).

then back to *Cosmopolitan,* so that the overall effect is similar to the regular schedule.

The seasonal schedule emphasizes seasonal sales opportunities by running irregular schedules that peak the advertising during the seasonal periods.

The build-up or step-up schedule starts out with small advertisements and eventually builds up to an all-out campaign of considerable intensity.

The blitz or step-down schedule simply reverses the previous procedure. Both of the last two schedule patterns are used to introduce new or established products to new markets. The choice is a matter of strategy preference.

Media Rebates to Clients

For many years, it was understood in the advertising business that agencies did not rebate to their clients any commissions. It was also illegal. Then a few of the major agencies started rebating media commissions or portions thereof to their most important clients, but did not lose any money because they received their incomes from professional fees.

A certain amount of controversy surrounds the practice of rebating to the client any part of the commission allowed by the publisher. Some publishers and agencies believe that this is unethical, while others do not. As an advertising agency owner, you are not legally bound to withhold any rebates you may wish to make to your clients. Nor need you do so. You may make any agreement you wish with respect to the manner in which you will be paid by your clients. Fees vs. commissions is discussed in Chapter 26 ("Agency Compensation") in greater detail.

Media Discounts

In the advertising business, media discounts are available that you must pass on to your clients.

First is the frequency discount. If you place an ad in a publication for a client every month and you know you're going to do so on a continuing basis, don't buy it every month; buy it by the year. Most publications have a 3-time rate, a 6-time rate, a 9-time rate, a 12-time rate. Some even have an 18-time rate. Every time you reach a larger gradation, you get a better discount. Frequency discounts are also available in broadcast media.

Other kinds of discounts available are ROP and ROM discounts. ROP means run-of-paper, and ROM means run-of-magazine. In this kind of discount, you buy space as such instead of specifying a preferred position. If you are running an ad and you don't want to specify a preferred position, you are an ROP—that is, the publication puts you in wherever it has the room.

Along the same lines is what is called the standby rate. After you have been advertising with a publisher for a while, you have developed a relationship, a rapport. The publication will have copies of your ads on file. At the closing deadline of a magazine or newspaper, the publisher may have an advertiser that cancels an ad. The publication then has two choices: to run an ad that will make money or put in some editorial content which is not profit-generating. All magazines are in business to make a profit. The publication sales rep will call you up and say, "Do you want an open page? I've got one, and you can have it for half the regular rate." If you have the authority from your client, you can say "Yes, I'll take it." Or you can call your client and get a clearance and then agree to the discounted ad. The advantage of a standby ad is that you can buy space for a small percentage of the full cost. A disadvantage to standby is that often, because the closing deadline may have already passed, the publication must use art materials that are on file, without giving you the benefit of making any revisions that may have become necessary since the ad last ran.

22

The
Media Plan

At the heart of media operations is the media plan. In many smaller advertising agencies, media planning can be directed by or handled by the account executive. But because this planning is such a key factor in the overall advertising and marketing strategy and accounts for the major portion of advertising expenditures, it is strongly recommended that this task be left to an expert, the media buyer or director.

Planning is by far the most important of all functions performed by media people. If the plan is a good one, and adhered to in all stages of the campaign development, the entire media program will be right, simple to carry out, and efficient.

The media plan itself is a written document that becomes part of the overall advertising plan, which is part of, and based on, a master marketing plan.

The objectives of any media plan define media goals. The goals must be positive, action-oriented statements representing an extension of the marketing objectives and, therefore, also be marketing-goal oriented.

The objectives cannot be innocuous. They must position the media plan relative to the market and the marketing plan. An objective that states "Introduce Product X in order to achieve high levels of awareness" does not provide direction. All it really is saying is: Advertise. A more realistic and actionable objective guides the planner in assessing alternatives, such as "Reach at least 80 percent of the potential market within the first month of advertising, ensuring that the average consumer will be exposed to a minimum of four advertising messages." Or, "Direct advertising to current and potential purchasers of Product Y by weighting current purchaser characteristics 60 percent and potential purchaser characteristics 40 percent."

Marketing Objectives

Because a media plan is an integral part of the marketing plan, the media objectives must reflect the marketing objectives. For example, we must ask if the product needs high levels of advertising that command the consumer's attention (as with new products) or sustained advertising (as with established brands).

Should advertising be scheduled in markets where the brand has its highest or lowest share? Are consumer promotions to be supported with advertising? Should media efforts be targeted to brand users, or nonusers?

Marketing Research

Marketing research can help define the advertiser's market and the consumer. There are a number of research resources available, such as Nielsen, and Simmons, to help with this investigation.

Creative Strategy

Creative strategy must be considered. If color is mandatory, the media planner would be hard pressed to rationalize the use of radio. The need for long copy versus short copy, or the knowledge that one advertisement will be created versus a pool of commercials, all have a bearing on media selection.

Promotion Strategy

The planner must be aware of the promotion strategy and, when appropriate, coordinate media activity with promotional programs. If consumer coupons are to be used, the planner must know timing and distribution requirements. How many coupons? How often? What kind of redemption is planned? What areas of the country? What target group of consumers?

Sales Data

Sales data are often a must. No product or service has a flat sales picture in every part of its marketing area. There are always areas of high and low development, areas where certain local factors or competitive forces play on the vitality of the advertised item. Sales data will also reveal seasonal sales patterns that may be important in scheduling advertising. The planner must also look at sales trends geographically. Seldom do the sales of a product increase or decrease in every market in the same way. Aberrations can usually be found and therefore acted on.

Competitive Activity

Competitive activity must be fully understood. The planner must analyze competitive efforts and ascertain: Which media are being used? How often? In which areas of the United States? To what levels? Investigating competitive media investment could reveal opportunities for dominating media not used by competition, or suggest increased spending in media used extensively by competition.

Basic Questions

The best approach to formulating media objectives is to answer basic questions that encompass the general areas of audience, geography, scheduling requirements, copy needs, reach and frequency and testing.

Audience

- Who does the advertiser want to reach?
- What is the relative importance of each group?

A thorough objective recognizes the importance, or lack of importance, of each demographic cell. The planner should analyze audiences on the basis of age, sex, income, education, race, employment status, family size, marital status, possessions, lifestyle characteristics and any other traits for which data are available. One must take care to ensure that the creative strategy addresses the same people as defined in the media objectives.

There are usually one or two key demographic groups for most products or services—for example, women 18–34 years old. Too often, however, a planner analyzes this group alone, completely disregarding all other groups. By limiting analysis in this manner, he or she makes the conscious decision that groups not analyzed have zero value, and that media reaching these nondefined groups are providing unwanted delivery. It behooves the media planner to analyze all demographic characteristics, including race, to set values for each group and thereby determine a target audience that encompasses all people.

Most market research generally reports on the value of each cell within a demographic category, such as women aged 18–34 within the category of age. But with the advent of computerized databases, much research is available to help in the decision of assigning values to each category, such as the value of age compared with that of income levels.

Geography

Where should the brand concentrate its advertising efforts? Are there markets which have minimal sales and how should one value these markets? Are brand sales changing disproportionately in any markets? Is national advertising mandatory?

The planner should establish geographic targets for the smallest possible universe. In order of desirability, targets should be based on:

- Neighborhood
- County
- Market (metropolitan area, TV market, etc.)
- Sales area

- State
- Region
- County size

The planner should recognize the sales or sales potential in each geographic area as well as any other ingredient deemed important, such as income, housing, and mobility. Often, we can use related data as a predictor of product sales: automobile mileage can be used to predict tire sales; temperature can be used to forecast sales of hot weather soft drinks.

It behooves the planner to establish a target for each geographic denominator and then allocate media delivery to each in accordance with these targets. Quite often it is necessary to do extensive sales analyses to establish targets by market.

Once all pertinent information is amassed, we need to decide which of two basic philosophies will be used to allocate advertising:

1. *Advertise where the business is.* This is basically a defensive posture. It protects the existing franchise and simultaneously seeks to develop more business on the assumption that increases in brand sales can be achieved most efficiently where the brand is currently strong. It is easier to build on an existing base where product distribution has been established and where there is apparent consumer awareness and acceptance of your client's product. Current nonusers in these areas have a greater propensity to become users than nonusers in areas where your client's product sales are low.

2. *Advertise where the business is not.* This philosophy is offensive. It is based on the belief that changing consumer demands, as well as changes in product formulation for your client's product or the competitive brands, result in brand-switching. Advertising in these areas would therefore announce the advertiser's presence and keep the product on consumers' minds should they decide to switch brands.

Scheduling

To what degree should the product or service recognize seasonal sales patterns? Are there any discernible patterns? How important is the introductory versus the sustaining period? Should competitive advertising efforts be countered?

The planner must formulate precise direction for each of these areas. Whenever possible, the most specific calendar units should be used (days, weeks, months). The extent of any effort must be quantified in order to show emphasis clearly. For example, clear direction is shown in the following kinds of objectives: "Spend advertising dollars in accordance with the percentage of sales each month." Or "Allocate no more than 60 percent of advertising expenditures during the introductory 13-week period." Or, "Increase advertising activity by 50 percent during each of the three planned promo periods. Precede the promotion by one week and run concurrently during the remaining four weeks of the promotion." Or "Concentrate all advertising from Wednesday to Saturday in order to reach potential Product X buyers immediately prior to the highest usage day, Sunday."

Copy

Some basic questions to ask concerning copy: What are the basic requirements for color, audio, visual? How does the complexity of the message affect copy length? What is the brand's creative experience?

Copy is obviously of extreme importance to any viable advertising effort. Regardless of the impact of the media plan, if it does not properly reflect the copy strategy, the entire campaign suffers. The media planner should, however, work together with the copywriter to create the best copy in the best medium, and this should happen in the early stages of planning. The copywriter should be made aware of the media ramifications of certain decisions, as should the media planner have a complete understanding of the copy needs.

Coupons

Will the media plan require a consumer promotion in the form of a media-distributed coupon? How many coupons will be distributed? How much reach will be required?

A number of advertising plans contain a promotional effort that can be either trade or consumer oriented. Trade promotions could take many forms, such as in-store displays, cost allowances (discounts) for purchasing certain quantities of product or purchasing at certain times of the year, sales contests, and so forth. These kinds of trade promotions do not generally require a consumer media effort.

A promotion directed to the consumer does require media support. Although the label of this effort is promotion, as opposed to advertising, the two must work in concert. If the marketing objective requires distribution of a cents-off coupon in order to counter competitive efforts or promote consumer trial, then this must be translated into an actionable media objective so the media planner can schedule appropriate media to deliver these coupons into the consumers' hands.

Reach and Frequency

What reach level is needed? How much frequency is required? Should reach and frequency levels vary by market? Should reach/frequency levels vary by time of the year?

The number of people you need to reach with advertising, and how often you need to reach them has the most demonstrable effect on a media plan. If it is possible to have a precise objective that clearly establishes how many people need to be reached and how often, this will significantly influence your choices of which media forms to consider, how much of each medium can be used, the number of weeks that advertising is affordable, or the budget that is necessary to achieve this objective.

Unfortunately, this objective is sometimes written after a plan is constructed and the delivery of that plan is determined. While this guarantees the objective will be achieved and will thereby make the media planner a genius at his task, it is a pointless exercise. If a predetermined level of advertising intensity is desirable or needed based on past performance, competitive pressure or judgment, then the planner should state that level in the objectives—prior to devising the actual media plan.

Testing

Should a media or copy test be conducted? What information can be garnered with a test?

Testing should always be considered in every media plan. There are too many unanswered questions to avoid testing. When one considers that an average media or copy test represents a negligible part of most large advertising budgets, the obvious conclusion is that testing should be continuous. Regardless of the media plan recommended, there is always room to conduct a test. For example:

- An unused medium—magazines if you are using TV, or radio if you are using magazines

- Media mix—magazines and TV versus either alone, or radio plus newspapers

- Copy length—ten-second commercials if the plan calls for :30s, or half pages instead of full pages

- Scheduling—flighting advertising with hiatus periods as opposed to continuous advertising, or concentrating in one television daypart rather than dispersing announcements through two or more dayparts.

Representative areas of the United States should be carved out in which to conduct testing. The areas should not only be a microcosm of total U.S. demography, but should also be representative of average product consumption, as well as having appropriate media availability in which to conduct the test.

Finally, give the test a fair chance to work. There is no magic timetable for a test after which period you can draw valid conclusions. But it is fair to assume that a media or copy test conducted in the marketplace will take weeks, or months, or perhaps a year before its thrust is felt at the consumer level.

In some cases, not all, objectives can be realistically met. For example, there may be an objective to reach at least 80 percent of a target group, and a second objective which requires advertising continuously throughout the sales season. Media availability and cost could prohibit the planner from accomplishing both of these objectives. It is therefore wise to give priorities to the objectives in order to have a clear direction in the decision-making process. If reach is given a greater priority than continuity of advertising, then the planner, when faced with the above situation, can elect to provide the needed levels of reach for as long a period as is affordable without necessarily advertising throughout the sales season.

Client Campaign/Media Plan Outline

1. *Start with a statement of the primary marketing objectives.*   These are established by the account executive after meeting with the client. The reasons for each objective should be clearly delineated in the overall marketing plan of which the media plan is only a part.

2. *Summarize essential market/product facts relating to selection and use of media.*   Include: sales figures and patterns by regions, county size, city-suburban, etc.; consumer data including age, income, family size, etc.; consumer purchasing data; consumer attitudes; consumer usage data; current competitive activity.

3. *Summarize creative objectives of the ad campaign that would effect the purchase and use of media.*   Is there color? What about product demonstration, visualization, product image?

4. *Statement of product's primary media objectives.*   These should be derived from the following sources: general marketing objectives, where they may be applicable to the selection of media; market and product data summary; and creative requirements. And they should cover the following information: Who is the advertising targeted at? Which markets should receive emphasis? What weight should the plan achieve in relation to the competition? Are there special times during the campaign period that should carry more emphasis? State the purpose of the campaign (to introduce a product, sustain or increase a product's sales, highlight new features of the product, etc.) What creative aspects of the campaign deserve special attention in relation to the media plan?

5. *Statement of media strategy.*   A summary of the methods that will be used to accomplish each individual objective and satisfy the marketing plan as a whole. The purpose of strategy is not to recommend or put down a specific medium, but rather to establish the major criterion by which all media will be judged and used. It would include reasons for: concentration in a limited number of media; level of coverage to be attained in various target groups; the reasons for using frequency vs. coverage levels; and timing of the campaign, among other things.

6. *Media techniques and plan.*   Include general media being considered. Details of specific media in each category (demographics), and the manner in which they will be used. Details of all media decided upon for the plan, with start and close dates of publication and airing, rates, special requirements, closing dates for materials, etc. (see Figures 22-1 and 22-2).

It should be obvious from the above outline that creating a workable media plan is no easy matter. It involves days, maybe even weeks of research, planning, figuring, refiguring, meetings with media people, meetings with agency creative and account people, going over media comparison figures, circulation figures…and on and on until a final, formal written proposal is ready for client approval.

One note of caution. A media plan should never be "set in stone." There should always be room to adjust it and make changes, if needed. Last-minute client marketing tactics or governmental restrictions imposed suddenly on the product, for example, might necessitate such revisions.

Krieff Advertising
3854 Sheridan Street, Hollywood, Florida 33021

CLIENT GREAT LIFE SAVINGS ASSOCIATION DATE_____

MEDIA SCHEDULE Newspaper/Bulletins APPROVED_____

PUBLICATION	AD SIZE	SECT.	RATE	JAN	FEB	MAR	APR	MAY	JUN	JUL	AUG	SEP	OCT	NOV	DEC	COST PER INSERTION	COST ALL INSERTIONS
*WEST-Ft. Lauderdale News	C 4x11 / CR 3x8½ / M 5x8	SUN WEST Twice Weekly	13.90													C - 573.96 / CR - 354.45 / M - 523.60	14,423.31
*WEST-Ft. Lauderdale News	C 3x8½ / M 4x6½	THUR WEST Thu-Tue	10.85													C - 276.47 / M - 282.10	8,408.27
Senior World-West	C 4x10 / M 5x7½ 13M	MTHLY WEST	300.00G									X	X	X	X	C - 300.00G / M - 300.00G	1,785.00
Plantation Mirror Sunrise/Tamarac Mirror	C 4x8½ / M 5x6½	WED	2/6.50													C - 221.00 / M - 211.25	581.00
*Jewish Journal	C 3x7½ / M 4x6	THUR	201.00													C - 201.00½ / N - 215.00	5,711.00
Sunrise Lakes Phase I	C 8x10	MTHLY	48.00							X	X	X	X	X	X	48.00	240.00
Sunrise Lakes Phase II	C 8x10	MTHLY	48.00							X	X	X	X	X	X	48.00 (34)	288.00
NOT AVAILABLE Sunrise Lakes Phase III																	

* Can Publish Current Rates
C=C.D. Means Custom Designed
M=More Money For Your Money
P=Passbook Account MM
R=Run Ad in Reduced Size

Figure 22-1. Sample of a media planning worksheet.

TV PRO FORMA – ACTUAL

Krieff Advertising

3854 Sheridan Street, Hollywood, Florida 33021 • Tel: (305) 987-9973 (Dade) 940-9973

SEALY PLANT:
TARGET MARKET:
AGENCY:

SEALY, INC. TARGET MARKETS

TV PRO FORMA

SCHEDULE DATES:
COMMERCIAL LENGTH:
RATING SERVICE:
DATE SUBMITTED:

WEEKLY SCHEDULE

ACTUAL

Station (Network)	Programming	Time	Day	ADI Rating (%)	Homes (000)	Women 25-54 (000)	Cost/ Spot	(*Sealy, Inc. Announcements)

Weekly Totals
Number of Weeks
Schedule Totals

SUMMARY

Station	GRP's Sealy, Inc.	Plant/Dealer	Total	Sealy, Inc.	DOLLARS Plant/Dealer	Total

TOTAL
PERCENTAGE

Figure 22-2. Sample of a television pro forma form.

Part 6 Action Checklist _____

✔ The main function of the traffic department is to assure that from the moment a new job is opened, to the time it is completed and billed for, all the elements and materials involved with that job flow through the various departments of the agency in an orderly manner, keeping to a strict time schedule, and within the approved budget. Interrelations between traffic and other departments of the agency are essential to the smooth flow of each job.

✔ An agency utilizes various traffic forms to keep track of each element involved with a particular job. Some of these forms include: a job log; a job work order; time allowance schedules; employee time sheets; client information sheets; job cost estimates; purchase orders; job status reports.

✔ The copywriter in your agency will have the responsibility of writing copy for the various types of advertisements your agency will produce. Being creative and effective with words, as well as being able to understand each client's marketing strategy is important. If your business plan does not call for an on-staff copywriter, you will want to consider using freelance talent.

✔ Every advertisement, whether it be for print, broadcast or whatever, is made up of certain elements. The headline or theme line, the illustration or visual action, the body or selling copy, the slogan or trade character, and the logo or signature.

✔ There is a logical order to all persuasive copywriting that carries the audience to the point of favorable action. There are many people in the business who believe this order is based on the theory known as "AIDA"—attracting *Attention*, creating *Interest*, stimulating *Desire*, and asking for *Action*.

✔ The copywriter must be able to thoroughly digest all the facts about the product or service being advertised, preferably by using it and comparing it to the competition. He or she must also understand the marketing objectives of the client as well as the nature of the targeted consumer—their buying habits, attitudes, and knowledge of the product.

✔ The ability of your art director may well control the fate of every campaign your agency produces. His or her layout skills, ability to attract attention, and awareness of what pleases other people can make the difference between a successful and unsuccessful ad.

✔ In creating an ad or campaign concept, the art director begins with a basic layout or outline of an idea. This idea is usually in collaboration with the copywriter, and is aimed at producing a clear, concise picture of how the final ad will look. Keeping the layout simple so as not to lose clarity, and interesting enough to catch and hold the attention of the audience, is the basic goal. The more elements added to an advertisement, the more confusing and disarranged it becomes. A good ad layout will emphasize the important product facts the client wants to get across.

- ✔ A variety of art media are available for producing the illustration portion of an ad. These include: still photography, videotape, or film; wash, line, or pencil drawings; color as opposed to black and white.

- ✔ The most important thing to remember about selecting a typeface for an ad is that it be legible. Type that is uninviting to the eye, and difficult to read, defeats the goal of the ad.

- ✔ After the creative portion of the ad concept has been completed and approved, the traffic department will send the materials to the mechanical production department which directs the conversion of the copy, layout, and art to the final mechanical which will be used by the media and printers to mass produce the advertisement.

- ✔ Media selection is the bridge that spans the gulf between what is created and what is seen or heard. To be most effective, the media selected by the media buyer must reach more of the right consumers, through the right media channels, with the greatest economy possible. The first step in selecting media is for the media buyer to develop a media plan for a particular ad or campaign. The use of research, creative and promotional strategy, evaluation of client sales data and competitive activity are all elements that are necessary to formulating an effective media plan.

- ✔ As in the case of on-staff versus free-lance copywriters, the same holds true for media buyers and planners. Your agency should also take advantage of information and services that are offered by the various media through their media reps.

- ✔ In making media selection decisions, make use of all the media information sources available to you. They provide important data concerning audience characteristics, market coverage and costs.

- ✔ In scheduling and placing media, consider that ad size, positioning, and mechanical characteristics can affect the effectiveness of a given advertisement.

- ✔ You owe it to your clients to take full advantage of all discounts allowed by media. These include discounts for frequency, discounts for positioning, discounts for standby ads, and discounts for early payment.

- ✔ The media plan must always reflect the marketing objectives of the client.

- ✔ Since last minute client marketing tactics, or suddenly imposed governmental restrictions may affect the selling of a product, the media plan should never be "set in stone." Always leave room for last minute adjustments.

Part 7

Production
and Printing

23

Printing: Nearly Everything You'll Need to Know

Art Directors, Production People, and Printers

Your agency is preparing a collateral piece for printing. The creative and production teams have designed and produced a mechanical that has fine line illustrations as well as heavy solids. Can they both be printed together, in close register, on soft paper on one run through a two-color press? Maybe on some stocks but not on others. Maybe the heavy solids on a soft paper will spread—or fan out—in the press. You may be better off using a smaller, less absorbent paper on a smaller press. You may have to redesign the piece or sacrifice a little bit of one to get all of the other. Your creative and production people need to know how they will get the best results.

It is important to remember that not all printers—or all printing presses—can yield the same results on a given job. Too often, the printer comes off as the bad person, if a finished piece doesn't give the result the art director had in mind. But the simple fact is that presses have physical limitations and paper has physical limitations and the artist or production person from the agency should have talked to the printer before the job was given out.

Ad agency creative and production people need not be printing experts. They need not know all the terms and expressions of the printing trade. That's what printers are for. But any collateral work put out by your creative department will be aided by at least a rudimentary understanding of printing techniques and press capabilities.

Types of Printers

The printing industry does not lend itself to strict definitions. There are many printers that specialize in one type of printing or another, and a large print house will not necessarily produce a better result on a particular job. It is best to know the capabilities of the printers you will be dealing with in your area.

Large Commercial Printers

Large companies generally provide a full line of printing services, including four-color. They usually have a sufficient mix of presses so that there's one that matches the requirements of your given job. Large print houses generally do a better job on long-run, high-quality, multicolor projects. Many large printers will not take on short press run jobs because the cost of press and art preparation will not be economical.

Small Commercial Printers

Smaller printers generally have both one- and two-color presses and work with papers that come in sheet sizes of 17" X 22" or less. They usually provide in-house services such as screens, stripping, and halftones, but will probably job out engraving, embossing, and other specialties.

Specialty Printers

These firms offer engraving, diecutting, embossing, foil stamping, pastel leafing, thermography, and other operations. Always make sure that any specialty printer or commercial printer you use can meet the needs of the particular job you are giving out. Ask for samples of similar work the shop has done. Check with the companies the shop did the work for to make sure the samples you saw were not jobbed out to another printer. Also make sure the printer was reliable on delivery schedules as well as sticking to the quoted price.

Quick Printers

Quick printers do short-run jobs on very quick turnaround. Most of their business walks in off the street. They generally work from camera-ready art, since most do not have the capabilities to screen or strip halftones.

In-House Printers

Sometimes your clients will have limited printing facilities on their premises, and will request that some of the jobs you create be printed on their own presses. In-house equipment can range from a simple duplicating machine to two- and four-color presses, complete with experienced press people. Before designing the piece to be printed by the client, it is absolutely necessary to find out the client's printing capabilities.

Designing for Printing

By simple definition, graphic design means planning and arranging type and illustrations to convey a message.

There is a tendency by nonprofessionals as well as experienced agency art directors to think of the design of a brochure or flyer, for example, as simply the working out of the aesthetics: making it look attractive, choosing the right colors, and so on.

The creation of any collateral piece should always be planned in the same manner as an architect plans houses or an engineer designs engines. If this basic functional approach is followed, there will be less chance for the type to be illegible, for the pictures to be poorly arranged, and for the person reading the piece to be ill-served.

Graphic design is a skill as much as it is an art, and it takes years of experience to learn how to do it well. It involves various ways to organize a collateral piece that includes such techniques as the use of symmetry (lines are centered); asymmetry (balance); flush left, ragged right (an uneven right-hand edge); and the modular "grid system" design technique. Chapter 20 discusses many of these techniques in greater detail.

A responsible art director can save a client money by correctly choosing type and size of type, creating sensible organization, and selecting the proper presses and bindery equipment.

Often, the aesthetics of a good design and effective format will help make an advertising printed piece more effective, thereby bringing higher returns to your client.

Good design is an accomplishment that the agency, the client, and the printer can all take pride in. Just as you care about your personal appearance, you should also have the same concerns for what you print for your clients.

How the Production Department Prepares for Printing

Your production department's concerns with printed matter involve such areas as determining costs, planning how the printed piece will be produced, and how long it will take to produce it. Since the range of production duties is covered more fully elsewhere in this book, we will only touch on some important production points to consider in planning a print job.

1. Get three or more quotes in writing on every job and make sure they are specific in what they include.
2. When figuring your costs for client approval, be thorough. Add a safe allowance for changes, embossing dies, shipping charges, paper price increases, and the like.
3. Select the right printer for each job, one whose size and capabilities best, and most economically, fit your needs. Get references and samples. Update your printing sources file regularly.

4. Try not to give all your work to one printer. On the other hand, you shouldn't use a new printer for each job. Working with printers is just like working with other vendors. The supplier and agency must get to know each other's procedures and business practices, and this takes time. We would recommend using two or three suppliers regularly, and occasionally trying someone new. If your suppliers are aware of the fact that they are not your only source for printing, you will find that their pricing will be much more competitive.

5. Visit the printers you work with. Look at their presses (even if you don't know what you're looking at). Ask questions.

6. Understand the trade customs that are generally used throughout the printing industry in the United States. Some important ones are:

    a. *Quotations*—A quotation not accepted within 30 days is subject to review.

    b. *Orders*—Verbal or written orders can only be canceled on terms that will compensate the printer against loss.

    c. *Preparatory materials*—Artwork, type, plates, negatives, positives, and other items when supplied by the printer remain the printer's property unless otherwise agreed in writing.

    d. *Alterations*—These represent work performed in addition to original specifications and therefore the printer is entitled to compensation at current rates. The printer should support alteration charges with documentation on request.

    e. *Proofs*—Proofs are submitted with original copy. Corrections are to be made on a "master set," returned marked "O.K." or "O.K. with corrections" and signed by the agency production person, the account executive, and the client. If revised proofs are required, the request should be made when proofs are returned. Printers are not usually held responsible for errors if the job has been approved by the agency and client or if changes are communicated verbally.

    f. *Press proofs*—Unless the cost is estimated in the quote, press proofs are charged for at current rates.

    g. *Over/under runs*—These should not exceed 10 percent on quantities up to 10,000 and/or the percentage agreed upon. The printer will bill for actual quantity delivered within this tolerance. If the agency or client requires guaranteed "no less than" delivery, the percentage tolerance of overage must be doubled.

    h. *Customer's property*—Such property will be insured by the printer against fire, vandalism, malicious mischief and sprinkler leakage.

    i. *Delivery*—Unless otherwise specified, the price quoted is for a single shipment, without storage, FOB local customer's place of business or FOB printer's platform for out-of-town customers.

    j. *Terms*—Unless other arrangements are made, terms are net cash 30 days from date of invoice. Claims for defects, damages, and the like must be made by the agency in writing within 30 days after delivery.

7. Small mistakes or defects are par for the course when it comes to printing. Though it is always good agency policy to hold a printer (or any supplier) to the agreement you have, if a mistake is something you and the client can live with, the

printer would probably appreciate not having to reprint the piece. And, should the situation be reversed at another time, the printer would probably return the favor.

You're Ready to Go on Press

Okay, now you've created the layout and charted your strategy of stock selection. You've steered the job through production and emerged with the finished art camera-ready for printing. The final challenge, printing, is about to begin. Shortly, something your agency conceived will be brought to life on paper, and whatever happens from that point on, will reflect in part, on your shop—the imagination of your creative staff and the judgment and knowledge of your production department.

Methods of Printing

There are three principal methods of printing: relief (letterpress), planographic (offset lithography), and intaglio (gravure).

In letterpress printing the impression area which establishes the image on paper is raised (in relief) above the areas from which nothing will be printed.

In offset lithography, a flat plate is treated so that it has an image area which attracts ink and repels water, and a nonimage area, which does the reverse. The inked image then transfers or "off-sets" to a rubber blanket and from there is printed onto paper. The image area is flush with the level of the nonimage area on the plate.

In gravure, the image areas are actually below the nonimage areas. Small pits or recessed areas arranged in a uniform, gridlike pattern on the plate carry the ink, which is deposited on the paper by means of great pressure.

There are many subgroups for each of the three printing methods, and possibly several systems that could be considered quasi-methods of their own, such as screen printing and electrostatic printing. However, we will examine the three basic methods in detail and see what each has to offer.

Letterpress Printing

Letterpress printing is the oldest form, originating in Korea as early as 1337 and in Germany with Gutenberg around 1440. A feature of letterpress is its tendency to squeeze the image into the paper. Compared with offset, the letterpress impression is darker and richer, and there is a tactile "impressed" appearance.

Offset Lithography

Offset lithography is a mere youngster in the history of printing technology, but has risen to be dominant in the United States. A mechanical outgrowth of stone lithography, offset printing was developed in the early 1900s, and was first used commercially to print tin sheets for cans and boxes. Today, it is the dominant method by which letterheads and envelopes are printed.

Even in the early days, the rubber blanket of offset triumphed in its ability to print images of every degree of delicacy—including halftones containing as many as 200 to 300 dots to the inch—on practically every degree of surface roughness. This is a big advantage, and explains why so much time, money, and effort went into the improvement of offset lithography. Letterpress does not allow fine-line halftone printing on rough paper surfaces.

Another advantage of offset, again associated with the rubber blanket, is its near-total elimination of the troublesome and time-consuming process known as *make-ready*, a necessary feature of good letterpress printing.

The short make-ready time of offset is one reason for the spectacular advances made in the technique known as web printing. In web printing, paper is fed to the press in rolls instead of one sheet at a time. The folding and gathering is done at the same time, at the end of the press. Web printing is thus highly automated and for long runs is efficient and economical. Web printing was once restricted to newspapers, magazines, and other forms of long-run work. With offset, shorter and shorter runs are now feasible, and web offset printing is making significant advances into markets long cornered by sheet-fed presses.

One-color offset presses are capable of laying down only a single color in a given press run. If two-color printing is required, the paper must be allowed to dry and run through the press a second time.

Also, registration can be difficult. Only partly does this reflect the skill of the printer or equipment. More, it's a matter of the paper used. Many letterhead papers are soft in composition, and can change shape as they pass through the press. In addition, since the paper must sit between press runs, there are dangers that it may take on or lose moisture, which will cause the shape of the page to shift. The second press run, therefore, is being done on a "different" sheet from the first run.

Two-color offset presses lay down two colors of ink in a single press run. Printing a second color on a two-color press costs relatively little more than printing a single color. In many cases, the cost of a two-color printed piece can be well within a client's budget.

Multicolor presses can lay down four or more colors in a single press pass, and can reproduce full-color illustrations as well as photography.

Gravure Printing

Gravure printing is best suited to long runs. It is too expensive for general short-run use, and so is not for the average printing shop. It is the platemaking process that makes gravure printing expensive, although efforts are being made to reduce this cost. The advantage of gravure is its capacity to lay down an unbelievably dense layer of ink. Silkscreen printing is gravure's only rival insofar as ink density is concerned, and silkscreen cannot print an adequate halftone. Gravure most certainly can. Black-and-white halftones and full-color halftones can be rendered with far greater contrast and "snap" than in offset or letterpress, because of the greater degree of color saturation (that is, the colors are deeper and more intense). You often see the result in luxurious art books and high-quality newspaper magazines: colors that are bright, intense, and attractive.

A disadvantage of gravure, besides the high cost of platemaking, is that everything, including type, must be rendered in grid or dot-structured form. Thus, type and other linear images that by their nature are meant to be printed with a clean edge are printed by means of a screen pattern. The choice of the right typeface—a type that is heavy enough—can minimize this problem.

Problems, Limitations, and Freedoms of Printing

This discussion will focus on offset printing mainly because offset has become the dominant printing method.

There is no excuse for poorly printed type. Sloppy presswork is usually the cause, but sometimes there are other reasons. The full name for offset lithography is *photo-offset lithography,* and it must not be forgotten that the end result is only as good as what gets exposed on film. Improper exposure or developing on film in the darkroom can ruin what would otherwise result in good printing.

Halftone reproduction, which is truly fascinating, is multidisciplined, involving photography, chemistry, mechanics, visual perception and judgment, and the study of the properties of inks, papers, and the kinds of presses used for reproduction. Some of the fundamentals are just as interesting as the technical complexities. A *halftone* is a reproduction of a photograph (or other subject containing grays or continuous tones). A halftone screen converts the original gray tones into dots of various sizes.

The screen is made up of crisscrossing lines on either glass or film. It is placed either in contact with the halftone film or in front of the film, and the picture is exposed through the screen. Each grid opening in the screen acts as a miniature lens and allows light to pass through and focus on the film. Thus each grid opening yields one dot, whose size depends on whatever degree of lightness or darkness comes through from the picture.

Why use a screen? Why must a photograph be broken into dots? The answer is that a press can lay down only solid areas of ink. Each halftone dot, no matter how small, prints as a separate mass of ink. But the masses are so close to one another that the eye is tricked into perceiving grays.

Screens come in different degrees of fineness, depending on the number of lines to the linear inch. Coarse screens of 65 to 85 dots to the inch are used for letterpress printing on rough-surfaced paper, and are common in metropolitan newspapers. Screens with 120 to 150 dots to the inch are typically used in general commercial offset work. Sometimes finer screens with 200 to 300 dots per inch are used for certain kinds of high-quality printing. A 300-line screen, of course, produces a printed picture with 300 dots to the linear inch, and you would need a powerful magnifying glass to see them at all.

When is a finer screen necessary? The most obvious answer is when minute details exist in the original and need to show up when printed. If there are twice as many dots, the detail will be defined approximately twice as well. You will also find 200- and 300-line screens used for high-quality "art" reproduction. Given the combination of an excellent printer, excellent original copy, and the proper paper, wonderful images can come into being through fine-screen lithography.

A disadvantage of fine-line screens is the difficulty encountered in the dark, shadow areas of a photograph. Shadow details are the trickiest to hold intact at any screen level, but when the screens climb to 200- or 300-line (particularly the latter), the shadow details are extremely difficult to retain on the printed sheet. Why? One of the properties of ink is the tendency to cling to itself. As a general rule, it is important to watch out for shadow detail in any picture. It's easy to lose some of it at any screen level, no matter how skillful the printer.

Getting the best photocopy to begin with is essential, and often overshadows any debate over fineness or coarseness of screen. All reproduction, including the making of a photograph, involves a loss of quality of some degree, or at the very best a change. The printed image is no less than four steps (generations) removed from the original. The picture goes from photograph to halftone negative, from there to the offset plate, thence to the rubber blanket, and finally to a sheet of paper.

What happens along the way?

Generally there is loss of contrast. The blackest black of offset ink cannot rival the darkest black of either a photograph or the real world. The whitest of white paper is not as "white" or reflective as the whites of the real world. There is also a loss of sharpness of detail. If the human eye can perceive a pine needle from a distance of 50 feet, a camera may retain the detail of that single pine needle, but the dot structure of the halftone will probably not.

Loss of contrast or detail is not necessarily bad. That is quite another question and depends on the situation. But we will assume for the moment that one criterion for good reproduction is that the printed image resemble closely its real-world counterpart.

Color Printing

Black-and-white halftones trick the eye by making solid black dots seem like grays. Color reproduction also relies on the dot phenomenon, but tricks us into seeing a full range of color from the use of only four inks. The colors of these inks are called *process colors,* and they are magenta, yellow, cyan, and black.

A halftone negative is made for each of the colors by interjecting a filter between the illustration and negative. These negatives are called *color separations.* A green filter is used to make the negative which will print the magenta color, a red filter for cyan, and a blue filter for yellow. Each halftone negative carries a different "record" of the image. Magenta and cyan together form purple; therefore magenta and cyan will be strong (through the large size of their dots) where purples will print. Cyan and yellow will be strong where green will print. Colored dots that vary in size combine to form colors when viewed from a distance. (The foregoing description grossly simplifies the concept of color printing and its perception.) The reason why black is almost always included as the fourth "color" is to add snap by increasing density in the blacks and grays.

Your clients should accept the fact that colors change from the original to the printed image. For instance, if you are printing a catalog as the only means of advertising your client uses—and the catalog pictures must accurately reflect the colors of the products shown—you may want the client to be present when the first sheets come off the press so that slight color adjustments can be made on the spot. Keep in mind that many colors in the visible spectrum can't be duplicated by the four-color process system. Occasionally printers run a fifth color on press, when a shade is critical and must be matched. Color printing is like every other graphic arts process. It is bounded by limitations, and the professional approach is to understand them so you can deal with them.

For the agency buying color printing, one of the first habits to develop is a common "color language" with your printer. It is wrong to examine a transparency by holding it to a window or light, send it off for printing, and expect the printed version to match what you saw. You and your printer must rely on the same light source when viewing a transparency. The industry standard is a 5000° Kelvin light source. There are devices (lightboxes) on the market that illuminate transparencies to the correct color temperature. They are within the budget of—and a must for—anyone who can afford to spend money for color printing.

Making separations is not an exact science. Whether the separations are made manually or by means of automated scanners, you will need to check the accuracy of what the separator has done and, if necessary, ask the separator to make color corrections. You have several options, in order of diminishing costs.

1. *Checking color on press, with no preliminary proofs.* If changes are needed, the press is stopped, the negatives remade or etched, and new plates made. Naturally this can be expensive. But it carries the advantage of running the color in place, with each picture in actual position. It is common to all printing situations that differ areas of the sheet need ink in uneven quantities. A heavy block of magenta in one illustration may drain this color away from another illustration. By seeing this, the customer and printer can make compensations.

2. *Press proofs.* These are proofs of the individual halftones only, made on a small proof press, and usually include progressive proofs as well as the finished proof. Progressive proofs show each color singly, and in succession, until the last proof entails the combination of all colors together, as they will be printed. They are useful to the printer. It takes a trained eye to spot a weakness or overabundance of color, and to know by what percentage a color should be strengthened or weakened to correct a flaw. If you have had no experience with progressive proofs, treat them with respect, look at and admire them, but confine your corrections to the finished proof (where all colors are combined on the same sheet).

Press proofs can do more harm than good if not made correctly. If the job will eventually run on a four-color press and one impression of ink is applied "wet" over another, then the proofs should be prepared the same way. Inks printed one after the other on a four-color press react with one another differently and result in different shades from those printed on a small proof press where the inks are allowed to dry between impressions. Be sure this common denominator for proofs and printing is made clear at the start of a job.

3. *Cromalin proof and transfer keys.* These are not printed on a press, but created chemically. A cromalin proof is a facsimile of the full-color halftone, made using dyes on a very glossy paper. Transfer keys are made on a single sheet of acetate.

4. *3-M overlays.* These are also chemically made. They are similar to transfer keys, since they are created on the same material, acetate. Instead of the dots coexisting on the same piece of acetate, each color—magenta, cyan, yellow, and black—is represented on a different acetate overlay. Since the acetate is virtually transparent, the combination of the four overlays will make a full-color image.

When asking for color changes, try to think as concretely as the subjective nature of color will allow. Printers are often puzzled and bedeviled by corrections which read "make this area browner." Much better to attach a color swatch of a particular brown to the area that requires change.

Finally, you should be aware of one way to avoid the hassle and cost of color correction, which is quite simply to do no color correcting and proofing whatever. This route is not as preposterous as it sounds. It is practical when high qualify is not expected or needed, when low cost is vital, and when you have confidence in the printer and the printer has confidence in doing justice to the original photograph or illustration. Of course, it must be quickly added that if you order no proof, any snafu of the printer will be quickly passed on as your responsibility. If the ocean is printed purple instead of blue, you must live with it. And given the relatively low cost of color proofing, some kind of proof is usually warranted.

Embossing

Embossing is a process for creating a raised, three-dimensional image on a sheet of paper. In some applications, the raised texture is printed; in others, such as blind embossing, no ink is used and the visual/tactile effect comes from the change in the papers shape and finish. The process may also be reversed, and an indented—or debossed—surface created instead of a raised one.

Embossing can have a unique effect on a high-quality letterhead, because the raised surface invites touch, and because the technique itself conveys a sense of richness. Embossing is an excellent way to modernize and spruce up an old logo without making a drastic change.

During the embossing process, both heat and pressure are applied to the paper, which is pressed between a "female" die and a "male" counterplate. The die may be flat, which means the etching was done to a specific depth, or sculptured, giving varying levels of depth for an added effect. Dies have a beveled outside edge to keep the paper from tearing under the pressure.

Creating an embossing die is a one-time expense and, given the effect of the technique, a very modest one. Dies may be hand-sculptured, machined in brass or other metal, or acid-etched on a photo-engraved plate.

For high-quality embossing, paper selection is crucial. Heavier sheets will take embossing of greater depth and detail, but weight alone will not determine the result. Heavily textured sheets add other design elements, because the embossing will press out the texture, creating a surface contrast.

The key to high-quality embossing depends in great measure on the printer's skill in making the counterplate and capturing the details of the original art.

Thermography

Thermography is a generally lower-cost alternative to embossing. Yet it adds three dimensionality to a printed piece and can be particularly appropriate in giving distinctive highlights to brochure covers, letterheads, envelopes, and business cards.

Two related processes are used to create this raised effect. In one, paper printed with a slow-drying ink is dusted with a resinous powder, which may be colored, clear, or metallic. The resin adheres to the ink, with the remains vacuumed away. The sheet is then moved to an oven where—at up to 1200°—the resin melts, fuses to the ink, and raises the image from the sheet.

The second approach allows four-color thermography. Here, a finished piece is overprinted with a clear varnish. The varnish is dusted with a clear resin which, once heated and dried, raises the entire printed image on the sheet.

When done correctly, thermography produces a permanent image which is chipproof and crackproof. It can be diecut and it can bleed from the page.

Using extrafine resin, fine type and line illustrations, thermography can be used to allow very detailed reproductions.

Not all paper works well with thermography. The sheet must be 20 lb and up. Many hard-to-print stocks may be successfully thermographed, including coated cover, vinyl, and polyester.

Hot Stamping

Hot stamping takes the heat and pressure process of embossing a step further by transferring an opaque foil material to the surface of the paper. The effect can be a vivid color statement, because the foils used have greater color density than ink.

While there are many different kinds of foils to choose from, the most commonly used are pigmented foils and metallics. There are also wood grains, marbled foils, and dusted foils that give a softer image. The foil you select depends on the effect you want to achieve, though deeply opaque pigmented foils are sometimes hard to cut cleanly.

In hot stamping, an extremely thin ribbon of foil is fed into a press, and it releases its pigment onto the paper when pressed between a die and a hard, flat surface and heat is applied. When combined with embossing, a relief die and counter are used. Foils can also be stamped over one another.

There are certain limitations to hot stamping. First, the temperature and pressure may discolor certain colored papers, especially browns, yellows, and oranges. Second, you will be limited in matching foils to standard PMS colors (Pantone Matching System—a color, number-coded guide that gives the printer the percentages of ink mixtures to obtain the desired final printed color). Third, pigmented foil colors may appear slightly darker or lighter, depending on the color of the background.

Pastel Leafing

A hot-stamping technique that is a good way to give shadings and tonings to blind embossing, pastel leafing adds the most color to the lowest point in the emboss and the least color to the highest point. It adds depth and definition to the design. For this reason, pastel leafing is most often used with sculptured or multilevel embossing.

Pastel leafing can be done with existing dies by shops that do hot foil stamping and embossing work. A heavy stock and a workable design are recommended.

Adding this effect is nearly in the same cost range as single-color printing, once the investment in the die has been made. It is an economical choice when you want to accent a small, intricate embossed design with a subtle color contrast.

The drawback, however, is that the choices of color are limited to pastel shades of blue, pink, green, peach, yellow, gray, and clear. The clear leaf adds a touch of glossy finish to a flat sheet.

Silkscreening

Virtually all letterheads printed today are lithographed, but there are times when silkscreening provides an alternative choice. Silkscreening is a refinement of the basic stencil process, consisting—from top down—of ink, a screen, a mask, and the printing surface.

Ink is forced through the screen and, where the mask does not block it, prints on the printing surface. The mask itself may be cut by hand from a film or photographically etched.

Because the technique involves substantial hand labor, it is cost competitive with lithography only for very limited quantities: 1000 or less.

As a printing method, however, silkscreening does offer certain advantages. The inks used are opaque, so a true white can be laid down on a dark sheet without the dark bleeding through. The same is true of heavy metallic inks.

In designing for silkscreening, avoid small detail such as delicate serifs and fine type. You are more likely to use silkscreening for printing on specialty items for your clients: T-shirts, binders, signs, and other materials that cannot be economically printed by other processes.

Diecutting

Diecutting is a strong visual technique used for special purposes and effects in printed pieces. Diecutting is a lot like cookie cutting, except that the design is punched out of paper instead of dough. Cuts can be straight, V-shaped, square, rectangular, circular, or any specially designed shape. The cuts are made on a letterpress as a sharp-edged steel die comes down on the paper and presses it into a flat, resilient counter.

Basic diecutting is roughly equivalent in cost to adding another color of ink—providing you already have your own die or can make use of a standard die that your printer has. If you are printing a brochure, for instance, and the back inside cover has a standard 3-inch diecut flap with slits for a business card, your printer probably has this die and may use it often for dozens of other customers. If you have to make a custom die, the cost will depend on how complex the design is.

When designing a diecut, use top-grade paper 22 lb or higher. Avoid delicate lacy patterns that tear easily, either on press or in use. Avoid tight registration between diecuts and printing, as they are hard to hold. Avoid cuts that get in the way of the printed message, prevent printed sheets from going into the typewriter easily, or cause filing problems.

Binding and Finishing

Binding and finishing printed sheets can be as simple as the single fold of a four-page flier. Or it can be as specialized as certain aspects of typesetting and printing. For instance, sheets intended for point-of-purchase displays must be trimmed, diecut, and mounted on cardboard "easels." Packaging is a trade to itself, characterized by intricate diecutting, creasing, and other complex operations. Of course, packages and point-of-purchase placards are everywhere. Without them, retail stores would hardly function, at least not within the merchandising tradition that exists today.

Binding

Not everything printed needs to be bound. Letterheads and many business forms are printed from pretrimmed stock and need no folding. But most printing must be converted from flat sheets to the finished form.

Sheets can be folded in many ways. Thanks to state-of-the-art equipment, the variations are endless. The buckle folders found in most commercial shops are usually equipped with three and sometimes four sections. A section is that part of a folder which stops the sheet and forces it to buckle, thereby creating a fold. Each section is adjustable. Despite the ability of these machines to handle all kinds of sophisticated folds, the customer should check with the binder to make sure the equipment can handle the folding requirements of the job. Binding equipment differs from one shop to another, and if printing is not done according to bindery machines, the end result may be a confused binder who receives 10,000 sheets of something that can't be bound. A printer should always be told to check with the binder for correction imposition.

The number of folding options may seem limitless. Actually, there are ways of categorizing folds.

Like all machine operations, folding is accurate only to within certain tolerances. For instance, if you flip through the pages of a book you will see that the page numbers and running heads on a page are not perfectly aligned with those on the facing page. This is normal. Folding is an operation where each step is one of diminished accuracy. If the first fold is not exactly perfect, the inaccuracy can't be remedied in the next fold. But it can become worse if the second fold isn't true.

The point is: Beware of losing the image off the page! What is more apt to happen, and is almost as aggravating, is for the image to wander too close to the edge of the page, where it will look peculiar even though it's still there. As a rule, you should keep type at least ⅜" away from the trimmed edge.

Another source of exasperation comes when material is designed to straddle the gutter between two facing pages. The problem of gutter crossovers tells us something on a broader level that is basic and axiomatic: namely, that folding (and binding and finishing generally) are the least accurate of the machine processes in the graphic arts. Commercial folding is accurate to units measured in sixteenths of inches. Offset printing is far more precise. The tolerances are measured in thousandths of an inch. A color halftone, for example, requires such accurate printing that each dot of a given color must be in register with the dots of the other three colors. Typesetting is equally precise.

Five generalizations on folding may help the print buyer or planner:

1. "Unbalanced" folds, in which the edges do not align corner to corner, (as in road maps), are difficult for the binder to execute.

2. Any piece with more than five folds may tax your binder's ability. If you reach

this level of complexity, you should also reach for the phone and consult the binder.

3. The grain direction of paper influences folding. Paper grain should run parallel to the binding edge or spine of the piece. If it doesn't, the pages will not lie flat. Covers printed on heavier stock will not lie flat either, and the surface of the cover stock will often develop cracks and wrinkles.

4. The range of paper weights a binder can fold easily runs from 50 lb. to 80 lb. Anything lighter or heavier costs more to fold.

5. When in doubt about any folding configuration, consult your binder. After folding, there are many different ways of assembling the printed pages.

Loose-Leaf Binding.   Loose-leaf covers many forms of binding. All of them are nonrigid. One of the "loosest" of all are pages held together by the do-it-yourself fastening devices that one can buy in stationery stores. Notebooks, ring binders, and post binders (the last are commonly used for ledgers) are other methods of fastening pages together. The many forms of loose-leaf binding comprise one of the two largest segments of commercial binding, the other being saddle-wire binding.

Spiral, Plastic, and Coil Binding.   Three methods of "mechanical" binding are commonly used for calendars, notebooks, and the like. Holes or slots are cut along the edge of the spine, after which the wire or plastic is inserted. All these bindings will allow the pages to lie flat. In fact, the spiral and coil bindings allow pages to rotate 360°. Plastic binding is almost as flexible. It allows the individual user to insert or remove pages through a device called a punching and closing machine. Spiral bindings will not allow for changing pages once the sheets are bound.

Saddle Wire.   Two or three wires, or staples, inserted through the crease of the spine hold the sheets together. Saddle wire is the common binding method for a small booklet, although it will accommodate 64 pages, and sometimes 96, if the paper is light enough. There are several obvious advantages to saddle-wire binding. The cost is low and the pages will lie flat when the booklet is used.

Side Wire.   Side wire is sometimes used when the number of pages is too great for saddle wiring, and when low cost is still desired, as well as great strength. Since the wires are placed about ¼" in from the spine, the binding is "tight" and pages will not lie completely flat. The page layout must be planned with a generous inside margin.

Perfect Binding.   Most paperback books are perfect bound. So are some hardbound books. Pages are folded and gathered, and the spine edge is roughened; an adhesive is applied, a cover is attached, and the pages are trimmed. This method of binding is less costly than sewing (see below). It is also less strong, although proper planning and proper use of materials can result in a binding of surprising strength.

Sewn.   The machine used to stitch books is somewhat more complicated than the ordinary home sewing machine. After sewing, and if the book is to be hardbound, the sheets are passed through a rounding machine, which imparts the characteristic curved back of hardbound books. Then, the case or cover, is attached. The indisputable advantage of a sewn book is its strength. Reference books and other books that need extra durability are usually sewn.

Finishing

Finishing is a catchall word to describe a variety of operations that are done after printing. They include inserting, padding, perforating, diestamping, punching, scoring, coating, varnishing, diecutting, laminating, embossing, and mounting.

Many of these operations are very specialized. This book will not unravel the finer points of such operations as padding and perforating, for instance, or most of the other finishing operations. But there are five kinds of finishing that come up in the everyday world of the print buyer often enough to justify further discussion. They are varnishing, plastic coating, film laminating, diecutting, and embossing.

Varnishing is usually done on press, sometimes even at the same time that the piece is being printed. The varnish is simply carried in an ink fountain, in place of ink. Varnish is applied to printed matter for several reasons. Varnish often enhances halftones, making blacks "blacker" or denser and by so doing increasing contrast and overall visual impact. Varnish will also protect the printed piece from scuffing and finger marks. Dense blacks and dark colors are unusually susceptible to showing the effects of wear and tear, particularly on glossy paper. Varnishing is usually reserved for high-gloss sheets. Any rough-surfaced paper generally doesn't benefit from it.

Plastic coating is a more expensive process than press varnishing; in return, greater protection and higher gloss are achieved. Plastic coating is done by a coating specialist. The equipment involved is too expensive for the average printer. The coating is applied by rollers. Each sheet is then passed through an oven on a conveyor belt so the coating will dry. As with varnishing, only high-gloss papers benefit from plastic coating.

Film laminating is a process by which a thin sheet of plastic film is glued to the printed sheet, using heated rollers. Items commonly laminated are menus and record jackets. Lamination gives ultimate gloss and ultimate protection. The surface is washable, which explains why so many menus are laminated.

As was covered earlier in this chapter, diecutting is the process of cutting unusual shapes into paper, sometimes by dies that look and perform much in the manner of a cookie cutter, sometimes by the use of steel rules. Diecutting can add enormous appeal to printed material. It can alter the rectangular shape normally imparted by traditional trimming. Holes and other shapes can be cut through a page, and when this is done, the reader usually wants to see what's on the next page! Diecutting is no cure-all for every piece of printing, but for some situations its potential is obvious.

Also covered in greater detail earlier in this chapter, embossing is to press paper into bas-relief. It requires male and female dies, and a slightly higher-than-usual budget. When embossing is effectively done, nothing can match its tactile properties. After all, we usually see a two-dimensional world on the printed page. The embossed image takes us by surprise because it introduces the third dimension.

It's easy to think of printing as a two-dimensional world of type, illustrations, or some combination of the two. But, of course, printed matter is physical matter that can be touched, not just seen.

Binding and finishing processes serve to remind us that every printed piece finds its way eventually into space, where it is manipulated and handled. Do the pages in a brochure lie flat? Will a flier with six folds prove dramatic and effective when opened, or only exasperating and unwieldy? These and many other questions are typically encountered when printed sheets are bound and finished.

Paper

A printed piece can be well written, well designed, typeset with skill and care, and printed beautifully, but all this comes to nothing if the paper is inappropriate. You cannot expect a full-color annual report to radiate its message on newsprint, any more than you can hope to make an oriental rug out of burlap.

Weight

Paper weight is calculated by the ream—500 sheets. For convenience, a fixed size is assigned to each type or grade of paper (for book grades, for instance, the size is 25" × 38") and the weight corresponds to how much 500 sheets of that fixed size would weigh. Thus, paper stock is "70 lb" if 500 sheets 25" × 38" weigh 70 pounds.

When weights are expressed in the metric system, the accepted standard is grams per square meter ("grammage"). If one sheet, one square meter in size, weighs 104 grams, the grammage of that paper is 104. (A paper of this weight has the same weight as 70-lb paper).

What weights are generally used for printed material?

Many pamphlets and brochures are printed on text paper of 50 to 100 lb. Covers usually run 65 or 80 lb. The basic size for cover stock is 20" × 26", not 25" × 38". Therefore 80-lb cover stock is considerably heavier than 80-lb text paper.

Opacity (Show-Through)

The heavier the paper, the greater the opacity (or the less one can see through the sheet). Lightweight papers generally exhibit some degree of show-through, whereas heavier papers are usually more opaque simply because they are thicker. The construction and ingredients used to make paper can also influence opacity.

Beware of the "show-through bug." It appears as a "ghost" on one side of the paper. Though barely visible, this occurrence takes place on paper with relatively few mineral fillers, which lack the opacity to withstand this eyesore. The only thing that will help is to use a paper with greater opacity.

Brightness

For halftone printing, a bright, white sheet—reflecting more light—improves the contrast range and, therefore, in many printing situations, improves halftone reproduction. However, if you're using a rough-textured stock—and you're counting on brilliance in the finished piece—you may run into what is known as the "light shadow." When the halftone dots settle down in the furrows of the rough-textured sheets, they are concealed in the shadows of the furrows which obscure the dots, depriving them of the light they need to look bright and lively. So the printed result may be less than expected.

Grain

On a paper machine the majority of the wood fibers lie in the direction in which the machine is running; the result is termed *paper grain*. Paper will tear and fold easiest parallel with the grain direction.

Grain is important for several reasons: The direction of paper grain should run parallel to the printing cylinders—that is, across the width of the press, particularly when two or more colors are run and their accurate register is required. Among the reasons is that pressure between blanket and impression cylinder (as well as moisture from the dampening solution) cause the paper to stretch. Paper stretches less with the grain than across it. Keeping the grain direction parallel to the printing cylinders allows the printer to make adjustments to counteract for the expansion of the sheet.

Binderies prefer the first fold of a sheet to run parallel to the grain direction. This makes the successive fold more accurate. Grain direction should run parallel to the spine of the finished piece. The pages will lie flatter and be easier to handle.

Bulk

Bulk is simply the thickness of paper, expressed in pages per inch. Paper thickness varies from the thinnest Bible sheets, which sometimes measure 1300 pages per inch, to thick card stock measuring 12 pages to the inch.

Two properties of paper affect its bulk: weight and finish. Generally a heavy paper is thicker than a light one. As for finish, a rough, toothy paper is thicker than a smooth one.

Surface

A rough or smooth finish, besides influencing bulk as mentioned above, affects the way images print—particularly halftones. Rich, dark tones can be printed effectively on a coated sheet, whereas a rough-surfaced, toothy paper will absorb more ink and leave the dark areas grayer and less intense.

Watch out for the "ink drinker": soft papers with low ink holdout which "drinks in" ink (that should have remained on the surface of the sheet) like a sponge absorbs water, robbing your job of hoped-for brilliance. Colors go flat, and blacks look gray.

The Printed Piece: A Reflection of Your Agency's Art

A primary goal in printing any advertising piece is to obtain a faithful replica of your finished art. Like a mirror, the finest printing job will reflect nearly exactly what is there on the original art. And if the printed piece is a true likeness of this art, it will exhibit both the good and the bad qualities with a mirror's innocent objectivity. Some flaws you may detect in the printed piece may represent not necessarily weaknesses in the printer's skill in reproduction, but shortcomings in the workmanship produced by your agency.

So take a long, hard look at what you give out to be printed, and try to catch in advance that which will let you down after it's too late.

Printing Can Mean Big Profits

When it comes to printing, nobody wins all the time. If you pick the right paper, the wrong typeface may ambush your job when you least expect it. Always check and recheck your final art against the printing specifications. Always look at proofs and try to catch mistakes or problems before they become very costly. Always have your clients approve each step of the design, production, and printing process. Make sure they see samples of the stock you suggest using and if possible, show them similar printed samples.

Before making any decisions about major print jobs, paper selection, use of complicated art, and folding procedures, ask your printer or your paper merchant for advice and guidance. If handled professionally, the printing end of your business can provide a major source of profits for your agency.

And don't forget, once a job is printed, chances are you will reprint it often. Reprints, especially those that don't need copy and production changes, require little more than a purchase order to the printer and a marked-up invoice to the client.

A Few Words About Envelopes and Business Cards

Envelopes

There isn't a client, an agency designer or contact person who hasn't at one time or another said "We'll need some envelopes, too!"

Contrary to the belief that envelopes are here only to carry the address and keep the letter dry in case the mailcarrier drops it in a puddle, you might find it surprising to know that envelopes are an important form of graphic communication. Consider the fact that the envelope is the first thing a recipient sees in a mailing. It introduces the communication. And just as the paper or the letterhead design gives tactile, associative messages, so does the envelope.

In selecting an envelope, two questions will help determine your choice. First, should the envelope paper match the letterhead stock, or do you prefer a compatible (but not identical) or contrasting paper?

The reason is this: Envelopes are either stock or custom made (converted). Stock envelopes are made in very large quantities, with printing subsequent. Converted envelopes are printed first, then cut and folded. There are advantages to using stock envelopes. In small quantities, they are inexpensive, and they are available on short lead times. But stock envelopes are not available in all paper grades and all colors. Converted envelopes can be made from any paper, but generally require a four-week lead time and quantities of 25,000 or more to be cost-effective.

A second consideration that affects your choice is your design. Some printing techniques and design elements such as embossing, thermography, and bleeds will not always work as well on stock envelopes as they will on converted envelopes. Check with your printer to make sure your design will work on stock.

Envelopes are divided into two general classifications depending on the location of the opening or flap.

- Open-end envelopes: opening or flat on the short envelope dimension
- Open-side envelopes: opening or flap on the long envelope dimension

Various types of adhesives or gums are applied to envelopes to seal the flaps. These include: remoistening gum (requires a moistening agent), Securoseal (adheres to itself), and adhesives that require no moistening agent.

Other styles of stock envelopes include:

- Commercial and official: applies to those envelopes most generally used in business and personal uses (correspondence, invoices, checks, direct mail, etc.) and range in size from style Nos. 6¼ to 14.
- Gusset: the sides of an expansion envelope which permit its taking on a box-like shape to accommodate bulky contents. The gusset is measured as one-half the total expansion.
- Window envelopes: with various standard window sizes and locations.
- Announcement envelopes: available in a variety of paper grades usually packed 1000 to a carton. Come in A-2, A-6, A-7, A-8, A-10, A-Long styles which represent different sizes.
- Peel and seal envelopes: adhesive remains free of dust or moisture. Sizes generally range from No. 10 to 12 × 15½". Also available in expansion styles.
- Catalog envelopes: opening on short dimension of envelope. Sizes range from 4 ⅛" × 9½" to 12" × 15½".
- Booklet envelopes: opening on the long dimension of envelop. Sizes range from 4¾" × 6½" to 10" × 13".
- Clasp envelopes: range in size from 2½" × 4¼" to 12" × 15½".
- Jumbo envelopes: sizes run from 11" × 17" up to 22" × 27".
- Special-purpose envelopes: include coin, proxy, oversize window display, double pocket, document, job ticket, safety fold, negative preserver, inter-department, remittance, and square.

Business Cards

While the envelope is the first thing the recipient of a mailing sees, the business card is often the first printed impression a company or its representative makes on a potential client or customer. That may be when the card is used as an introduction by a person making a business call, or when the card accompanies a letter or piece of collateral.

A business card design should reflect two considerations. First, the card should provide continuity with the company's visual image in general, and its letterhead and envelopes in particular. Second, a business card should be durable and easy to carry. Because the card is liable to be handled frequently, it should be printed on a heavy weight of paper (at least 65 lb cover stock). Some companies print, thermograph, or engrave their cards on colored vinyl or thin plastic for durability and effect.

The standard size of American business card is 3½" × 2", but through folds and die cuts, many different styles of cards can be produced. If the card contains a fold, it is preferable to have it scored on the press to ensure accuracy.

Some of the many different styles of business cards include:

- Horizontal (no fold)
- Vertical (no fold)
- Short fold horizontal
- Short fold vertical
- "Z" fold
- Tent fold
- Gate fold
- Book fold

The value of a business card as a first impression cannot be overstated. It is one of the best entrees to getting new business.

Part 7 Action Checklist

- ✔ In order to get the best printing results and cost efficiently, your production department should have a knowledge of printing techniques and know the capabilities of the printers you are dealing with.
- ✔ Plan your printed piece so that it will be easy to read with all type legible and illustrations attractively arranged.
- ✔ Get three or more quotes on the printing of any piece. Make sure all printers are bidding on the same specifications.
- ✔ Before quoting a price to the client, allow for changes and other contingencies such as overruns, delivery charges, and changes.
- ✔ Have the client approve every step of the design, production, and printing process.
- ✔ Make sure the client sees samples of the stock you suggest using.
- ✔ Don't be embarrassed to ask your printer or paper merchant for advice on a job. Printers will know if your artwork is prepared properly and if you have chosen the right stock for the job.
- ✔ Submit printing orders in writing with all terms and special arrangements spelled out.

✔ Be sure to ask for a printer's proof on every job before it goes on press. Check it against the mechanical to be sure nothing has been omitted. Have your client okay the proof before it goes back for printing.

✔ If your printed piece is being done in the offset process and has photography, make certain the photos you are using are sharp. The final printed image will be four generations removed from the original and some quality will be lost. So the better the picture you start with, the better the reproduction you'll end up with. Remember that in photo-offset the end result is only as good as what is exposed on film. Be sure your printer is competent in the darkroom.

✔ Make your client aware that sometimes colors change from the original to the printed image. If accurate color reproduction is essential, having your client okay the color proofs may not be enough. The client should also be present when the first printed sheets come off the press in order to make color adjustments if necessary.

✔ When using thermography, remember that not all paper weights work well with this process. The sheet must be 20 lb weight and up.

✔ If your printed piece is to be silkscreened, avoid delicate serifs and fine type, which will not reproduce well in this process.

✔ If your printed piece is to be diecut, use top-grade paper 22 lb or higher. Avoid delicate, lacy patterns that tear easily, and hard-to-hold tight registration between diecuts and printing.

✔ Beware of losing the image off the page. Prepare your artwork so that when the finished piece is bound (folded), all type is at least ⅜" away from the edge to be trimmed.

✔ If your printed piece has a lot of dark ink coverage or many pictures, have the job varnished. It will enhance the pictures and protect the printed surface from unsightly finger marks.

✔ Beware of "ghosting" and "show-throughs," which occurs when the opacity of the paper you are printing on is not great enough.

✔ In general, the brighter and whiter the paper, the better the halftone reproduction.

✔ Tell your printer to run the paper grain parallel to the printing cylinders so that adjustments can be made to counteract the sheet expansion and make for better folding. The pages will also lie flatter and be easier to handle.

Part 8

Toward a More Perfect Agency-Client Relationship

24

Getting
New Clients

Landing a new client is like fishing. You need the right bait, the right equipment, and the right technique. You also have to know where and when the fish are biting!

But it is neither as easy nor as simple as the fishing parallel makes it sound. Because ever-hungry agencies in your area are continually after just the kind of accounts you are going after. And many of these agencies, which may act "friendly" toward you at industry functions or through mutual vendors, can be fiercely competitive when new business is at stake.

Because much of your new business will be local in origin, it follows that you will have all those other local people fishing in your area out there trying to catch "the big one," who as a result of all this attention, has a chance to be highly selective.

So what is the secret in bringing in new advertising billings while keeping and expanding the billings you already have? One thing is certain: In the history of advertising, few agencies have had the good fortune of being able to just sit there and wait for new business to come to them. Most must have an organized plan to go out and get new business, not only to grow, but to offset the business they may lose from time to time.

Working hard and working smart is one way to get new clients. Seeking unaffiliated firms, by recommendations and by invitations is another. Expertise in a particular area of advertising is yet a third. But what about the agency just starting up? Where does it start?

Go After Business You Know You Can Handle

Sometimes, people in advertising are not realistic. They will go out and spend a good deal of time and often a good deal of money making a pitch for an account they don't stand a chance of getting. But good luck if you try telling them that. Whether it be the ego of the agency principal or the overenthusiasm of the agency's staff, more often than not, agencies do not see the true picture of what they have to offer a potential client.

If, for instance, you have no knowledge of a technical business, and can't even speak the "universal discourse" of the business, don't waste your time going up against agencies that do have track records in that field. If you put yourself in the client's shoes, it may become painfully clear that if you were the client you wouldn't let your agency (as nice as it may be) in the front door. Of course, you may be the world's greatest salesperson, and all the other agencies pitching this client may be the world's worst, but don't count on an astute advertiser taking a risk on an unknown, untried new business.

You Can't Be All Things to All Clients

Take a good look at your strengths and weaknesses. Are you good at creative writing? How about art? Marketing? Promotions? Media planning and buying? You can always find experienced free-lance talent to fill in your weak spots. Outside expertise added to your own can make for a stronger presentation. Many agencies overlook using outside talent primarily because they don't want to spend the extra money, or because it may appear as being internally weak if they have to bring in outsiders. Don't make this mistake. First of all, even the giant mega-billion-per-year agencies use outside talent as needed, on a regular basis. If you feel as though you have most of what it will take to be successful with a potential account, taking a chance and bringing in outside guns can be the best move you could make. And chances are, if you land the account, the extra expenditures will pay for themselves many times over.

Outside expertise can give your presentation a depth of experience it would be impossible for a newcomer like you to have otherwise. And while in the beginning you may not be able to afford these talents on a full-time basis, you could be taking advantage of their experience at modest cost. It is possible that many free-lancers will be happy to work with you in making a presentation on a speculative basis: They get paid if you get the account. By building their costs into your fee to the client, you could actually find that using outsiders costs you nothing if you get the account.

Don't waste your time going after accounts that are looking for larger agencies. Spend your valuable time seeking out accounts that will best fit your size and style. There's always time later, when you're larger, to go after the bigger accounts.

Select companies that you believe can use your expertise or those that will be impressed with the track record you have with other clients. If you have no track record in that particular field, perhaps your experience in another field can be adapted. For example, if you have a bank as a client, other accounts in the financial industry could become good prospects: mortgage companies, stockbrokers, investment firms, and the like.

Find out as much as you can about potential clients you want to solicit. Which agency are they using now, and who have they used in the past? Do they pay their bills promptly? Are they open to new ideas? Are they worth putting time and effort into developing? Do they expect too much in the way of a presentation?

Selecting prospects by reading trade publications can be another method of building a list of new business prospects. Pay particular attention to announcements about employee changes at a company. Sometimes a new ad manager will get rid of all the vendors his or her predecessor used. Of course, the reverse of this is true as well. Your agency could be on the wrong end of a personnel change, too. Should this scenario take place, and you feel your position with a client is in jeopardy, you might put out the word to competitive companies that your agency is available. If the former employee you worked with is going to another company in the field, keep in touch with that employee.

Another method of locating new business prospects, often overlooked by most agencies, are those companies that announce the appointment of a new agency. Why go after an account that just hired someone new? you ask. Many times companies make snap judgments when they go through an agency selection process. They find out later that the new agency is not what it represented itself to be. Or the agency may have oversold itself and is unable to deliver as promised. Also, the agency may have lost a larger account and had to cut back drastically on personnel. Or the company may have hired a new ad manager after selecting new agency and that person wants his or her "own team" to work with. Whatever the reason, it never hurts to make an inquiry. All any company you are pitching can say is "No, we are not interested at this time."

Once you've selected your "target" account, develop a creative marketing approach and implement it. Make contact via the telephone and mail and in person. Make sure you let your prospects know that you are familiar with their business and the problems that face their industry.

Approach Every New Prospect as You Would Every New Campaign: Be Creative

Instead of telling new prospects about how "great" your agency is, tell them what they really want to hear—how you can increase their sales. If they ask you why they should change the good thing they have going now, tell them "to make it even better!"

Try to be as creative as you can in your approach. Getting the attention of a target market is of prime importance in any ad or campaign you will produce. The same principle holds true for your "campaign" to get new clients. The more you stand out, the better you will be remembered.

And whatever you do, don't give up. Try to make a date for a formal presentation. If you can't at that time, try again in a few weeks. But keep trying. Persistence often pays off. You may never know the real reason you are being put off. It could be that the current agency is related to the president of the company, and though the ad manager might want to give you a chance, his or her hands are tied. But one day the manager may be in a better position, at that company or at another, where he or she *will* give you a chance. Better late than never.

When Time Is Scarce, Who Comes First: Current Clients or Prospective Ones?

With only 24 hours in a day, when will you have time to pitch new prospects if you barely have enough time to take care of the clients you already have? Obviously, a bird in the hand is worth two in the bush. Your current clients always come first. In fact, you should do everything in your power to let them know that they come first and are important to you, and that you appreciate their business. The fact of the matter is, the best way of increasing your billings is to increase the sales of your present clients so they in turn will increase their advertising budgets. By increasing your billings from within, you are less likely to lose accounts and may not have to spend a lot of time seeking new ones.

Often, clients that have been with you for some period of time may go into other businesses or recommend you to friends of theirs who need a good agency. The agency business is a service business and the more service you give your clients the more likely you are to keep them—even if you're not the most creative agency in the world.

However, if a sustained program of seeking new business is part of your business plan, there are a number of ways you can handle it without taking time away from current clients and risking their loss.

One way is to assign one or more people to the task of going after new business. This could be in addition to other jobs they have at the agency. The creative director, for example, may be just the person to come up with an approach that will impress a new prospect. As the principal of the agency, you will still have to be available to go to some meetings and possibly help make the presentation. Most clients like to deal with the agency principal if not on a regular basis, at least occasionally in case problems arise and they have to complain to someone with authority.

One advantage to having a group work on new business development is that more time and talent can be channeled to the task than if just one person were doing it. And when more people are involved, they provide a broader range of knowledge and expertise.

In order to keep a person or group continually involved with the process of new business development, it is necessary that regular meetings be held to both assign new prospects to go after and to discuss progress on prospects in development.

If the agency is very small at the outset, the most economical way to handle new business development is if the principal is the one doing it. If such is the case, allocation of time becomes an important factor. The agency head will have to set priorities and devote whatever time is available to the task.

Another method of getting new business is by using outside people. There are free-lance "account executives" and "new business developers" who will seek out prospective new accounts for your agency, solicit them, and help work on the presentation your agency will make, and if you get the account, they may take a finder's fee or percentage of the billing as their payment and drop out of the picture. Or they may service the account for you for a fee or percentage. Be sure that if you use outside solicitors, they are working exclusively for you. Also make sure that they are knowledgeable in all facets of advertising and marketing—as they will be representing you. They should be completely familiar with the background, policies, capabilities, and operations of your agency. As the principal of your agency, you will find it in your best interest to be present at one or more meetings that a free-lancer has with a prospective client—not only because you are the head of the agency and your presence will be impressive, but also because you will be in a position to discover any exaggerations or untrue claims about your agency made by the free-lance person that could become problems later.

Another alternative is to work closely with the various media reps who call on all types of accounts every day. They are out there in the business world and are usually the first to know when a company is not happy with its agency. Media reps can be an excellent source of new business leads as well as a source of information about what is going on around town and in the advertising industry in particular.

Often, agency media people don't have the time to spend with reps who have been known to pop in without an appointment. Try to make it a policy to make time for them. If your media person is busy when they come in, they might be just as happy with a hot cup of coffee and passing the time of day with your receptionist. If time permits, a few minutes of "shooting the breeze" in an air-conditioned office could be the best public relations move you could make. Being nice to everyone who comes into your office should be standard policy. But being especially nice to media reps might someday pay off. Who knows? They may be close enough with the person in charge of advertising at a potential new account to recommend a new agency—like yours.

Use whatever method of developing new business is best for you, but don't forget to budget for it.

Putting Aside Dollars for New Business

If all is going well at your new agency, setting aside dollars for future account development may not seem necessary. Never let your guard down—in good times or bad. You can lose a major account and a major source of income when you least expect it and for reasons you'd never guess. Then you'll find yourself in the position of having to make severe staff and expense cutbacks in order to remain in business. It's always safer to have some good prospects in various stages of development "waiting in the wings."

But in order to have a program for new business development, you must have a budget for it. And it all goes back to the original business plan for your agency. Some provision for getting new business, no matter how small the amount may seem, is better than no provision at all. Setting aside a reasonable amount of money every month or every quarter for mailers, PR releases about your agency, telemarketing, research and entertainment expenses, travel, free-lancers, and a host of other items may be the best "investment" you'll ever make—because it's an investment in the development of your own business.

It is not necessary to add on payroll expenses before you get the new business. Rather than anticipate, hire those you need only when you are sure you will need them. Or reshuffle existing personnel to help cover positions that are short.

Now, Put Yourself in Your Prospects' Shoes

By way of helping you approach new business prospects with a better perspective, the following scenario will give you an idea of what the advertiser looks for when selecting an ad agency. It is presented strictly from the standpoint of the advertiser—the new client you might hope to get.

Let's say you are the ad manager or head of a company spending somewhere in the neighborhood of $750,000 per year on advertising. (Three-quarters of a million is a good cutoff place. Under that, you're considered small; over that, you don't solicit or appreciate advice from anyone.) So this primer is primarily for small to medium-size advertisers—from innocents who may never have worked with an agency, to the jaded and cautious who have already worn out several.

As a business owner, you have always had some degree of difficulty in finding a good professional. This is true whether you were looking for a doctor, a law firm, an accounting firm, a stockbroker, or an advertising agency.

Now let's say you already have an ad agency, but for some reason or other, it's performing badly. That campaign you were talked into last year isn't working. Sales are sluggish. Profits are down. And the stockholders are screaming.

You're still committed to your agency, and you still have to work with it. Looking could create a problem, because no matter how large a city you may be located in, every city is small when it comes to advertising gossip. For this reason, some advertisers give their agencies notice of termination before they start looking. But it leaves them little time to screen, study, and select.

Dossiers: Should You Keep Them?

Some advertisers keep an up-to-date file on the agencies in their area. When the time comes to consider a change, they've got a file to help them, plus a dossier on each of a handful of agencies they'd be willing to consider. Thus, their preliminary screening has been done over a period of time, and they have been able to study the performance as well as the promises of the agencies involved.

Consultants: Should You Use Them?

Some advertisers hire consultants, experienced agency professionals, to help in the selection of an agency. Their recommendations are usually well above average, since they are based on a full-time search and a lot of homework and research.

The "Top 10" Method of Selection

The "top 10" method of agency selection would be laughable, if it weren't so serious.

It starts with the advertiser going through a list of the 10 or so largest agencies in an area, and working down until some agencies that do not handle conflicting accounts are uncovered. If this sounds like the natural thing to do, consider this: Every one of the agencies in the top 10 has been rejected or fired by at least two of your competitors. Settle for one of these agencies, and you've got second or third best.

There's more. Suppose you start at the top, and you find a big agency billing really big bucks. Take your $750,000 account into this megabuck agency, and it may represent 0.1 percent of its billings. How much personal attention do you give to one of your accounts which represents 0.1 percent of your business?

The Who-Actually-Did-the-Campaign Agency

You've heard stories about it from other advertisers and media reps, even from ad agency people. The one about the $800,000 campaign handled by the media buyer's secretary at XYZ Agency. Or the one about the banking campaign written by the despairing person in the traffic department. If the clients only knew what was going on, no doubt they'd fire the agencies. If they had thought about it in the first place, they wouldn't have hired them.

Stay Away from Agencies with Firefighters

So, the top accounts go to the top people in the agency, and the small accounts go to whoever is left. Typically, what's left are the junior creative people, until the advertiser starts to complain loudly, and the noise reaches the ears of top agency management, which assigns enough people to put out the fire and appease the client, for the time being—until it starts over again.

Watch Out for the Agency with Cookie-Cutter Campaigns

When an agency keeps the same headline, but changes the illustration from time to time while running the campaign into the ground, the process is fondly called cookie cutting. Now there may be a valid reason that an agency would run advertising like this, but be warned, it's more likely that the agency's well of creativity has run dry.

Another version of cookie-cutter campaigns are the "do three ads and run them to death" technique. Here the agency convinces the advertiser that repetition is the way to go. The ads are done at the beginning of the year, and the agency collects for the rest of the year.

The Interview

Five people per million. That's the average number of people an average agency claims to employ per every million dollars worth of billing. So, theoretically, if you walk into an agency billing, say, $10 million, you can assume that it will be able to find a dozen or so people to attend the interview.

Don't be fooled. This does not mean that these people will work on your account. Remind yourself of that several times during the interview. In fact, regardless of its size, you should assume the agency will have to staff up for your account.

There are four basic questions you want answered when you interview an ad agency for the first time. You already know that the agencies you've selected for your account can advertise to your satisfaction. You've seen their ads and television spots, heard their radio, and so on. They know their craft. So what else do you need to know?

First, Do You Like Them?   This criterion is so simple and so obvious, too many advertisers overlook it. Do you like to be with these people, talk to them? Are they your kind of people? Do they think the way you do? Do you feel comfortable with them? If the chemistry is right, the relationship with the agency can be right.

Do They Know Anything About Your Business?   They don't have to know everything, but they should know something. Maybe someone in the agency worked for a competitor. Maybe they worked on something similar.

If they don't have experience or knowledge in your field, they still may do a good job for you. Especially if they're smart, innovative, eager, and daring. They are not aware of the taboos, the no-nos, and the myths that sometimes stifle good work. Often, all that's needed to rejuvenate a tired business is for someone to forget everything that's been done before and start with a fresh, new approach.

What Do Their Present Clients Think of Them?   How well has their advertising worked for their present clients? It's not enough for them to show you some ads, then say "and sales for this client are up 24 percent."

What was the problem these ads were designed to solve? What was the strategy, and where is the documentation of how well it worked? You can tell a lot about how an agency will approach your problem by its presentation. If all you hear during an interview is fluff and vague generalities about what the agency may or may not do for you, it's time to wind up the meeting and leave. The agency is wasting your time. Don't give it a chance to waste your money.

Do They Pay Their Bills?   This means, do they pay *your* bills? Never forget an agency is acting as your agent. If you make it a practice to pay your bills on time, your agent, acting on your behalf, should do the same. An agency's reputation for slow pay can rub off on your company because people assume the agency is late in paying because you were late in paying.

Of course, if you, as the client, string out your payments to hold onto the cash longer, to earn interest on the money, to boost inventory, to meet payrolls, or for whatever reason, the agency you want may not want you. Your relationship with an agency can offer lots of fun and excitement—except where money is concerned. While you're checking out the agency and its financial reputation, chances are it will be checking you out, too.

Where Do You Go from Here?

Well, you could check out the agencies you have interviewed with media reps who call on them. They may not know how well the agency's campaigns are working, but they will know if the agency is made up of professionals, if they pay their bills, if they are sharp buyers, if their management is strong, and if they are easy to get along with.

Now let's say you've narrowed your choices down to two agencies and you want to know exactly what they can do for you. The next step is asking them to prepare a presentation. They want your business; they should be more than willing to do this, right? Wrong.

Unless your budget is very large, or agency professionals are absolutely sure they are going to get your account, they may not be willing to gamble on a speculative presentation. It means taking their people off work they are doing for existing clients and spending untold hours and money gambling on the possibility that you'll like what you see.

For small to medium-size accounts, presentations are a total waste. The agencies that don't win the account will have disrupted their entire operation for nothing but an exercise; the agency that gets the business may spend a year or more recouping its presentation costs. If you can possibly make your decision on the basis of past work the agency has done plus a little faith, do so. But if you feel that a presentation is the only way to be sure, ask your finalists to make their presentations—and pay them for it.

Give them a budget (say, $1000 to $10,000) to work with, and a deadline to do it by. Give the competing agencies enough information to do an intelligent job. Each agency should be given the same background information, so everyone is working from the same base. Your market, competitive information, pricing problems, distribution, and anything else that contributes to your sales effort and problems should be spelled out.

You may think your advertising account does not justify the time and expense put into a presentation. Just remember, there's something unique about any business, no matter how small it may be. Many times, the small advertiser presents more challenge than the big ones. Your account is tougher to handle because you don't have the dollar clout the big boys have.

Buying an agency presentation accomplishes several things: It says you don't expect something for nothing. Also, you can ask the competing companies to account for your money—which will give you an idea of how well they utilize time and dollars. What you will get back from them in presentation form will be a marketing plan that includes ad layouts, broadcast ideas, media suggestions, and promotional ideas. If the competing agencies stayed within your advertising budget and gave you good, sound ideas, that tells you a lot about them. If they overspent (with some of their own money) trying to impress you with how much that want your business, they may do the same with your money once they have your account.

So the speculative presentation which you are paying for can be highly educational. It gives you a base from which to judge an agency's ability to meet deadlines, the caliber of its creative work, and how it spends money.

You, Not the Grapevine, Must Tell the Winner

Once you've made your decision on which agency to hire, call the winner with the good news first; then call the runners-up and tell them whom you have selected.

It's better that they hear the bad news from you rather than from someone else.
End scenario.

Some Final Thoughts About Getting New Business

The success of your clients is the only commodity on which your agency can grow and prosper. If you truly believe an advertiser's approach is wrong, say so. Don't present yourself as a "yes person" agency; there are already too many of them around.

It is important for advertisers to understand that advertising "pulls," it does not "jerk." While advertising can accelerate the success of a good product or service, it can also accelerate the death of a poor product or service. It is only part—a vital part, to be sure—of successful business.

Lastly, there's an adage in the business that's worth remembering when pitching for new clients: "Stopping your advertising to save money is like stopping your watch to save time." When you run up against prospects who disagree with this, it may be best to run the other way.

25

New Business Presentations, or It's Show-and-Tell Time, Folks

It's an art, a science, and a game—it's also something that just about every ad agency has to go through: making a new business presentation.

Is the Gamble Worth It?

Your agency is one of two or three that have been selected as "finalists" for a big new account. The advertiser has looked at past work done by all the finalists and now is asking each agency to make a presentation. You want the business. A presentation can be costly. Even if the advertiser is willing to pay for the presentation, you will have to take people away from work they are doing on existing accounts. Your office will be disrupted. Is the gamble worth it?

If the advertiser is paying for it, the answer is yes. If not, you may have to do it anyway in order to keep pace with the competition.

Unless your office is in a storefront, business doesn't walk through the door. So to get new clients you'll have to do one of the things you do for your existing clients: solve a marketing and communications problem—in this case, your own. And the problem will require the presentation of your credentials along with specific advertising and marketing campaign ideas to a qualified prospect.

Competition among agencies seeking new business in the advertising field has intensified in just about every part of the country. Landing new business has helped many survive recession. Boosting their billings geared them for recovery. Now, many are selling their sizzle to attract new accounts. The new business proposals used by advertising agencies to sell their marketing abilities is like a show-and-tell ritual, with some wild variations of how much to show or how little to tell! It also has led to some memorable presentations as agencies try to outdo one another in impressing the prospect and sometimes find themselves coping with the unexpected.

It Starts with People

The agency new business presentation starts with people—the personalities of those who represent the agency, the feelings of mutual respect and trust they generate, and the way they relate to the people they are presenting to.

It develops with expertise: the way an agency confronts a challenge, identifies a problem, suggests a solution.

It culminates with talent: the idea that dazzles, the concept that captivates, and hopefully a new client.

Be Creative

As mentioned in the previous chapter, be creative in your approach. The principle of catching attention and creating interest, desire, and action, which holds true for every campaign you will produce for your existing clients, also holds true in your "campaign" to get new clients.

As the owner of an aggressive young advertising agency, you are in the business of selling creativity, brain power, and marketing expertise. Combine that with all the background information the prospective client is willing to give you, plus all the information you can get through media reps, competitors, and other sources. Then do all your homework—and create a presentation that sizzles with exciting ideas and says something important to the advertiser.

It's a Team Effort

Putting new business presentations together requires a team effort—including, of course, your own creative staff members and/or free-lancers. Preparation has many facets: understanding the prospect's products or services; analyzing the market situation to reveal market opportunities; developing a marketing strategy; articulating that strategy creatively; budgeting the program accurately; and finally, presenting the package coherently.

Along with the background information you will require, the prospective client will most likely give you a deadline date on which you must make your presentation and the location where the presentations are being held. If it is possible to hold them at your office, that might prove more convenient and beneficial for you, since your staff is already there and you can control whatever audio and visual equipment you may need.

If the presentation is being paid for by the prospect, you will be given the maximum amount you can spend. Never go overboard and spend your own money to impress prospects; they will only think you will do the same with their ad budget if you get their account. You may also be given a time limit on your presentation (30, 60, or 90 minutes) as well as limitations on the type of presentation you can make (slide, flip card, video, etc.).

Preparing for the Moment of Truth

The first phase is the prospect-conducted "input" session. Here you ask questions and take notes. You find out all you can about the prospect's market and competition, pricing, and distribution. Get samples of ads done before. Find out what problems the prospect has. The battle among agencies for clients is often won or lost at this stage.

The next step, after picking the brains of anyone you can find who has had dealings with this advertiser, is to develop a new definition for the prospect's product, and establish measurable marketing objectives as well as a marketing and creative strategy for the presentation.

With the basic strategy in place, your next step is preparing the visuals which summarize your key points, the ad layouts that visualize the marketing concepts, and all the other materials that may be part of the presentation, such as spec TV and radio spots, comprehensive layouts of promotional items, and a media recommendation.

Then it's D-Day. The day of the presentation. Your charts are lettered. You've rehearsed the presentation team as to who says what, when, where, and how. You tell your prospective client what you've learned and you spell out, in brilliant marketing terms, how you and the prospect can "beat the pants off the competition."

Your new business presentation, if done right, will help the advertiser make a sound, considered decision, just as your advertising for other clients gives the prospect an opportunity to make an intelligent choice.

By being creative and making memorable, sensible, well-orchestrated presentations, your agency should be successful in your bid for new business.

Some Points to Consider Before You Get to the Presentation Stage

Have one or several of your clients send letters of praise to your new prospect. Most clients will be happy to serve as a strong reference for you, if they are happy with your work, and many will write letters on your behalf. Advertisers like agencies that are successful. It reinforces their good judgment in hiring you. Don't be afraid to ask for help from existing clients.

Send an overnight letter reminding the prospect of your interest. If the decision to narrow down to the finalists takes a month or more, send a second letter.

Send the ad manager or top executive some information about his or her business—a clipping from *Business Week* or the local newspaper, for example. The executive may already have seen it, but will be impressed to know that you took the time and interest to send it. Do your homework. Learn about the client and its problems, and let the prospect know that you have done so.

These are but a few examples. There are as many good ideas as there are creative thinkers. The point of it all is to stand out from the crowd. You must be remembered in a positive way to get into the finals. From the client's perspective, all agencies are alike. You need to prove that you are different, aggressive, bright, and remembered.

Dos and Don'ts in Making Presentations

- Don't make presentations too rigid.
- Put warmth into them.
- Use your allotted presentation time efficiently.
- Be organized.
- Do your homework about the client, its position in the market, and its objectives.
- Answer all questions a prospect may ask of you.
- Present yourself well.
- Don't be dull.
- Rehearse before you present.
- Don't promise things you can't deliver.
- Focus on the decision maker.
- Ask for the account.

Putting Together a Hot A/V Presentation

What is an A/V presentation? Theoretically, any combination of sight and sound qualifies as audiovisual. That includes video, motion picture film, 35mm slides, even a flip chart.

Who doesn't remember an audiovisual presentation from his or her school days? That is often the problem. When you tell someone you're planning an A/V presentation, memories of those old school shows come back—most of them not necessarily favorable.

But with today's modern technology, no A/V presentation has to be dull. Not when there are so many devices and techniques to use, like computer-synchronized, multiprojector, multi-image slide walls, huge video screens, and wraparound sound.

Creativity, though, is the secret element in every exciting audiovisual presentation. Slide presentations, in particular, need all the creativity they can get—good photography, a great music track, strong narration, and superior sound effects as well. When you mix these elements successfully, you come up with a slide presentation filled with pizzazz.

The Importance of Visuals

For communicating the fully dimensional message, a picture is worth a million words. The right pictures are essential for memorable and effective presentations.

Begin by thinking visually about your subject. Develop bar graphs, pie graphs, picture symbols, size comparisons, simple diagrams, and key words to punch home your ideas.

Choose the right visual aids. Flip charts work for small groups and can be self-drawn. Make them bold enough to be read at the back of the room. Overhead projectors have great flexibility for large or small groups. Unlike many slide projectors, overheads will allow you to keep the room lights on, a big advantage. Slides are best for formal, structured presentations where full visual professionalism is important.

Remember that you are a visual aid yourself! Use your face, arms, hands, even your fingers to illustrate what you mean. Your words stimulate pictures. Use action verbs, color words, taste, sound, touch, and feeling words. Use physical demonstrations, examples, samples, or physical analogies to extend and embody your message.

Using Slides Successfully

1. Make one point per slide. If you put 10 points on a slide, your audience is going to jump ahead of you. Slides enable you to focus the attention of your audience on a single thought or idea.

2. Please, never over 10 words per slide. Slides should be regarded as billboards. They are not pages in a text.

3. Make your words as big as your ideas. With 10 words or less per slide, you can give your words some size. They'll be easier to read, and they'll look important.

4. Slides should trigger your thoughts. They are not substitutes for scripts. Too many presenters dutifully read slides as they appear, slide after slide after slide.

5. Don't make every slide look like every other slide. Surprise your audience. Vary the content—words, charts, simple graphs, cartoons, photographs. Don't always do the expected.

6. Lots of statistics on a slide are a sure-fire turnoff. Most charts and graphs can be simplified. Long rows of figures or statistically overpowering graphs are turnoffs for most audiences.

7. Slides are a visual medium. If you use pictures to pick up your slides, don't assume you have to label or title everything you show.

8. Give every slide a focal point. Cluttered slides discourage interest. The disciplines of good layout apply in slide design as well as advertisements.

9. The bigger the advertisement looks on a slide, the better the response. If you want your audience to really see your ads, put them on slides. And go all the way. If you're showing a spread, use a horizontal slide. If you're showing a page, use a vertical slide.

10. Use color functionally, for emphasis, not ornamentation. Color for color's sake is an extravagance.

11. Operate the slides at a pace that gives you the absolute freedom to say exactly what you want to say about each slide, then move on to the next one.

12. Don't leave a slide on screen after you have discussed it. Never have a subject on the screen that doesn't correspond to what you are saying. It splits attention in two.

13. Always check your slides. Know what's coming up next. Don't stand there with egg on your face when slides suddenly appear upside down, backward—or both.

14. Rehearse with everything exactly as it will be. Say every word. Make every move. Don't leave anything to chance. This is the most important—and most often violated—principle of persuasive presentation.

15. Read the words on the slide exactly. Don't rephrase. Don't inject new thoughts. Read the slide as it appears. After you have read the slide, you can add commentary of your own.

Presenting with Flip or Presentation Cards

If you're going to be presenting with flipcharts and/or presentation cards, keep these fundamentals in mind:

1. The lights will be on. Plan for more comments from your audience. Cards stimulate conversation. So allow for more time to show cards and charts than for slides.

2. Be simple, telegraphic. Generally, the same design rudiments that create good slides also produce good cards and charts: one thought or idea per card. Make sure your cards are big enough for everyone to read easily. Use the cards as thought joggers for yourself. Don't just stand there and read. Vary your cards. Surprises are spice—and hold attention. Use color, but sparingly.

3. Cards are bulky. Plan to get rid of them gracefully. There's nothing more amateurish than a presenter who presents a splendid posterior view every time he or she bends over to put away a card or a chart. The secret: Don't bend over. Dispose of cards by placing them behind the cards you have yet to show (if you are using an easel). Or place them on a nearby rack or stand at the same level as your other boards.

4. Arrange your lighting. Make sure your cards are positioned in a pool of light. This is a touch of theater that can make a significant difference in the "atmosphere" surrounding your presentation.

5. Consider using a pointer, which has two distinct advantages. It makes you look professional, and it enables you to "get involved" without your cards getting in the way.

6. Write notes to yourself on the cards if your memory needs help. Keep them on the side from which you are operating.

7. Place cards around a room to reprise a thought sequence you want to register. Or use them to illustrate a variety of ways to execute an idea. For exam-

ple, the potential of a campaign idea can be vividly demonstrated by putting a lot of headlines on separate cards and surrounding your audience with them.

Some General Tips

1. Pace yourself to a conversational tempo. Get yourself a cassette and put your presentation on tape, then play it back privately. Most people talk more slowly than they think they do. Also, most people talk in one tone. Listen to yourself.

2. Don't wait for laughs. If the laugh comes, fine. If it doesn't, don't break stride.

3. Don't wait for heavy, profound thoughts to sink in. The audience will think you've forgotten your lines.

4. Don't jingle coins in your pocket, play with a necklace ornament, or continually scratch your head and fidget.

5. Prepare for questions. It takes work, but it's easy. Use the presidential press conference technique. Spend at least an hour anticipating the questions you may get. Write them down. Make sure you've got strong factual answers.

6. If you don't know the answer to a question, don't guess. This can be fatal. Write the question down. Then answer it fully by calling the prospect the next day.

7. Know the members of your audience. Try to find out how they usually act at meetings. If they're likely to interrupt, be ready—and don't be jarred out of your thought sequence. Do some digging on the key people. The more you know about your audience, the better able you'll be to control the situation.

8. A little nervousness is a good thing. It happens to everybody, gets the adrenaline going, and gives you an "edge" you wouldn't have otherwise. But if your voice shakes—and your knees shake—you're going to generate more pity than confidence. Rule number one on nervousness: Know your material. Uncertainty is what causes most nervousness. And your audience will sense it in the first 60 seconds.

9. If possible, rehearse in the room you'll actually use. You've got to feel comfortable when you get up to present your material.

10. Psyche yourself up with a pep talk before you go on. If you tell yourself you're the world's best expert on the material you're presenting, you'll probably look and sound the part.

11. If someone criticizes you, don't act mortally wounded. It embarrasses everybody. The best attitude is one of good-natured confidence. If you're good-natured, your audience probably will be too.

12. Don't let your temper get away from you. This creates an atmosphere in which it is impossible to sell anything.

13. Don't memorize your presentation. This will make you nervous before you

get up to speak. You may want to memorize key parts or key lines, but if you memorize the whole thing, your presentation will sound "canned."

14. Don't go overboard on "show business." But being persuasive doesn't mean being dull. A bit of "theater" in your presentation will keep your audience alert and attentive.

15. Time your presentation. The important people in your audience will have other meetings to attend. If you push them off their schedules, you're going to lose points. Stay within your time allotment. It's businesslike. It's considerate.

16. Become a student. Learn something from every newscaster, performer, and speaker you see. Watch their hands. Note how they register key points. Listen to the range of their voices. Pay particular attention to the length of their sentences. How they close. Be sensitive to their mistakes. You'll learn a lot.

Things to Avoid

Don't allow fear to block you. Fear can be controlled by confidence. Confidence comes from knowing what works. It comes from experience: by knowing your material cold, by knowing yourself and how you come across, and by knowing why you're up there talking. Have a clear, focused point of view.

When there is a chance to volunteer for a presentation, take it. Find out when the next meeting, convention, or presentation is coming up and play a part in it.

Practice in front of people—your family, friends, and coworkers. Get used to being on your feet. Realize that nervousness is normal. Don't panic when you feel it. Just double your interest in giving your listeners the best of your experience and knowledge.

Use Your Natural Energy

Speaking in front of groups is just like having a conversation, except you can have more impact, if you choose. The secret is to be as comfortable and natural when you are presenting before groups as when you are conversing.

Use your natural gestures. Monitor how you talk when you are in a comfortable conversation, and try to use those elements in your presentations. Use your hands to emphasize and clarify ideas.

Move when you talk. There is nothing as boring as a lifeless statue. Keep your legs relaxed and flexible. Moving off the mark helps to release nervous energy as well. Have steady eye communication with individuals in the audience when you are speaking to them.

Know your posture. A strong base is crucial for breathing, gesturing, and your whole nonverbal message of confidence. Take a position in which your weight is forward, knees flexed, aligning you in a natural posture of action. Relax your voice. Nervousness constricts your vocal muscles.

Use your sense of humor. Many people take business presentations so seriously they can't even crack a smile. You don't have to be a stand-up comedian. Don't even try to be funny; simply relax and join the group. Treat your subject seriously, but take yourself lightly.

Complicating the Simple

Many business presentations, especially technical ones, fail because they are too complicated. Don't let convoluted explorations into data obscure your message. People want to know how your information relates to their needs. Tell them.

One of the most important elements is to always have a strong point of view in speaking. Any time you open your mouth, you are persuading your audience of something—even if it is only the importance of your information. Here are some tips:

- Keep it short. Don't ramble. Make your point and get on with it.
- Keep visual aids simple.
- Keep to your time limit. If you have too much material, throw it out rather than rush to cram it all in.
- Repeat your key points more than once, in different ways. People need to hear them more than once. Don't assume everyone is listening attentively.

Remember the "week later test." What one, two, or three main points do you want people to remember one week later? They won't remember much more. Emphasize those, and toss out distracting side issues in your presentation.

Don't make your presentation like a written report. Don't drone on and on. Your points may be well rehearsed, even well written, but they are almost always boring. Many speakers and business presenters make the same mistake. The spoken medium is very different from the written medium. Both use words, but there the similarity ends. Notice how your attention wanders the next time you hear a scripted presentation read out loud.

Work from note concepts when you prepare presentations. Use them when you present. Note concepts are the fewest number of words or pictures that will trigger an idea you can talk about for 30 seconds to 5 minutes. Your concepts should take up a page or two, or a dozen note cards, tops. Don't forget to tie in your visual aids.

Develop your spontaneity. Realizing that you never need to freeze up or worry about blocking again will change your approach to presentations. If you need a printed handout of your speech or presentation, give your talk from note concepts, but hand out the formalized version at the end.

The Lack of Preparation

Practice makes perfect—but only if it's the right practice. The wrong practice only gets you in deeper trouble. People respond to, and remember most, *how* something is said. So spend a proportion of your time preparing yourself along with your message. Don't assume that content alone will carry you. It never does! Good preparation compensates for a lack of talent. Good speakers aren't born that way, so plan to prepare. Preparation gives you confidence, which beats talent by a long shot.

Start now for your next presentation. Begin the thinking process today. Prepare yourself to speak polish your skills. Volunteer at community and business groups, take a seminar, or join a club or association. Jot down noes, clip out magazine and newspaper items, and begin to keep track of ideas that relate to your subject.

Rehearse all the way through. Don't stop because you get stuck midway. Do it in front of others, or audiotape, on videotape. Get feedback. As a rule, rehearse at least two but not more than four times. You want to sound spontaneous and organized, not memorized.

Remember the 75 percent rule: If the total out-loud rehearsal time is 15 minutes, your actual presentation will be about 20 minutes. In front of a group, you will have more to say as you warm up and respond to it.

Think presentations. Picture yourself in action, smiling, having a good time, giving people information that is useful and interesting. Finally, research your audience. If you're speaking to an unfamiliar group, find out all you can about it ahead of time. Tailor your ideas to meet those interests.

Use Today's Technology

Today, most people have the opportunity to see themselves as others see them. This is the active age of television: interactive cable; home videotape; teleconferencing. There is no reason for anyone to lack confidence and feel ineffective as a speaker. The power of video allows you to see how you come across, and gives you the power to control your own effectiveness, your own self-confidence.

First record your presentations, conversations, even telephone calls. Watch yourself speak in everyday situations. Be an observer of yourself. Begin a videotape library of yourself. Arrange to be videotaped as often as possible. Use the tape feedback to monitor and reinforce your progress.

Creativity, Showmanship, and Humor

In a business which lives by its creativity, most ad agency presentations are dull. Prospective clients, too, are human. They like to smile, they like to be sold—so put some humor in your presentation where it fits. An appropriate smile or chuckle loosens everyone up.

There are several points to be made about the subject of humor in presentations:

1. You need to know something about the prospects. Again, this is a matter of homework.

2. Humor can be broad or light and subtle, depending upon the interests and sophistication of the client. It should always be topical and current.

3. While there are times when humor is not appropriate, there is never a time when a light, friendly touch is inappropriate. Clients should not be considered as ogres, and agency presenters should not perform as plastic people.

4. You have to be confident enough and relaxed enough to employ humor. If you can't do that comfortably, don't push it and come off as strained and forced. Perhaps your personality is such that you play it straight, leaving a cre-

ative person, account exec, or media person with a different kind of personality to inject humor or lightness into the pitch.

Skip the Presentation If the Best You Can Do Is Only Half-Hearted

Your new client presentation gives every new business prospect a chance to be introduced to the agency and its staff and made aware of its capabilities. If the lack of time, personnel, or ideas prevents you from putting your best foot forward, forget it!

In addition to the ideas you are presenting to your prospective client, your presentation should include the following points about the agency:

- Agency philosophy and uniqueness; how the agency positions itself
- Capabilities and areas of special expertise
- Agency growth
- Staff—thumbnails of top management and key personnel
- Creative work, including a few case histories
- List of clients

Always update agency case histories and creative work with current examples.

Getting the New Account

Generally speaking, the average ad agency will get a worthwhile new account through a combination of perseverance, experience, innovative thinking, and plain hard work.

But there are exceptions. Take the 6-month-old agency that carefully put together a truly great and memorable new client presentation. It hired the best freelance talent its budget could afford. Agency staff spent weeks researching the account and more weeks preparing their visuals. Getting this new account became an obsession. Then the phone rang. It was the new prospect, who simply begged off. The client didn't want a presentation. It just wanted the 6-month-old agency, and right away.

It's a lovely story. And who knows—perhaps in your lifetime it may even happen to you.

26

Agency Compensation

Over the years, the advertising agency's traditional compensation system of "15 percent commission plus markup on production" has produced plenty of pro-and-con debate. Though it is still the most widely used method of compensation in the industry, many agencies in recent years have given up media commissions in favor of receiving compensation for their work on a "fee" basis, or a combination of both fee and commission. In addition to there being variation in the way different agencies are compensated, the method of payment by clients within an individual agency may also vary.

Why does the agency business hold the commission system so dear? Just what relationship does this method of compensation have to the kind and amount of effort necessary for your clients? Does it make good business sense for an agency to risk a 100 percent loss if a client does not pay for a commissionable ad, in order to make a 15 percent gross profit which may yield a net profit of just 3 percent? Will an agency working on commissions paid by media have a tendency to "push" its clients into using commissionable media when some other advertising medium might be better?

Some accounts with well-defined markets will do a lot of media advertising from the start. They can be profitable for an agency working on commission. They don't need intensive preparatory work. On the other hand, you may have accounts that need a wide range of services, and considerable preparatory work, to get them started. They may need the assistance of marketing and merchandising experts, counseling, direct mail, research, telemarketing, package and product design help, and 101 collateral services before they require much media advertising. Should an ad agency just starting up have to go through a period of famine—supporting the effort, in actual fact, with the profits from other clients?

The key to billing your services properly is to first understand the process involved in the placement of advertising. Only then will you be able to decide which is the better system of agency compensation for you: fee or 15 percent commission. Advocates for each system can be found among both advertisers and agencies.

Percentage Compensation

Most media, both electronic and print, allow advertising agencies a professional 15 percent discount for placing ads with them. They do not grant individual advertisers this kind of discount; at least, they are not supposed to. Theoretically, media would rather deal with advertising agencies as media professionals than with advertisers on a one-to-one basis. This is why they will accept ads from advertisers directly, but bill advertisers at gross retail rates.

The media bills the advertising agency according to their retail or national rates, less the 15 percent commission. This commission is retained by the advertising agency and it in turn bills the client at the gross rate. Thus, if the rate for one page in a magazine were $10,000, the agency would be billed by that magazine for $10,000 less $1500 (15 percent) for a net amount of $8500. The agency in turn would bill the client for $10,000 and pay the magazine $8500, retaining $1500 as its gross income.

Typically, terms are net 30 days on the payment of media bills. However, a discount of 2 percent on the net bill is often available to those agencies that pay within 10 days. Some agencies pass this discount along to their clients; others do not.

There are print media that do not offer discounts to advertising agencies. Local small newspapers are an example. In such a case, the common practice is for the agency to add on 17.65 percent to the net amount billed by the media so that the agency, in effect, earns the equivalent of what 15 percent commission on the gross would have been.

Some advertising agencies do not charge for writing copy and preparing layouts in connection with commissionable advertising. Others do, however, and there are also many other expenses which are incurred by the agency in the preparation of advertisements. These are charged to the client at cost plus a percentage—generally 17.65 percent for larger agencies and a higher figure for smaller agencies. The reason for this difference is that the smaller agencies usually place advertisements in less expensive media, their smaller commissions give them a smaller gross margin, and they argue that the higher percentage is necessary in order for them to have a sufficient gross margin to cover their expenses and realize a profit. In the example above: If the cost of the artwork, photography, copy, type, pasteup, mechanical, and color separations for the magazine advertisement came to $3000, the agency would bill the client $3000 plus 17.65 percent, or a total of $3529.50.

Clients frequently request agencies to do other work in addition to preparing advertising for commissionable media. This collateral work may include the creation and production of point-of-purchase material, leaflets, catalogs and brochures, videos for sales and training, sales manuals, and similar material. For such work, an hourly charge is generally made for creative time, and out-of-pocket expenses generally are billed to the client at cost plus a percentage of 17.65 percent or more.

The argument for the 15 percent commission compensation system can be summed up as working best for agencies with clients that have large enough budgets to compensate the agency through media commissions and production markups.

Fee Compensation

In general, smaller agencies with smaller clients who expect full agency services but do not have the media and production budgets to support such services are the agencies most likely to use the fee compensation system. Cyclical accounts too, whether at a small or large agency, should be on a fee basis, since it may not be economically possible for the agency to reduce or enlarge its staff to accommodate these "peak and valley" clients. A fixed fee allows the agency to remain stable staffwise with planned income.

Agencies billing on a fee system will receive a set fee, usually paid monthly, but based on an annual budget projection. The fee covers certain specific services the agency will provide. All out-of-pocket expenses as well as expenses for services not covered by the fee are usually billed to the client at the agency's net cost. Media commissions earned by the agency can be applied to the fee or rebated to the advertiser.

Some agencies working on a fee basis prefer to have the media bill the advertiser at net rates directly, thereby eliminating costly agency bookkeeping expenses. If the media will not do this, the agency can forward its bill to the client with instructions for the client to pay the net amount due.

The amount of fee an agency will charge is determined by such factors as the nature and size of the account; the amount and kind of services to be provided by the agency; the amount of commissionable income that will be lost. Some agencies prefer to work on a guaranteed profit basis or a costs-plus basis.

There are many reasons that both agencies and advertisers prefer the fee system over the commission system:

- Media inflation is often the main reason fees have gained in popularity. Double-digit rate increases created a windfall for agencies, which many clients felt was unfair.

- Advertisers today are more cost-conscious and don't mind rolling up their sleeves and learning the agency business. This mind set is more important when compensation is by fee rather than commission.

- More agency-type work is now being performed by boutique specialists and in-house by advertisers, partly to save money and partly to have more control over marketing functions. Consequently, many companies are finding that they don't need all the services an agency provides under a commission.

- Agencies are doing more nonmedia work, such as public relations, research, sales promotion, and direct marketing. All these tasks require a fee billing.

- Small accounts often are not profitable. Fees can be set to guarantee the agency a profit.

Variations of Compensation Systems

There are many variations of the fee and commission systems. These include guaranteed fee with commissions completely retained; guaranteed fee with commissions credited against the fee; work done on a time basis with an annual minimum agreed upon; work done on a time basis with no minimum; and cost plus markup.

Some agencies charge fees for new-product development because so little media are involved that the agency can't make commissions that will cover the time and costs put into the project. On the other hand, some clients may do some of their own media buying, and they would rather be charged a fee for just the work the agency performs instead of paying a full 15 percent commission on the media used.

Alternatives to the traditional 15 percent commission are more widespread than are obvious. The big advertisers with few products don't pay the traditional 15 percent; they negotiate the commission lower to 10 percent, 7½ percent, and even 5 percent. Agencies will accept less when the budgets are large, the company prestigious, and the opportunity for growth present. The commission system always has been and always will be open to compromise.

Fees Require More Time and Work Than Commissions

Operating on a fee system has its shortcomings in terms of more time and work, in the lengthy negotiations a fee system usually necessitates (an advertiser and its agency have to agree on whether fees, charges, markups, and profits are reasonable), and in the paperwork required. It takes a lot of time to administer a fee system, including keeping daily time sheets and submitting reports regularly to the client. For these reasons, some agencies don't get into it.

The agency has to put together a fee estimate based on projected costs for labor, overhead, and profit. Some factors, such as overhead and production costs, are always changing and any time the cost of something changes, it has to be negotiated. But despite all the drawbacks, the fee system is growing because it works

Who Profits Most from the Fee System?

There are two schools of thought concerning which method of compensation is best for both client and agency. One side feels that under the 15 percent commission system an agency has more incentive to do a good job. The better a job it does, the more the budget grows and the more the agency will earn. Also, these advocates believe that the commission system provides greater ease of administration with more services available to the client.

Conversely, advocates of the fee system argue that fees are the most equitable way of compensating agencies. Fees enable the agency to give an unbiased recommendation on what media to use. The fee system also allows clients to change their order of priorities easily, since the agency makes the same amount of money regardless. The fee system can eliminate the need to negotiate compensation when new projects arise. And it helps keep up with agency costs and trends.

It all comes down to this: The needs of each client and each agency are different. No two are exactly alike. It will be up to you and your client to determine the compensation arrangements that suit you both best.

Creative Fees and Markups

It's a fact that the standard 15 percent media commission has stayed the same for the last 100 or more years, while operating costs seem to rise every day. It follows that the standard commissions from media will most probably not be sufficient to cover all the costs of running an agency at a profit. You will need to supplement that income with additional charges for a variety of services that an agency commonly performs for its clients.

Suppose a client decides that in addition to its schedule of ad production and placement, it needs telemarketing to sell its product. This may be a departure from what the 15 percent commission or fee billing covers, and may require special, separate billing under a category such as "special services" or "creative consultation." This kind of service fee can vary enormously. Just as business consultation fees vary from $30 to $100 per hour and more, so do creative fees. A creative fee, however, is usually quoted as a flat sum on a per-project basis.

Since the telemarketing services you provide will not produce media commissions, you may bill the client a fee for your consultation and preparation time, actual hours spent on the phone, and follow-up time, plus a markup on outside costs. There are no universal standards for what items are marked up or how much the markup should be. Some agencies use different markups for different kinds of jobs. In any case, the markup is seldom less than 17.65 percent and may be as much as 25, 50, or even 100 percent, depending on the complexity of the job. Since the agency's income is derived from commissions, retainer and creative fees, hourly charges, and markups, there can be trade-offs. A small creative fee combined with a high markup can yield the same bottom-line profit as a monthly retainer fee in conjunction with a low markup. Markups, therefore, cannot be judged as high or low in isolation from other agency fees. They are just one element within the whole pricing system.

Using different markups for different kinds of work is usually preferable to adopting a single markup that you apply to all work. In this way, the compensation you receive will correspond more closely to the nature of the work the client requires, and your charges will be easier to justify. Whether you do a small job in which you quote the client cost plus commission (i.e., your markup) or whether you do a big one for a "package price," the procedure for determining the final price is the same.

While it is customary to mark up materials and services you purchase from outside suppliers, you should not mark up charges for time spent by any of your staff. Clerical services, research and marketing services, and media coordination (interviewing models, photographers, etc.) can be billed to the client on a hourly basis. If you quote an hourly rate to a client for a particular job, the rate you quoted should already include the pay rate for that employee, plus the overhead rate for your agency, plus a factor of profit for you. If you establish hourly rates for different categories of service that your agency supplies, your clients will know better where they stand.

There is one other category of charges that are seldom marked up. These are the out-of-pocket expenses that you incur on behalf of a client in the course of performing your services. These expenses might include long-distance calls and faxes, postage or overnight delivery charges, and other project-related expenses incidental to the assignment. You should have an understanding with your client at the outset as to what kinds of expenses will be reimbursed and what limit, if any, will be placed on the total amount.

Because each advertising project tends to develop a "life of its own," the criteria for billing each project can vary tremendously. As your agency grows, you will determine how best to charge for your services. The key is flexibility and the ability to develop your own standards for billing your various services.

Extending Credit: Don't Finance Your Client's Campaign

Though the subject of collecting funds is treated elsewhere in this book, it should be noted here that most agencies, especially those working on a commission basis, pay the media and then bill their clients when the ads have been placed or after they have run. Clients usually pay the agency 30 days later. This represents a potential negative cashflow situation for you.

One way around it is to bill clients well in advance of their ads being placed or running. This approach is especially recommended with new clients that have not established a track record of keeping current on what they owe you.

It is not recommended that you pay media in advance. Often, ads run incorrectly and it is much easier to get "make-goods" when you owe the media money.

Agencies working on the fee system most often bill the agency fees at the start of each month, and for production and other costs at the end of each month. It is not uncommon to bill in advance for media expenses since on the fee system, you are not earning commissions and the client is either paying you or the media direct at *net* rates. This way you are not financing your client's campaign, which you are not expected to do in any business—except maybe in the advertising business.

Keeping Time Sheets and Reviewing Your Compensation

When you are working on a fee system with new clients, your primary basis for determining charges will be the time spent on each job. The keeping of meticulous time sheets is important. Your clients have a right to know not only who worked on their project, but exactly how many hours were spent. Time sheets provide the necessary documentation you will need if a client questions or challenges your charges.

Time sheets will also provide you with much of the information you will need to review your fee compensation on a client-by-client basis. A portion of your fee was based on an estimate of the time you expected to spend on the account. The time sheets will give you a clearer picture of how close you were and whether or not you want to renegotiate the fee if it is not fair to you. It is recommended that you conduct a compensation review of each account at least every 6 months.

There is one other consideration you should have concerning working with new clients on a fee basis. Since most fees are based on a full year's budget and then billed monthly, you might want to get new accounts to pay half the yearly fee within the first 3 months. The reasoning here is that you will spend more time in the first 3 months on a new account than you may in the last 9 months—and there is always the possibility that a client may terminate your services before 6 months. Unless your agreement calls for fair compensation, you would not be properly compensated for the time you put in with this client.

One final thought on fees versus commissions: No matter which compensation system you use to bill your clients, your foremost job is to operate an efficient and creative machine.

Collecting Delinquent Funds

In the early stages of delinquency send another copy of the outstanding bill, with the notation "past due" or "overdue notice" stamped on the front. If this does not bring payment or arrangements for payment, the second step in the collection process is to send a letter with a friendly, courteous tone. The purpose is to maintain good relations with the customer, realizing that your invoice may have been overlooked, or your client may be temporarily hard-pressed for the cash to pay its bills at the moment. These reminders should be routine with any late payment of bills, and will let your customers know that you are aware of their lateness. While these reminders should be friendly and sympathetic, they should also be firm and short.

Since sending a letter, or series of letters, each a little less friendly and a little more threatening than the last, is a "soft" approach, it may not always evoke response. There is no demand for acknowledgment from the debtor. Therefore, you may need to initiate stronger methods in the collecting process.

Confrontation by telephone or in person is more effective than the letter because an immediate response is forced from the debtor. The initial confrontation should be in private and should appeal to the debtor's sympathies, sense or justice, and pride. This is the opportunity to make the debtor's embarrassment work in your favor. Get a firm commitment as to an amount and when you can expect to receive the payment. If your pleas don't have the desired effect, then threats are in order. Inform the client of your intended course of action if payment is not received by a certain date.

Some of your credit clients may be totally immune to polite and gentle approaches. The customer has been warned that its company reputation and credit rating may be damaged; you have done your best to maintain consideration and respect for the client's situation. Not it is time to give up the client as a customer—as it is probably not worth the trouble—and to take the measures required to collect the money owed you. You have several alternatives open to you.

1. Notify other creditors of the client. It is possible that they are also owed money, and this knowledge will tell you how quickly you must act to collect your share. It will also prevent the client from receiving further credit extensions elsewhere.

2. Send a sight draft to the client's bank with the instruction to pay the amount owed you. While payment of this draft requires the debtor's consent, the client may approve payment of the draft just to avoid embarrassment with the bank.

3. A collection agency may be useful as a final resort. While an agency will take from 25 percent to 33 percent of the amounts collected, or even up to 50 percent on amounts under $50, it is better than writing the account off as a total loss. You will find collection agencies listed in the yellow pages of your phone book. If you do try an agency, and it proves ineffective, don't hesitate to take your accounts to another agency after your contract with the first expires. Agencies use various methods of collection, and one may realize better results with your customers than the other. A point to keep in mind when hiring a collection agency is that any monies paid by a debtor while an account is signed over to the agency is credited to the agency against its fee, regardless of whether that payment is a direct result of the agency's efforts or yours. So be sure you have already exhausted your own collection methods.

4. Garnish the debtor's wages, savings, or checking accounts, or any other assets you can find. The legal expense makes this approach impractical unless you are seeking collection of several thousand dollars or more.

5. Some lawyers have a good deal of experience in collection proceedings. However, a lawyer's time will be an expense whether you receive payment on the account or not.

6. Small claims court is an inexpensive and informal method of seeking payment from a debtor. But even if you receive a judgment in your favor, this does not always guarantee payment. Keep in mind also that because of the absence of legal technicalities, you may be legally right, but if the judge or referee is sympathetic to the story your debtor tells, you may not receive a judgment in your favor.

As we will see in the next chapter, the other side of getting existing clients to pay their bills—and equally important—is paying the costs of securing new or additional business.

27

Paying for
New Business

Increasing Your Business

The lifeblood of any advertising agency is, of course, its clients. For an agency to grow and be successful, it must not only be good at solving a client's problems and increasing client sales, it must also secure new business.

Generally speaking, there are a number of ways an advertising agency can increase its business: It can produce advertising that helps clients achieve solid, lasting growth. As these clients get larger, so will their advertising budgets, and so to, will the agency billings. As an agency's business develops, many new clients can come from referrals of one kind or another. An agency can buy new business by merging or affiliating with smaller hot agencies that are in a growth stage—or it can do what most ad agencies do: go out and solicit new clients.

Who Gets New Business?

The first question to ask is: Who is the person who gets new business? Is he or she already on your staff in another position? Is the agency principal the prime source of new clients? Are there a number of people in the agency involved with new business? Do you use free-lance new business developers?

There are situations in which an advertising agency will pay a finder's or referral fee to an outsider who brings in a new client. It is more common among small agencies for someone on staff to be compensated partially, or even totally, because of his or her ability to generate new business. It is this person, usually the account executive, whom the agency principal has in mind when the question is asked, "How much should we pay for new business?"

The Account Executive and New Business

The liaison between the agency and its clients is the account executive. It is the job of this person to sell the agency's recommendations to the client, and to be aware of the needs and desires of both the client and the agency. It is also the account executive who will most often be charged with the responsibility of finding and bringing in new business.

There are two kinds of account executives in the ad agency business. There's the aggressive sales type who enjoys making cold calls on new advertising prospects, brings them in as clients, and services them with an eye toward building up their expenditures with the agency. Then there's the less aggressive type who may prefer not to go out and get the new business, but rather service it once it has become an agency account.

If your agency is just starting out, you would be better off with the more aggressive of the two, since you will have relatively few contacts in the business community and will need an aggressive person who can go out and hustle new business by selling the creativeness of your agency. If you are coming into agency ownership from another area of the business, you may already have an account base and a number of good business contacts built up over the years. Even if this is the case, you would still do better with the more aggressive account executive, as building up your business quickly and on a solid base the first year can be crucial to your future success.

Be sure that before you employ any account executive, you examine his or her background carefully. He or she must be experienced in advertising agency procedures or related fields such as print and broadcast sales, or as a public relations account executive, and should be knowledgeable about all aspects of the business—from the creative end to the cost of services. The account exec should be able to answer any questions a prospective client might ask about the agency or campaigns in general and should be willing and able to make cold calls on all types of new prospects. The exec should also know how to "line up" good prospects and get them interested in using your agency's services. Though this person should be a good hustler, don't forget that he or she is representing your agency, and the first impression a prospective client gets of your agency will be that of the account executive.

There are a number of ways to compensate account executives, including straight salary, salary plus commission, salary plus bonus, or a percentage of gross profits on the new business they bring in.

Some agencies believe that offering a straight salary attracts a more solidly based, better-quality account executive, even though they may be paying more money up front on unproven ability. Other agencies prefer to pay part or all of the compensation on a commission basis, theorizing that the more an account executive can talk a client into spending, the more the account executive—and the agency—will make.

What Is the New Business Worth to the Agency?

Whatever compensation plan an agency uses to pay for new business, it cannot pay more to the person who brings in the business than is affordable and still return a profit to the agency. So the next question is, "How much can the agency afford to pay for a new client?" To determine this, you must first know what your operating profit is. As pointed out earlier in this book, gross profit (the difference between the amount billed to a client and the hard dollar cost of that billing) is 100 percent of all the money available to pay all operating expenses and return a reasonable profit to the agency.

This example can help you determine the operating profit of your agency:

Gross profit	$40,000	100%
Operating expenses		
Salaries	$20,000	50%
Overhead	$12,000	30%
Total operating expenses	$32,000	80%
Operating profit	$ 8,000	20%

When compensation for new business is based on a percentage of gross profits on the new business brought in, a key consideration is the amount of operating profit that will be earned from the billing. As shown in the above table, if an agency can hold total operating expenses to 80 percent of gross profit, there will be an $8000 operating profit to the agency.

The question now is, "How much of the $8000 can the agency afford to pay for the new business that produced $40,000 gross profit?" If you agree that one-half is fair, it means that for every dollar of gross profit, you will pay 10 percent of that amount to the person bringing in new business.

What If Your Operating Profit Is Less Than 20 Percent?

Your operating profit may well be less than 20 percent, especially if yours is a start-up operation. The more you spend of your gross profits, the less operating profits you will have left. So how much of what's left are you willing to pay? If you continue with the 10 percent of the gross profit to the person bringing in new business, then the operating profit to the agency will be drastically cut.

Suppose, though, that the compensation for the new business finder is based not on the gross profit, but rather on the operating profit and that it be split evenly on whatever the operating profit of that new client's business is. However, a new or mismanaged agency may not show an operating profit at all, so how can the new business finder be fairly compensated?

The Pro Forma Profitability Statement

Whether the business brought in is a one-time project or an annual budget, you should prepare a pro forma profitability statement, based on current operations, to determine how much operating profit can be expected from the new business. Then you can determine how much you are willing to pay for the business. The amount you decide upon is expressed as a percentage of gross profit.

Using the $40,000 example, if your pro forma operating profit shows that you can pay $4000, then the agreement is 10 percent of gross profit. Or if you can afford only $2000, the agreement is 5 percent of gross profit. How much you can afford is your individual decision.

Don't Pay for New Business Before You Get Paid

Be sure that your agreement with a new business developer includes the understanding that he or she will not receive compensation until the new client has paid the agency. Since most clients pay monthly, compensation to the new business finder should be on the same basis, after the client's checks have cleared.

The Finder's Fee: How Long Do You Keep Paying?

If the new business brought in is seasonal, a special project, or a series of different projects, the payments made to the finder should be based on the total gross profits derived from those billings. But if the new business represents an active, ongoing account, compensation to the finder should be based on the gross profits of that client for the first year only. If the account grows, you might want to continue paying the finder's fee in the second year on that amount of gross profit in excess of the first-year gross profit. This can be determined only at the end of the second year, at which time the fee is paid, if earned.

Off-Staff New Business Developers

There are individuals and companies that specialize in developing new business for advertising agencies and related businesses such as public relations firms, package and art design firms, and other companies in the communications field. These new business developers prefer not to work for a particular agency and usually do not get further involved with servicing the accounts they bring into the various agencies they work with. Because much of the new business that is acquired through these off-staff finders is business that they refer to an agency, their compensation is usually considered a "referral fee." The referral fee is a negotiable amount, since the off-staff person most likely will not provide the servicing of the client that you would get from a person on staff. Usually it is a one-time fee based on a much smaller percentage of the gross profits than a typical finder's fee.

The methods and arrangements for compensating those who bring in new business are numerous and vary with the size, operating methods, and philosophies of each agency. However you structure your new business compensation plan, the bottom line for you, the agency principal, comes down to how much you can afford to pay.

28

Losing Clients

Some Reasons That Agencies Lose Business

One reason could be that your client has a sluggish sales curve. Or the ad manager at the client's office has left and the new person wants his or her "people" to act as the agency. Or no one's talking about your advertising. Or everyone is talking about your competitor's advertising. Or the work being turned out by your agency is especially bad. Or you're doing such a good job for your client that you've attracted the interest of some hot new agency which wants this great account and has come up with a better approach that your client feels you should have thought of. Or your prices are too high. Or your prices are too low and your client thinks your work isn't as good as another agency's because it charges so much more. Or there have been rumors in the business that you are losing accounts at a fast rate. Or there have been rumors that your top creative people are leaving. Or there is talk in the trade that you're in financial trouble. Or the client has just grown too big for your small shop. Or the client is fed up with your billing errors, missed deadlines, and lack of account supervision and direction. Or it could be something as simple (and face-saving) as the client has decided to go in house with advertising.

Whatever the reason, the fact is that during your career as the principal of an advertising agency, you will more than likely lose accounts. And no matter how stifflipped and unconcerned you may appear about each loss, unless you really hated working with the client or lost money servicing the account, every loss will be upsetting—to you as the head of the agency and to your staff who put in untold hours of creative effort working on that account.

It should be noted that there are many advertising agencies that keep their clients for years and years. Unfortunately, you don't hear very much about them. A client staying with an agency for 20, 30, or even 50 or more years makes for interesting storytelling, but it isn't nearly as newsworthy as the announcement that a good advertiser has fired so-and-so and is moving its account to a new agency. And too often, when a client decides to leave an agency, the agency is the last to know—or finds out about it through the grapevine.

So, what can you do to hold onto your clients?

The Advertiser-Agency Relationship

It all starts with the relationship you have with your clients. Obviously, they all expect you to deliver successful campaigns that will increase their business. But many other factors enter into this relationship.

Do your clients look upon your agency as a marketing partner or simply as a vendor? Are they satisfied with what you're giving them or do they want more creativity, service, and help than you originally said you would or could give them?

Unfortunately, many advertisers and their agencies tend to be fickle, and as a result their relationships are short-lived, despite the fact that the ever-increasing complexity of the marketing task makes it costly for both parties when changes occur frequently. The cost in work hours and dollars spent by the client selecting and orienting a new agency can be substantial, as is the cost borne by the agency that has spent time and money soliciting, researching, and pitching the client—and then going through the "getting to know you" phase.

One sensible method of building a lasting relationship is for both advertiser and agency to take the necessary time and effort to make sure they are right for each other before they start their relationship.

Building a Flexible Relationship

A good client-agency relationship should not be solely dependent on two people (usually the ad manager on the client side, and the account executive on the agency side). Both the advertiser's management and the agency's management should strive to make a flexible relationship that includes the diffusing of authority and decision making to other levels for execution. And both companies should be wary of a relationship that depends too heavily on the compatibility of two individuals.

In a situation where both agency and advertiser are small companies, diffusion of authority may not be possible. The agency head may work directly with the head of the retail store, manufacturing, or service company. In any case, if both client and agency strive for a full understanding of each other's needs, goals, and problems, there will surely be a positive effect on their relationship.

One fatal mistake every agency should avoid is to present top management as part of the "team" when they make their new business presentation. Then, once the advertiser has become a client, the "big guns" disappear and the account is left to the junior members of the staff. By the way, if an agency is large enough to have junior staff members, the agency management has the responsibility to keep in close contact with the client and take care of any problems that may come up.

In a well-planned marketing relationship, the client should take the agency into its confidence and disclose all the facts of its operation that would be helpful to the agency. If the advertiser fails to make these disclosures, it cannot expect the agency to do the best possible job.

It is important, also, that the client allow its agency to participate in its annual planning process, and should encourage it to contribute to the advertiser's strategy. The advertiser should recognize that an important reason for using an advertising agency is for the creativity, expertise, and unbiased point of view that agency people will provide in successfully marketing the client's products or services. Thus, the client should encourage the agency to be uninhibited in presenting its views. This does not mean that the agency should expect the client to accept all agency recommendations. On the other hand, the agency must recognize that it is working *for* the client, which has the right to make any final decisions.

The agency should maintain not only normal contact with the client, but be fully aware of what is going on in the client company at all times—by checking regularly on sales, meeting and speaking with new personnel, and finding out about client expansion plans, new products coming up, or maybe a company event that will generate good PR or become the basis for an ad campaign (such as an anniversary or expansion sale). The more time that agency people spend learning about their clients, the more secure their positions with those clients will be.

Accepting Accountability

The agency should always accept accountability for its actions, as well as provide justification for its compensation. Making a wrong decision or purposely putting a client in a position that can cause financial loss or other problems is not uncommon in the advertising business. Like a doctor or lawyer who causes such a situation, someone (in this case the agency) has to be accountable and responsible.

The agency should be up front with its clients about what it does in house and what it "farms out." An agency should not represent itself as a full-service, one-stop shop if it merely acts as a referral service for sales promotional and other marketing services that the client believes the agency is providing.

In a good relationship, the agency and client should have mutual consideration for each other's operational procedures. If the client has a cutoff day each month for the payment of invoices, the agency should make sure its invoices are sent on time. The client should be considerate of the fact the agency has extended credit and may have laid out moneys on its behalf, and should pay the agency's bills on time.

If the agency gives its client an estimate on a job that comes in at a higher cost, the agency should notify the client in advance of sending the bill and explain why there is a difference in price. If notification can be made before the job is started, all the better. This way the client has the option of not doing the job if it is too expensive.

Though there will more than likely be a contract between the agency and client, and though most contracts usually make sure the interest of both parties are protected, a good client-agency relationship will go beyond the contract and rely more on goodwill and mutual respect.

It Can't Hurt to Use the Client's Products

You may not be able to afford a million-dollar home, if that's what your client sells, but if your client is a retail store, or bank, or automobile dealer, or supermarket, you will rack up points by patronizing the client's products. After all, your clients think enough of you to use your services. Besides, patronizing your clients shows them that you think enough of their products or services to use them yourself. And by using them, you are in the best position to create campaigns that will be successful for them.

What Advertisers Consider When Selecting an Agency

In a 1990 study conducted by Rhine and Hayes Research, major advertisers were asked to indicate the factors they considered when going through an advertising agency selection process. These are the considerations, ranked in the order of their importance:

1. Honesty and integrity
2. Results
3. Creativity
4. Talent and staff
5. Responsiveness
6. Easy to work with
7. Professionalism
8. Marketing expertise
9. Competitive pricing
10. Media expertise
11. Strategic planning
12. Scope of services
13. Size of agency

If you look at each factor, you will see that the majority relate to the agency personnel. So an agency should consider personnel issues of critical importance in its relationship with clients. The study showed that competitive pricing as well as internal agency financial problems were also important factors that advertisers considered in their selection of an agency.

In an April 1991 article in *Advertising Age* magazine quoting excerpts from a client-agency relationship study by Professors Bruce Smackey and James Maskulka of Lehigh University and supported by *Advertising Age* and Thomas Ferguson Associates, it was pointed out that "frequent justification of an agency's expenses can be the cause of unnecessary friction between the client and its agency." This was the conclusion drawn from interviews by client and agency personnel. The article also pointed out that conflicts were caused as the result of ad campaigns being canceled as well as the agency's having to absorb too much of the cost of special projects. The article suggested that through the development of client-agency people scheduling and the application of creativity to agency compensation some of these problems might be eliminated.

Client-Agency Shortcomings

A 1982 research study by Holtz, Ryans, and Shanklin of 100 advertising managers from the top 100 advertisers and 100 account executives from agencies that managed these accounts showed that many shortcomings were perceived by both sides.

From the Advertiser's Point of View

1. Lack of cost-consciousness
2. Failure of agency to meet deadlines
3. High personnel turnover within agencies
4. Poor communication between agency and client
5. Poor agency follow-through

From the Agency's Point of View

1. Lack of clear-cut objectives from the client
2. Client indecisiveness
3. Too many approval levels
4. Poor communication to the agency
5. Client lack of knowledge about marketing and advertising

Keeping the Client Happy

Agencies that consistently ask themselves the following questions have the best chance of keeping a client happy.

- Is the account executive fully knowledgeable about the client's operation?
- Is there good rapport between client and agency?
- Do you have confidence in the recommendations the account exec makes to the client, and are these recommendations more often right or wrong?
- Does the account executive move quickly to meet deadlines and solve problems?
- Does the account executive keep to client budgets and communicate accurately with other agency members?
- Have you contacted the client to see if it is happy with the account executive?
- Are new campaigns fresh and creative in their approach and look?
- Have new campaigns accomplished what they were intended to accomplish?
- Are the creative people assigned to an account fully familiar with all the client's needs, goals, and problems?
- Do you feel your creative people are coming up with consistently good ideas?

- Are you happy with your creative and general reputation?
- Is your media department current on the most up-to-date rates, special offerings, and research available?
- Does the media department notify your clients of specials, short deadlines, or documentation that may be required to verify claims the advertiser is making?
- Is the media buyer a good negotiator who looks out for the client's interests?
- Is the media buyer respected by the media?
- Are print and production costs kept in line with the client's budgets?
- Is each job estimated by at least three sources?
- Are clients notified if estimates turn out to be lower than actual costs?
- Is the quality of the work produced by the agency consistent?
- Does the agency have a good relationship with suppliers?
- Does top management at the agency keep in close touch with the client?
- Does top management at the agency respond quickly to client concerns?
- Does the agency pay its bills on time and maintain good relations with its vendors and the media?
- Does the agency have abnormal personnel turnover?
- Is the agency accomplishing its goals in relation to growth and other philosophies set forth in its agency plan?
- Are your invoices to clients thorough in their descriptions, leaving little or no doubt about what you are billing for and why the costs are what they are?

Key Words to Remember That Will Enhance Client-Agency Relationships

Communication. Make sure that everyone at the agency fully understands what the client wants, and that the client fully understands what the agency plans to give.

Consistency. Be consistent in the quality and creativeness of the work you produce. The client should, by the same token, be consistent in its requests of the agency. Don't ask for one thing today, and change your mind tomorrow.

Accessibility. Because of deadlines, and times of opportunity, quick decisions often have to be made by agency and client. Both should make themselves reachable by beeper, portable or regular phone, fax, or whatever communications means are available.

Understanding. If both client and agency try to understand the complexities of each other's business, a more tolerant relationship will result.

Promises. Agencies should not promise things they can't possibly deliver. Clients, on the other hand, should never put their agency in the position of having to make exaggerated claims about client products or services; nor should they make promises to their agencies that they have no intention of keeping.

Listening.   Both parties should listen carefully to what the other is saying, always keeping an open mind.

Records.   Both client and agency should write down the "minutes" of each meeting and send each other copies to verify that they both saw, heard, and understood the same things. Records also come in handy when someone is asked to back up an invoice charge or verify a purchase.

Time.   Stick to schedules. Don't be late for meetings. Everybody's time is valuable.

Respect and humility.   Respect each other's shortcomings. Go out of your way to help each other so both of you can benefit.

The Ad Agency "Self-Audit"

To help reduce the risk of account disenchantment and possible loss, advertising agencies, like most businesses, should regularly review their internal programs and methods of operation, their relationships with clients, their creative strategies, and their effectiveness in the marketplace. Such reviews, if done in a comprehensive, systematic and periodic manner, will provide valuable information that can be used to adopt new planning procedures and adjust to changes that may have occurred in the marketplace.

What Will an Audit Show?

Economic and other circumstances make it more than likely that your client's needs have changed since you first started your relationship. It is also likely that during this same period there were internal changes within your own company—new employees; new vendors; new clients; lost clients; and more competition, not only from other advertising agencies, but from related industries such as printers, marketing consultants, graphic designers, and even the media. By reviewing your procedures and relating them to the situation that exists now at your agency, you will have a basis for making modifications in your objectives, strategies, and programs for clients as well as for your own company.

An "audit," used as an examination of your business, will point out the strengths and weaknesses of the agency, suggest ways to correct existing problems, and structure preventative policies for the future. It can act as sort of a diagnostic tool for evaluating the effectiveness of your agency.

Factors to Review in Your Agency Audit

The agency audit should cover the following:

- Current personnel situation and turnover rate
- Current financial situation and potential financial problems

- Current management procedures
- Current agency marketing and creative orientation
- Current client relationships
- Agency performance and results of campaigns
- Changes in client marketing strategies due to new products or strategies
- Current agency pricing and changes in vendor prices
- Market and trade trends that may create new problems in marketing (the impact of direct-response advertising, database marketing, and telemarketing; the effect of cable television and sales promotion; an increase in postal rates; zipping, zapping, and 900 telephone numbers; interactive and high-definition television; voice mail; computer animation; etc.)
- Economic considerations (wars, hikes in oil prices, recessions, demographic and cultural trends, geographic changes, etc.)
- Competition from ad agencies and others
- Regulatory changes affecting the client's and agency's businesses, such as new FTC, FDA, EPA, FCC, and BBB regulations
- Harmony within the agency—how well the account people get along with the creative people
- Agency standing and image in the community and trade
- Scope of agency services
- Agency ability to meet deadlines

If it is possible to use an outside, unbiased person or company rather than your own staff to conduct the agency audit, the results and suggestions will be much more objective.

Part 8 Action Checklist _____

- ✔ Have a plan for acquiring new business.
- ✔ Solicit clients in businesses that you or your key personnel are familiar with. If not, consider using outside expertise.
- ✔ Don't waste your time going after accounts that want a larger agency.
- ✔ Find out as much about the potential client as you can before making your pitch.
- ✔ The number-one reason a client is considering any new agency is to increase its business. You must convince the client that you can.
- ✔ Don't risk losing current clients in your quest for new ones.
- ✔ Set aside dollars in your budget for new account development.

- When approaching new prospects, put yourself in their shoes and present your agency accordingly.

- Be creative when making a new client presentation. Be warm, not rigid. Be organized. Do your homework on the prospect. Prepare for possible questions you will be asked. If you don't know the answer to a question, don't guess. Call back at a later time with the answer.

- Know the materials you are presenting. Use audiovisual aids whenever you can.

- Keep your presentation clear, short, simple, and within your time limit.

- Once you've acquired a new client, establish the basis for compensation at the outset. Make sure it is spelled out in detail in your agency-client agreement.

- The range of services a client will need is a key factor in determining which system of compensation (fee, commission, or some combination) is best for you.

- When charging for production or outside purchase markups, remember that small gross margins on a job may require higher markups.

- If you are working on a fee basis, consider having the media bill the client directly. This will save you bookkeeping expenses on that phase of account servicing.

- Unless you want to finance your client's promotions, bill in advance of ads running, and always pay the media after the ad has run—and run correctly. If not, negotiate with the media for a credit or make-good.

- If you are working on a fee system, keep accurate time records and review them periodically to determine if the fee you are getting is adequate for the amount of work performed.

- Be strong with clients that are delinquent in paying their bills. Don't hesitate to seek legal action if all else has failed.

- Your agency's relationship with a client is determined in part by the person servicing that client. Be sure he or she is experienced in agency procedures and knowledgeable about the client's business.

- If you are compensating someone who brings in or services one of your clients, be sure you are not overcompensating. You must determine the operating profit from the client and pay a percentage of that to the person servicing it.

- Never, never pay for new business before you get paid.

- A good agency-client relationship is maintained when the client makes the agency a part of the "family," disclosing all factors concerning company operations, and allows the agency to participate in its planning.

- The agency in turn should keep in constant communication with the client, be cost-conscious on its behalf, meet all deadlines, use the client's products if possible, and make sure the client is happy with the job the agency is doing and accomplishing the results it set out to accomplish. It doesn't hurt to check from time to time to make sure that the client is also happy with the person servicing the account.

Part 9

Important Developments and Trends

29

Computers and
Your Agency

The trouble with jumping into the latest technology is that it's nearly always ancient history barely 6 months later.

Nowhere is this more evident than in the advertising, marketing, communications, and graphics-related businesses, where the need to acquire, upgrade, and replace computer systems keeps computer vendors very busy and fills the meeting rooms of computer seminars.

The question is not whether or not you should computerize your agency; it's how far you should go when investing in equipment and software packages.

Agencies of all sizes have discovered that they must stay current in order to stay competitive. Often they're competing not only against other agencies but against advertisers as well. They have found that if they want to keep their clients from performing many services themselves, they have to stay one step ahead of them.

Desktop publishing, computer-based word processing, graphic design, production and creative, layout, and basic business programs have become key factors in helping an agency grow, cut costs, improve flexibility and turnaround, and take advantage of an increasingly technical-base employee pool, as well as keep current with marketers' capabilities. And while equipment and software are expensive, many agencies, especially the small ones, are finding it cheaper in the long run to keep as much production work as possible in house.

Agencies are finding that there is a whole new generation of designers and production people who use only computers, and if you want to attract good talent, you must have the equipment.

Computer makers are always developing faster and more powerful machines, yet their brawn isn't much good without the programs that make them operate—the software. Software contains the hundreds of thousands of detailed instructions computers need to perform their countless tasks. If hardware is like the human body, the software is the brain.

General Types of Programs Available

The software choices available to the communications industry in general, and the advertising business in particular, are as diverse as the human imagination. Here are a few of the most common.

Productivity: Includes general business programs, even software that helps executives manage projects. These programs can help your agency enter a new world of increased profitability and fiscal control. Some applications include job costing, billing and profitability, media management, print and broadcast schedules, design and generation of media insertion orders and purchase orders, traffic management, production management, client profitability, database reports, comparisons of target profit and income, billing forecasts, general ledger, accounts payable, accounts receivable, payroll and personnel, and direct marketing.

Word processors: Convert computers into electronic typewriters with great versatility.

Spreadsheets: Display long rows and columns of numbers and perform rapid calculations and "what-if" scenarios easily. They can also produce graphics from the numbers used.

Graphics: Can provide layout, art, typography, and animation; incorporate slides and photographs; create special effects such as 3-D; retouch, enhance, and modify artwork; produce overheads with the click of a mouse; and even print to a Linotronic or other typesetter for camera-ready art or final film. From simple pie or bar charts, graphics programs have become amazingly sophisticated.

Databases: Derive their appeal from their ability to quickly access, sort, classify, and print massive amounts of data. Applications can range from generating a simple mailing list to storing, sorting, and analyzing research results that can form the basis for future ad campaigns.

Desktop publishing: Offers the ability to merge text and graphics into an attractive package. The cost of high-quality laser printers, scanners, software, and computers that can handle large data loads means desktop publishing is usually restricted to serious users.

Integrated: "All in one" software that brings together various functions, such as word processing, databases, spreadsheets, graphics, media, and communications.

The list of software packages and their applications to advertising is endless, and when these programs are used with modems, the applications are greatly expanded, since the users can be linked to extensive outside databases and services by merely making a phone call.

Putting a Computer System to Work in Your Agency

Computer systems can be complicated and expensive, so it is important that you select the right system for your business. There are numerous computer makes and models, hundreds of accessories available for them, and literally thousands of software titles out there. That means time and effort researching equipment, interviewing consultants, and training employees on new systems.

You don't have to understand the complex circuitry of a computer to make it work effectively for your business. All you really have to know is what you and your staff are doing now—on a frequent basis. Once you know that, you'll know what you want your computer to do for you. And, depending on the exact tasks, you'll be able to key in on those peripherals (monitors, keyboard, disk drives, software, scanners, printers, etc.) that will fit your present and future needs, too.

If you're just beginning to look at computer systems, use the worksheet provided at the end of the chapter to evaluate your agency's needs. If you're already familiar with using a computer for certain business functions, but are considering enhancing or upgrading your system, use the worksheet to make the most of your next buying decision.

Tips on Buying a Computer System

The following tips for buying and using a computer system are designed to help you avoid pitfalls, ensure the added productivity that computers can bring to the workplace, and help reduce the trauma involved in the process.

Educate Yourself

Buying a computer system for your agency requires a sizable financial investment; it deserves similar investment in research time.

Read as many books and trade magazines as possible to give yourself a head start to a smart business computer purchase. Learn as much as you can about basis terminology (see the computer glossary at the end of this book), product comparisons, software applications, manufacturer profiles, and service and training package offerings.

When comparing technology, find out about the manufacturer's service record and the equipment's ability to accommodate any planned upgrades.

Be a Snoop, Investigate

Your best resource for computer information may be another ad agency or the company right next door. Has any business in your area recently installed a system? What is it used for? Is the user satisfied? What would the company do differently if it had to be done over again?

After checking with other businesses, visit computer retailers. Take time to talk with sales representatives, to gather product literature, and to "test drive" the different models and brands.

Speak with consultants. Just make sure they're not affiliated with a manufacturer.

Evaluate

Take a real close look at your business and determine what functions can be computerized, and in what order they should be computerized. Computers can be used for hundreds of tasks. Determine the areas where a computer could improve productivity and profitability the most for you. You will probably want to start with one high-priority (primary) function and add more as you and your staff become comfortable with the system.

Don't forget to evaluate the human and environmental aspects of computerization. Who will actually be using the computer? How do they feel about working on computers? How many fonts will your art department need? How many come with the package? If the copywriter needs a word processor, is it for ads and correspondence or a 500-page manual? Is there a spell checker? An automatic hyphenator? A dictionary complete with definitions? Can the package automatically generate an index and a table of contents? Make your employees part of the buying process and get their ideas on how to improve work flow at the same time.

What is the memory capacity of the equipment? The more intricate and advanced the programs you use, the more memory space you will need.

Where will the equipment be located? Are electrical outlets and lighting adequate? Microcomputer systems don't require highly controlled environments, but temperature, static electricity, and dirt can damage them if not controlled.

Plan

Consider the future. Review your long-range business plan to allow for growth or any major upheaval. If you're thinking of moving your office in the near future, consider a system that operates over phone lines (not cable). How do you expect your business to change in the next year or two or three? What changes will your business need to make to keep up? Businesses can experience tremendous growth or discover new markets—all in a relatively short period of time. You can avoid costly overload problems by projecting these possibilities and making sure the system you buy will grow as your business grows.

Select

Buying a computer system is not a chicken-and-egg dilemma. The process is clear: First, you select the software programs to match your business needs; then you buy the computer hardware (including monitors, keyboards, disk drives, printers, modems, and scanners).

The availability of software programs is tremendous; and the selection grows every day. You'll want the assistance of an experienced sales representative to help you determine what programs best suit your needs. Read the trade journals for software manufacturer ads. Take a copy of the completed worksheet at the end of this chapter with you to your local computer retailer to give the sales representative an accurate picture of those needs. Look into systems that were developed by ad agencies.

Set companywide application standards. That means, whenever possible, have employees in each agency department use the same version of software. This will ensure that documents or graphics created anywhere can be used by anyone. Problems can occur if only some receive updated versions of programs.

Buy tried-and-tested equipment. Avoid getting exotic hardware if something less exotic will do the same job. Computers are like building blocks: You can always build and add on equipment at a later date when you may better be able to afford it.

Protect

As a businessperson, you should protect your computer investment and the productivity of your business by purchasing from a full-service source. Be sure to get a warranty service if it is available. Buy a service contract for routine maintenance and technical assistance. And, since many repairs are done by retail technicians, chances are you won't have to wait for your equipment to be shipped to the manufacturer, serviced, and then shipped back to you.

Don't scrimp on protective supplies, either. The cost of a good interruptible power supply for your system can pay for itself the first time it saves your data. There are UPS devices that will guarantee that the power supply to your system will never shut down. Power companies are notorious for "brownouts" or "blackouts," and for dropping line voltage to save on their fuel supply. Surge protectors are another must in times of electrical storms. A direct hit by lightning or a major power surge can "melt down" your entire computer network along with the telephones, printers, and scanners that are connected to it.

Whether to Buy Outright, Finance, or Lease: These Are the Questions

Price, of course, plays a role in your computer system buying decision. Once you've determined what system you need, you have to figure out how you're going to buy it and how you're going to pay for it. Of course, buying for cash is one way. But do you want to tie up a goodly sum of money in equipment? Credit financing is one option; leasing is another. Leasing allows you to conserve your capital as well as possibly obtain advantageous tax benefits. Ask your accountant about what is best for your agency.

Another option is to purchase used equipment. Often, you can get top-of-the-line hardware and software at tremendous savings. The problem is that buying used computer equipment is like buying a used car. You don't really know what you're getting until you own it. And that may be too late. If you decide to buy a used system, have an expert or two check it out very thoroughly.

It's Installation Time, Folks

The day of installation will be a success if you and your employees are prepared for realistic results. Peak efficiency can't occur overnight. It takes time for employees to acquire computer skills and to input all the information the software requires. Make sure your computer source has the capacity to help train your employees.

You may want to consider hiring a manager of computer systems, rather than throwing computer responsibilities on someone who has another function in the company. Either that person's original work will suffer or the computer system will. An experienced computer person—someone with a knowledge of programming, networking, operating, instructing, and taking care of technical difficulties—can be a valuable asset, especially if you're just getting into the computer age.

When It's Time to Add On

As the months go by and you become familiar with your system, and you discover all the amazing programs being offered, your computer abilities will not seem adequate and you will probably want to expand them. You may want to buy more software to increase the system's usefulness, or enhance the system's capacity to store and display information by adding disk drives, color monitors, scanners, and printers. Fine-tuning and improving the system pose an ongoing challenge as your business shifts and changes.

Be objective, however, if you're thinking of linking your computers on an officewide or outside shared network.

Networking isn't necessarily for every agency. Most computers already come with simple printer-sharing software. Some use switch boxes, printer add-in boards, or printer-sharing boxes. Make sure that confidential information is available only to those authorized to use it. You may want to consider a "pass code" protection system that will not allow unauthorized individuals to tap into confidential data.

Enjoy Your System

It's hard to imagine the satisfaction a copywriter derives from being able to totally eliminate retyping corrected manuscripts—until you introduce word processing. It's hard to imagine an art director clicking a mouse to give an intricate color layout an entirely new look without having to redraw, recolor, and re-layout the piece on an art pad—until you purchase an advanced graphics program. With a computer system, your agency's productivity and efficiency will increase and, perhaps most important of all, so will your profits.

COMPUTER ASSESSMENT WORKSHEET:
Evaluating the Computer System Needs of Your Business

1. Agency Background
Company Name
Address
City, State, Zip Code
Year Founded_____ Number of Employees_____ Number of Clients_____

2. Expectations

Every businessperson has expectations of what a computer can do for his or her company. Listed below are some commonly expressed reasons for installing a computer system. Check the ones that apply to you and then rank them in order of importance by circling the corresponding number (5 = high priority, 1 = low priority).

	Rank
I want a computer system to provide me with more timely operational information.	5 4 3 2 1
I want a computer system to provide me with more timely creative capabilities.	5 4 3 2 1
I want a computer system to reduce my overall labor and operational costs.	5 4 3 2 1
I want a computer system to provide me with accurate client need projections.	5 4 3 2 1
I want a computer system to provide me with follow-up and trafficking information.	5 4 3 2 1
I want a computer system to provide me with financial reports and projections.	5 4 3 2 1
I want a computer system to produce professional-looking collateral and correspondence.	5 4 3 2 1
I want a computer system to produce invoices and statements.	5 4 3 2 1
I want a computer system to improve my business customer relations by increasing the speed and accuracy of all outgoing and incoming projects.	5 4 3 2 1
Other_____	5 4 3 2 1
Other_____	5 4 3 2 1
Other_____	5 4 3 2 1

(Continued)

3. Current Business Applications

Check the business activities your company now handles manually that you would like to computerize (any activity on this list can be enhanced by a computer system).

__ Budgeting
__ Job costing
__ Cost accounting
__ Cashflow, amortization, depreciation
__ Creative
__ Agency-client profitability reports
__ Production
__ Electronic worksheet
__ Graphics
__ Media planning, estimating, buying, following up
__ Traffic control
__ Investment analysis
__ Bids, quotes, proposals
__ Payroll
__ Billing
__ Accounts receivable

__ Accounts payable
__ General ledger
__ Tax reporting
__ Employee records
__ Purchase order creation and entry
__ Order scheduling and tracking
__ Sales and business forecasting
__ Database and direct mail
__ Sales monitoring and analysis
__ Client-prospect lists
__ Materials handling
__ Supply purchasing
__ Production management
__ Inventory management
__ Word processing
__ Contracts administration
__ Other

4. Projecting Future Needs

Which of the activities listed above might your business get involved in during the next year: _____

In the next five years: _____

5. Personnel

List below the names of the people in your organization who are most likely to use the computer and the primary function of each.

_____   _____

_____   _____

_____   _____

_____   _____

_____   _____

_____   _____

(Continued)

6. Environment

Describe your company facility (number of rooms, type of outlets, power supply, etc.).

_____

_____

Then rate it (1 = good, 2 = fair, 3 = poor) in terms of:

	Rating
• Space for computer hardware	1 2 3
• Availability of computer stands, desks and chairs	1 2 3
• Location of electrical outlets	1 2 3
• Number of electrical outlets	1 2 3
• Stability of temperature inside building	1 2 3
• Cleanliness of general environment	1 2 3

30

Telemedia: Move Over Print, Broadcast, and Outdoor Advertising

It's been said, "Create a new medium that helps advertisers move their products, and the advertising world will beat a path to your door."

Enter the telephone. The telephone? A *new* medium? You better believe it. Telemedia systems—using the telephone (800 and 900 national numbers and 540 and 976 local numbers) and an interactive voice information service—have become a major tool for advertisers and their agencies to market, advertise, promote, entertain, and inform on both local and national levels.

Utilizing the same creativity and strategic thinking that goes into traditional advertising and marketing programs, telemedia present marketers with unique point-of-sale and instant-response opportunities, especially with target audiences that are hard to reach through traditional media such as print, broadcast, outdoor, and direct mail.

Telemedia Agencies: A New Breed of Direct Marketers

Expertise in the use of this competitive marketing tool has spawned a new breed of telemedia advertising agencies and media service bureaus knowledgeable about the complexities of interactive telephone technologies. These agencies specialize in creating and implementing telemedia marketing campaigns for their clients as well as for other advertising agencies. Through telemedia agencies, businesses are effectively utilizing the telephone as a medium for marketing and information gathering and dispensing—and are taking advantage of the instant, targeted reach this medium offers. It is a reach they cannot obtain from traditional media.

With recent breakthrough applications in both voice technology and database marketing, telemarketers have made the telemedia approach an everyday technique that has changed the way both advertisers and consumers interact.

Telemedia Systems and How They Work

First, you must look at the telephone (along with state-of-the-art telephone technology) as an advertising and sales promotion tool used in conjunction with other forms of advertising, such as TV, radio, and print. When a customer responds to an advertised offer by calling a 900 number (and paying a specified cost for the call) or a toll-free 800 number, the interactive voice information service that the caller connects with becomes a direct link between the advertiser and that customer. The call is answered immediately (seldom put on hold) and the caller is identified and receives prerecorded, personalized information, and/or is routed for the most effective order processing by making suggested press touch-tone selections on the home phone.

Some telemedia systems provide large-volume call capacity (400,000 or more calls an hour) 24 hours a day, 7 days a week. Callers are handled by an all-electronic system that treats them in a pleasant, personalized manner. The caller can activate the system to provide just what the caller needs, and even place orders. If necessary, the system can connect the caller to a live operator.

The interactive voice information system automatically gathers statistics about each caller (consumer demographics, preferences, etc.), which are reported to the advertiser in printouts and used later for targeted direct-response campaigns.

The 900 Campaign

The benefits of a 900 number are broad ranging and should lead every quick-response advertiser to consider launching such a campaign.

Self-Liquidating Costs—Even a Profit

A 900 campaign can be a way to self-liquidate advertising and other promotional costs. Since the person responding to the advertised offer pays for the 900 call, it is possible, if priced properly, to self-liquidate the promotional costs and make a profit before the customer buys the product or service. At worst, a portion of the advertising expenses can be recouped.

Detailed Databases and Qualified Leads

Interactive phone response systems enable advertisers to qualify each respondent through a series of questions, and then customize the manner in which the sales messages are delivered.

With the interactive voice information system, a database of detailed information about respondents is gathered each time a call comes in. This information gives the advertiser the ability to pinpoint specific individuals in their target audience, and have the information needed to effectively sell them in future campaigns. Customers and prospective customers can be profiled and qualified, and large savings can be realized from following up on direct-selling and promotional efforts. Collecting databases in this manner is less expensive than other methods of information gathering because live operators are not being used.

Savings are also realized because the cost of gathering the information is self-liquidating through the use of the 900 number.

Enhancing Consumer-Advertiser Relationships

It is a generally accepted fact in the industry that the 900 number response enhances the respondent's relationship with the advertiser.

Respondents have the opportunity to express their opinions, while advertisers can carry on previously unaffordable "loyalty and brand building" dialogues with large numbers of targeted individuals at an affordable cost.

Instant Orders

When people see an advertised product on TV or in print that interests them, they usually act on impulse and want to buy it quickly—much the way they do in stores. They also want as much information about this product as they can get, and that information should be available while the interest is at its highest point. It is important for them to know:

- Where they can buy the advertised product
- How much it costs
- How they can make an immediate purchase

Telemedia provide this kind of quick response to an advertiser's message. The telephone becomes an instant order taker each time a call comes in. If the call is for information only, the caller is automatically routed to the source for that information. If the information needed is where to buy the product, the call is routed to a dealer locator that tells callers where to buy. And don't forget, because the respondent is paying for the 900 call, all or a portion of the expense in getting the order comes back to the advertiser.

A Vehicle for Sales Promotions

Innovative marketers have created new and exciting "teletechniques" to enhance direct-marketing campaigns. Promotions include:

- Games
- Contests
- Sweepstakes
- Coupon dissemination and product sampling
- Fund raising

Using the telephone for couponing, cash refunds, and product sampling, marketers are able to measure the results of campaigns more accurately because they find out immediately who responded to a particular offer.

They also find that running contests, games, and sweepstakes on the telephone delivers interactive "instant win" excitement that is not possible through other forms of media.

A large cosmetics manufacturer ran a 900 number direct-response beauty-care sweepstakes promotion that targeted women 18 to 49 years of age. The company advertised the sweepstakes to 52 million households by using a color insert in hundreds of newspapers throughout the United States.

Readers called the 900 number and gave the 4-digit code on their insert to find out if they were "instant winners" in the $2 million sweepstakes. A mail-in coupon was included in the insert. The self-liquidating sweepstakes not only generated a database of phone-responsive names and demographic information; it also provided a short phone commercial for its products. And by donating a portion of the revenue from the 900 calls to a charity, the cosmetics firm created a "corporate-community" tie-in for building brand loyalty.

Many television and radio stations use interactive 900 number telemedia for instant polls on current situations in the news. Television networks use interactive 900 numbers to provide viewers with the opportunity to answer questions as well as voice their opinions about their favorite programs.

With a single 900 telephone call, respondents to an ad can hear variable messages or upsells based on their locations, demographics, and buying histories. They can be immediately connected to the nearest dealer selling a product. They can receive faxes on demand with coupons, contest details, product information, and other ad-enhancing information—all within minutes and all at self-liquidating costs.

Telemedia Can Be Used
Locally or Nationally

Once you've decided to use telemedia as part of your client's overall marketing campaign, you will have to decide whether to confine yourself to local or national telephone response numbers.

The answer, of course, depends on your target market and the purpose of the campaign.

If your product or service is being offered locally or regionally, for instance, you wouldn't want to use a national (800 or 900) number unless you are interested only in getting a database for future sales in other markets.

Another reason for using local telemedia is if you are running a test program in one of several major markets. Remember, the cost of advertising in local media (radio, TV, newspapers) is much less than going network or into national publications. Add to that the use of local 540 and 976 response numbers, and you have substantially lower costs to test a campaign before going all out nationally.

The Telephone—Part of a Well-Rounded Media Mix

There is no doubt that the telephone has become an integral part of the advertiser's media mix. Both 800 and 900 telephone numbers, faxing telemarketing, and computer and other information activities over telephone lines have affected virtually every facet of the advertising industry—complementing campaigns in traditional media and serving as the centerpiece of innovative product promotions, contests, and electronic couponing and rebate programs.

And just as toll-free (800) calling has become an accepted way for respondents to react to an advertisement, the 900 number, even though there is a usage cost involved, has followed the same evolutionary path.

The Effectiveness of Telemedia

In a competitive environment, with advertisers demanding tighter targeting and more accountability, telemedia emerge as an effective advertising tool that goes beyond the bounds of ordinary mass media.

- Interactive telemedia are much more personal than other media which simply address mass audiences. Also, with database knowledge of a caller's demographic characteristics, telemedia are capable of directing a "personalized" message to that caller.

- Interactive telemedia are less costly than traditional media because the consumers pay to participate. In addition, since 900 numbers employ automated voice information services, they are less costly than using live phone operators.

- Customer reaction time to an offer is faster, because people have a reason and a way to react on impulse to telemedia promotions. The responses can also be instantly measured.

- Telemedia, unlike other mass media, provide high-quality interaction with customers. Callers receive personalized information merely by pressing touch-tone selections on their telephone. Callers also have the opportunity to express their opinions in many promotions.

- Interactive telemedia add an additional and personal dimension to campaigns in other media, generate and qualify consumer leads, build databases of prospects by profiling customers, and help promote long-term customer loyalty.

- Telemedia have been successful in getting competitive users to switch brands.

- Telemedia allow consumers to respond to advertising around the clock, as long as they are close to a telephone.

The Future of Telemedia

In the late 1980s telemedia and the use of 900 numbers were closely associated with phone-sex lines and other dubious types of advertising. Nondisclosure of phone charges was a major issue, as was false and misleading advertising. However, federal regulations protecting consumers, policing of 900 numbers, and the rapid rise of legitimate 900 number telemarketing revenues have fueled the growth of the industry as major advertisers use telemedia for more than just information dispensing and gathering, and become more sophisticated in developing applications.

During the same time that telemedia were taking foothold as an effective new advertising tool, the use of sales promotions as a marketing tool was also experiencing rapid growth. According to Robert Lorsch, president of Lorsch Creative Network (Los Angeles) and of the 900 number marketing firm Teleline, in an article entitled "900 Numbers: The Struggle for Respect" in *Advertising Age* (February 18, 1991): "Sales promotion was only 20% of the marketing mix during 1974–75." However, Lorsch adds that in 1991 sales promotion was "more than 50%…and the reason is agencies and companies got educated—and excited—about what sales promotion could do."

With sales promotion becoming such an important marketing tool, it follows that the promotions have to work harder in order to make themselves heard. That's where interactive telephone response, telemedia, comes in. By giving consumers the opportunity to respond immediately on impulse via an interactive telephone number, promotions become more exciting and more personal to the consumer and more effective for the advertiser.

According to the *Fourth Annual Guide to Telemarketing, 1990,* telemarketing revenues were approximately $500 million in 1989, practically doubled to $900 million in 1990, and are projected at nearly $3 billion in 1995.

Unlike many nontraditional advertising media that crop up from time to time and end up being flashes in the proverbial pan, the telemedia approach looks like it's here to stay.

Telemedia and Agency Compensation

In general, according to an Alan Radding article, "Agency Compensation a Hangup," in *Advertising Age* (February 18, 1991), for each typical 3-minute, $1-per-minute 900 call an advertiser receives, "the phone carrier takes an average of 35% of the call fee ($1.05); the service bureau, playing a purely technical role, 10% ($.30); the client, 55% ($1.65)."

The question is, "How should your agency be compensated for diverting a client's money away from commissionable media, as well as spending time developing and working on a 900 number telemedia project?"

First, many telemedia service bureaus pay 15 percent commission to advertising agencies that place 900 programs with their service. It is then up to the ad agency and its agreement with the client as to how the commission with the client will be handled.

If you work on a fee or cost-plus basis for the creative time put into a 900 number program, you can't get hurt for time and expenses. If you work on commissions based on the income generated by the 900 calls, and stop collecting commissions when the number generates enough profit to cover the cost of the promotion, chances are everyone will be happy. In other words, if you create a successful 900 campaign that not only is self-liquidating but makes a profit, commissions can stop when the client stops laying out money.

31

Direct-Response Marketing and Telemarketing

Advertising with a Personal Touch

Do you remember when many of the storeowners in your neighborhood knew you by name and always managed to save the best apples or the last magazine just for you?

You went out of your way to shop at those stores—and even recommended them to friends and relatives. Why? Because by treating you as an individual, they found out what your specific needs were and they gave them to you. In other words, they applied the *personal touch*, a concept that sometimes gets forgotten in our high-tech world of mass marketing.

However, people have come to expect and even demand this personal kind of service from the companies they deal with—no matter if those companies serve 1000 customers or 1 million customers. Progressive companies like your clients have learned that without some form of personal service they will not keep their present customers or attract new business.

Direct-response marketing is a form of marketing that targets in on precisely the right buyers for any given product or service. Based on the idea that no matter what you are selling, people respond best when they are treated as individuals, direct-response marketing attempts to understand the desires of your clients' customers and prospects through the use of a continually updated database and then create personally targeted communications programs to meet their individual needs. Sometimes referred to as personal marketing, this concept has been the inspiration behind the rapid growth of the multibillion-dollar direct-response industry.

The Methods

The most often used means of getting direct response through direct marketing on a mass basis are direct mailings, television, print, and the telephone (telemarketing). With the proper blend of creative advertising and the advanced technology available to reach your clients' customers through these media, direct marketing can be a very powerful, cost-efficient, and successful means of selling your clients' products and services.

The trick to using direct marketing successfully is to know how to identify and where to find the most profitable targets your clients wish to reach. Then you must create a sales approach that will satisfy the prospects' reasons to purchase and motivate them to respond. By feeding the responses you get back into your database and continually updating each prospect's information, you not only can establish ongoing relationships with customers and prospects, you can also communicate with them as individuals, not just as names on a mailing list.

An updated database allows you, over time, to sharpen your targeting of customers and maximize efficiency in selling them. A well-targeted and creatively conceived mailing of 10,000, for example, can easily outperform a mass mailing of 1 million.

Creativity

Much of the creative side of direct marketing suffers from a lack of vision as well as aim.

By carefully researching and analyzing your prospect database, you can identify the most profitable segments within your total audience and then, from the information you have on that segment, determine the most important product benefits and the right appeal and message that will stimulate purchase.

As an example, suppose your client is a builder selling condominiums to the senior market. Your database information shows that a primary reason for many seniors not buying at this particular time is because they can't sell the home they are in. Your creative approach could address this problem head on with a number of alternative marketing plans that would allow a potential buyer to feel better about buying now: A "you buy ours, we'll buy yours" approach is one; a "buy now, don't make payments for 3 months" program is another.

By sending out a mailing to a list of people who have visited your client's sales office before, you can get even more personal—since they have been there, are familiar with the products, and have met the staff.

If your media buy includes television, you would of course purchase time on those stations whose demographics show the greatest number of senior viewers who would be of interest to your client. Your message, in addition to addressing what you already know is a major reason for prospects not buying, should include a toll-free number for viewers to respond to immediately. Because of the age of the audience, you would want that phone number to be in large readable type on the screen and repeated a few times on the audio track. There should be a program created to accommodate the calls that come in. Operators should know what questions to ask callers. They should encourage a personal visit, and get as much personal information as possible: Are you interested in a condominium for just you or you and your spouse? Where do you live now—in a home or rental apartment? What price range are you interested in? How many bedrooms do you want or need? Do you own a car? Are you interested in recreational and social amenities? If so, what kind? Do you know anyone who already lives here? How soon do you need occupancy?

From the information you get for marketing input, you can then look at your database as a whole and see how it can be broken down into a number of segments, each motivated by different reasons for purchase. Those potential condominium buyers who are now renting don't have to worry about selling a home. In future campaigns that address that problem, that segment of the database can be eliminated or sent a different message.

Whether you are selling condominiums or child care, food or Fords, by feeding the responses from your campaigns back into your database, you can track and qualify leads, help retail clients acquire and retain customers, induce prospect trial, and build brand loyalty for packaged goods.

Direct Mail

As an advertising agency, you can provide a myriad of services to clients who want to reach their prospects and current customers through the mail.

First, it will be your job to design and produce a mailing piece that appeals to the particular reason a customer wants to buy the product or service you are advertising. Such pieces usually include a mail-back card or toll-free phone number for direct and/or immediate response.

Second, it will be your job to isolate the individuals you want to reach. If you are selling condominiums to retirees, as in the example given above, you wouldn't want to send the mailing to teenagers. If your client is introducing a new product, you may want to cross-sell to existing customers as well as the customers of competitors.

Third, it will fall on your agency to get the mailing out, usually through the services of mailing houses that specialize in large mailings. Though most mailing services use the U.S. Postal Service to deliver, a number of companies are now providing private mail delivery service. This method of alternate delivery began when magazine publishers hired their own carriers or private delivery services to deliver their magazines.

Large mail-order-catalog marketers have also used alternate delivery and have found that it produces higher response rates and no mailbox clutter. Many newspapers already have private delivery systems in place.

By using the databases they've developed in their markets, dailies are combining with fledgling delivery services to target home deliveries of magazines, catalogs, samples, and a variety of ride-along ads. Alternate delivery gives newspapers a way to use their often extensive databases to fend off saturation mailers and other direct marketers, which have been taking away an increasing amount of advertising from newspapers.

The papers also make money by selling additional advertisements to go in the home delivery package. This includes very targeted ride-along ad pieces. A newspaper can, for instance, group magazines delivered by the segments they want to focus on. A sporting goods company could advertise only to households that receive sports-oriented publications.

The products most often used in private delivery are magazines, catalogs, and third-class letter mail. However, companies selling pet food, video cassettes, sunglasses, and record albums are among the many using private services and bypassing the U.S. Postal Service.

Telemarketing

Reaching customers and prospects by telephone has long been an effective way to market products. As outlined in detail in Chapter 30 ("Telemedia"), the telephone is more personal than mailings because you (or a recorded message) are actually talking to the prospect.

Using WATS lines that are toll-free to the prospect, computerized message machines, and touch-tone voice response, it is possible to reach your target customers at home or in their place of work, give them a sales pitch over the phone, and take their orders 24 hours a day without the use of "live" operators.

The advantage of toll-free response when telemarketing a product is that prospects usually respond more quickly because there is no cost to them. All they have to do is pick up the phone and place an order or ask for more information. There is little delay from impulse to order.

Direct mailers and retailers, whose direct-marketing business is done mainly through catalogs and print ads touting toll-free phone numbers, have faced the problem of credit-card fraud for years. Now, many large companies are starting to use databases that will help eliminate this problem. One database—the Bin Number Directory of All Visa- and MasterCard-Issuing Banks—contacts the card-issuing bank and verifies names and addresses to determine whether a buyer is the cardholder.

Many databases like the Visa and MasterCard Bin Number Directory are available to advertisers. The Directory of All Mail Drop Addresses & Zip Codes allows marketers to see whether an order is being shipped to a mail drop location. The Directory of All Prison & Jail Addresses & Zip Codes allows the marketer to see whether an order came from or is being sent to a prison or jail. These orders often involve stolen credit-card numbers.

Advertising That Delivers

There's a theory that "nearly 80 percent of a company's business comes from just 20 percent of its customer base." That theory is not necessarily fact, but one thing is certain: Although a product or service may have mass appeal, only a small portion of your audience is comprised of brand-loyal consumers. It is important, therefore, to know who these people are and communicate with them frequently, on a one-to-one basis, addressing their unique needs. If you can accomplish this, you will be creating successful direct-marketing campaigns for your clients.

Part 9 Action Checklist

Computers

- If you know what functions your agency will perform frequently, you will know what you want a computer system to do for you.

- Purchasing a computer system requires a substantial investment. Be sure you thoroughly educate yourself about available technology before you buy anything.

- Your best source for computer information, other than consultants and retailers, may be other ad agencies or service companies with needs similar to yours. Find out what system they are using. Are they happy with it?

- First select the software programs to satisfy your business needs, then buy the hardware.

- Purchase your equipment from a full-service source. Make sure you get a warranty and service contract that covers routine maintenance and technical assistance.

- Put surge protectors on your equipment and remember to shut down during power company "brownouts" and "blackouts."

- Consider financing or leasing your computer equipment if cash is short, or possibly buying used equipment. If you buy used equipment, have an expert check it out very carefully.

Telemedia

- Telemedia utilize the telephone as an advertising and sales promotion tool in conjunction with other forms of advertising, such as radio and TV.

- When a prospective customer responds to an advertised offer by calling a 900 or 800 number, the interactive voice information service becomes a direct link between the advertiser and the customer.

- Used locally or nationally, interactive telemedia systems are more personal than other media, collect database information from callers, profile them for future targeting, are less costly than traditional media, and require less customer reaction time.

- Many telemedia systems can accommodate large-volume call capacity, all day, every day.

- Campaigns using a 900 number (where the caller pays for the call, usually by the minute) can be self-liquidating and even profitable—and result in instant orders. They are most often used for games, contests, couponing, and fund-raising campaigns.

- Telemedia systems have made the telephone an effective tool for gathering and dispensing information and achieving instant target reach and response that cannot be obtained from traditional media. They are also another source of income for your agency.

Direct-Response Marketing and Telemarketing

- ✔ Your first goal in using direct-response marketing successfully is to properly identify and locate your target audience.

- ✔ You must next create a sales approach that will motivate the targeted prospect to respond.

- ✔ If a prospect doesn't respond and/or buy, don't give up. Add whatever new information you have gathered on the prospect to your database, and try again.

- ✔ Make it easy for a prospect to respond. Utilize toll-free and 900 numbers as well as postage-paid, preaddressed reply cards.

Part 10

Surviving a Recession

32

Recession!
What Do You Do?

Recession and the Ad Budget Ax

Cut now, catch up later! That is usually the attitude of clients toward budgeting during recessionary times. And when clients attempt to reduce their operating expenses, they often start with their advertising budget. While this approach may seem the most sensible way to go, research and experience has shown that in the long run it may cost the company much more than it saves.

In many cases, the economic downturn that occurs during a recession does prompt companies to prune off deadwood, trim fat, and tighten fiscal control. These measures often pay off when things pick up again. But as the 1986 McGraw-Hill research analysis of business-to-business advertising expenditures during the 1981–1982 recession shows, those who maintained or increased their advertising in a recession reaped a major sales advantage over their competitors. And this advantage continued to expand long after the recession was over. There are two important points to remember when recessions take place: First, they are a normal occurrence in most types of economies; second, recessions can create tremendous opportunities for those with courage.

Don't Panic—It'll Go Away
in About 11 Months

The United States, with its cyclical type of economy, alternates fairly regularly between periods of recession and expansion. According to an article entitled "To Cut or

Not To Cut" in *Marketing & Media Decisions* magazine (April 1981), there have been 28 recessions since 1854, about one every 4 or 5 years. And according to "Duration of Post-War Recessions," published by the National Bureau of Economic Research, these recessions are relatively short-lived. Over the past 45 years, in fact, recessions have lasted only an average of 11½ months.

In a 1991 ad campaign entitled "In a Recession, The Best Defense Is a Good Offense," the American Association of Advertising Agencies (AAAA) cited the McGraw-Hill study as "demonstrating that nervous advertisers lose ground to the brave and can't gain it back."

The AAAA campaign also cites the Center for Research & Development's October 1990 study of consumer advertising during a recession and points out that "advertisers who yield to the natural inclination to cut spending in an effort to increase profits in a recession find that it doesn't work."

Of course, it should come as little surprise that ad agencies and the media would endorse such a campaign in a time of crisis. Convincing your clients' CEOs or boards of directors may not be as easy, especially when many of them come from nonadvertising backgrounds and do not understand the effectiveness that advertising can have during a downturned business period.

Generally speaking, advertising as a category is looked upon in some companies as a variable expense as opposed to a fixed expense—something that can be increased or decreased in relation to the current market status. While it may be difficult to cut lights, rent, and employee expenditures during a recession, these companies find it relatively easy to lower the ax on the advertising budget.

So where does all this leave you and your clients? It leaves you in the position of having to cope with the situation—to try to get your clients to at least maintain their current levels of advertising if they are not willing to take the chance and increase their budgets. It leaves you, the advertising expert, with the job of helping your clients get more targeted in their advertising approaches, and refocusing their advertising budget priorities.

Present them with new and exciting ad ideas. Gather all the research and current information you can find that shows that larger, more experienced advertisers are not sitting back, cutting budgets, and waiting for the storm to pass. Get copies of AAAA studies and ads and send them to your clients highlighting the success stories of aggressive advertisers. If your clients have multiple products and some are doing better than others, recommend budget increases for the products doing well.

This May Be the Best Time for You to Start Pitching

Odd as it may seem, recessions can create opportunities not only for your clients but for your agency as well. During times when nothing seems to work for most advertisers, they are more vulnerable to changing agencies. Many get fed up with dull, borax, and flat advertising. They are up to their ears with agency excuses that blame the economy rather than provide the direction that will increase their sales. And because many agencies are forced to cut back on services when their clients cut back on ad budgets, clients often feel that they are no longer getting the services and attention they originally contracted for.

An account can be a good prospect in a recession if:

1. Its sales curve is sluggish or downturned

2. The work being turned out by the current agency is especially bad

3. You've heard rumors that the current agency is in financial trouble and the client is looking at other agency presentations

Learning from Lean Times

It has been said that those who forget history are condemned to repeat it. Surviving a recession can provide some very useful lessons.

The most obvious, of course, is that good times don't last. So be adaptable. Service your clients properly. Hold the line on the pricing of your services. If you feel very secure with your clients, you might even increase your prices. If your clients are happy with your agency, they will go along with normal price increases. One important thing to keep in mind, especially during good times, is the need to look ahead. Lulled by growth, many companies don't anticipate a downturn and are not able to adapt quickly when one occurs. Follow the old scouting motto and always "be prepared!"

The second most obvious lesson to learn is that recessions always end. So start thinking past the recession you are in, and start planning for the next four-year cycle of business upturn.

Try not to cut your costs at the expense of your clients. This is not always easy when you are in a service business, but try to find other areas where you can cut—such as having employees share in the cost of medical plans if you are now assuming the whole burden yourself. Sit down and figure out the true cost of doing business, with correct margins and other figures. Many agencies do not know what their true cost of doing business is. As a result, they cannot make fully informed decisions concerning their business.

Look for good deals, especially on people. Recessions mean high unemployment, and smart agencies can find highly motivated and highly skilled employees at salaries these people would have turned down 5 years earlier. Negotiate your media buys. In recessions, print and broadcast companies are hurting the most and they are the most likely to offer large discounts and money-saving packages. The same holds true for printers and other vendors serving the advertising industry. Don't be embarrassed to ask for discounts and favors. You'll kick yourself if you don't, because these vendors are happy to have your business at almost any cost. During a recession you will be able to negotiate discounts on everything from banking services to courier services. It is also a good time to buy the equipment you need at huge discounts. Watch the classified for troubled companies selling equipment.

Don't sit back and wait for new business to come your way. A recession creates big opportunities to pick up new business. Be sure to put presentation dollars in reserve so you can be aggressive when the opportunities present themselves.

In your business plan, always leave a margin for error. Plan for less-than-expected sales and, please, concentrate on debt collection. Your own accounts receivable are a fantastic source of funds. You may want to put one of your employees on full time to do nothing but collect receivables if they are slow in coming in. Focusing on IOUs is almost like making money out of thin air. And always remember, you can be out of business in no time just by being paid late by clients. You can also be out of business quickly if you continue to do work for clients that continue not to pay.

Employee Stress During a Recession

In the fast-paced, high-tech world of advertising there are any number of factors that can affect the job security of your staff: mergers and acquisitions of both clients and agencies; loss of clients; changing competition; and economic recession. These and other, less noticeable factors affect employees' ability to cope with the prospect of job loss.

During a recession, when clients cut back on their budgets, their agencies are sometimes forced to cut back on their services and their staffs. Some agencies will lay off staff members that work directly on those accounts that have cut back. Other agencies may put willing employees on a 4-day work schedule rather than lose them completely. For employees to live with the threat of losing their jobs or losing a portion of their income is to experience unpredictability, which can be a root cause of anxiety.

According to the well-known Social Readjustment Rating Scale of S. C. Holmes and R. H. Rahe, first published in 1967 in the *Journal of Personality and Social Psychology,* "job loss ranked eighth in stressfulness after loss of family members, health setbacks, and incarceration." The study also showed that "those who lose jobs are at risk of becoming depressed, abusing substances, and abusing their spouses or children as well as others."

In the ad agency business in particular, where tight deadlines, tough competition, even tougher marketing challenges, creative egos, big budgets, lots of tension, and insecurity are an everyday thing, mixing in the effects of a recession can result in increased stress and psychological problems with employees that could have a negative reaction on the overall productivity and effectiveness of your agency.

While some employees successfully cope with their anxiety, others do not—and the more a recession affects agency operations, the more it is likely that these employees will experience adverse reactions.

As the principal of an agency, it is important that you involve yourself with the situation. Often when employees have job insecurity on their minds they are not as effective in their jobs. You might want to double-check figures in client estimates, for instance, or contact your clients to make sure they are happy in their dealings with your account executives. Go over client invoices to make sure everything that should have been billed for was billed for. Go over your accounts payable to make sure you paid everything you owed, once!

Never underestimate what seemingly rational and stable employees will do under stress. If they are people working with numbers and their minds are not on their jobs, watch out for mistakes. If they are production people working on highly involved ad mechanicals and they are affected by negative office situations, technical errors could be made that will be costly to the agency.

On the positive side, it is important for employees to receive a lot of support and encouragement from management. Let everyone at the agency know when something good happens. If the opportunity arises to improve an employee's job situation, do it.

Try to get all employees to share in agency concerns, so they won't feel alone in their fears. Encourage them to come up with positive adjustment strategies. Keep the lines of management-employee communications open and, whenever possible, try to reduce uncertainty about any situations that employees may be concerned about. For example, if word is out in the office that there may be cuts in personnel by a certain date, make that date known.

In the face of an uncertain job future, suggesting the right coping strategies and giving proper management support may not eliminate, but can help combat reduced employee motivation, commitment, and productivity.

Some Final Lessons to Learn

Okay, so you're in a recession, and maybe this isn't the year you went to college for— but before you set your diploma on fire, there are a few constructive lessons to be learned in times like these.

First, if your business was heading downward before a recession, don't hide the fact by blaming it all on the recession. Be honest with yourself and try to find out what you are doing wrong and correct it.

Second, don't blame the recession for the problems your clients may be experiencing. Even though they know why their sales may be down, they don't want to hear "it's the recession" over and over again.

Finally, lighten up.

Look at a recession as being sort of like corruption or taxes. It's *so* big, and so everywhere, you're not going to do a whole lot to stop it. So do the best you can—hit where all the others are cutting back. Heavy up where it will do your clients the most good. Make advertising the workhorse for the results your clients need today, and build for their tomorrow with long-term identity-enhancing strategies. Who knows, you may just find that your business is way up in a way down market.

Recession does not mean the death of advertising, no matter how bad it may seem at the time. Keep your staff well oiled and ready for the turnaround. Chances are, you and your clients will come out of it a whole lot smarter and better.

And when it's all over, everyone will feel great again. You may even want to have a party or something.

Part 10 Action Checklist _____

- ✔ Recessions usually last just under a year, are a normal occurrence in most types of economies, and often create great opportunities for agencies and clients with courage.

- ✔ It is a fact that companies that maintain or increase their advertising in a recession experience greater sales than those that don't.

- ✔ It is important to convince your clients to at least maintain their current budgets. Show them exciting new ad ideas, more accuracy in targeting their market, more creativity in your media priorities. Point out more experienced advertisers that have not cut back. Prove to them that since there are fewer advertisers, their ads will have greater visibility.

- During recessions, advertisers often change agencies for a number of reasons. This presents opportunities for your agency to pick up new accounts.

- Try not to cut your agency expenses at the expense of your clients.

- Keep your eyes open for bargains—in media buys, printing discounts, equipment deals—and for skilled employees recently let go by other agencies.

- Your employees will need support and bolstering during hard times. Let them share in agency concerns. Keep the lines of communication open with them.

Part 11

Establishing a House Agency Within a Company

33

The House Agency

As the American society ages, demographic, social, and economic changes are transforming many consumer markets from being relatively easy pickings to highly elusive targets. With segmented markets becoming more difficult to predict, much harder to reach, and tougher than ever to sell, advertisers are looking for greater efficiencies in their marketing and advertising efforts.

The focus of many advertisers has shifted from trying to achieve more efficient manufacturing and distribution operations to selling more products with fewer advertising and promotion dollars. And some advertisers, for a number of reasons, have reverted back to what was a once popular marketing setup: the in-house advertising agency.

Simply defined, a house agency is an advertising agency formed by an advertiser for the purpose of handling the advertiser's own products or services. There may be times when a house agency will also handle the products of other, usually small, noncompetitive clients, but its dominant concern is with the products of its parent company.

The house agency has several advantages over an independent agency. It does not have to worry about soliciting new business. Establishing credit will more than likely be easier. Office facilities, equipment, and other supplies will be made available by the parent company, and the "buying power" of the agency will already be established by the company products it will be handling.

Why Advertisers Prefer a House Agency

There are several reasons that an advertiser would prefer a house agency instead of using outside services. One reason, as you might guess, is financial. The advertiser would hope to save the compensation normally paid to an independent agency and get rebates on media commissions. Another reason is that the advertiser would hope a house agency could provide the same services at lower cost than could an independent ad agency. But there are reasons of late that apply more to the changing market situation.

Advertisers that favor house agencies feel that their company's products receive fuller attention than would be possible in an agency serving many different clients. The advertiser also has greater control over media expenditures, discounts, and operating costs. With a house agency planning and placing the advertiser's media, the company would not be "pushed" into certain media and collateral situations that mean profits for an independent agency. Bartering is a good example of a marketing form that some independent agencies do not recommend to their clients, mainly because there may not be a fee or commission in it for them. In addition, some advertisers feel that their products have unique marketing requirements which a multiclient ad agency could not or would not want to handle. There is also the "control" factor. Because the advertiser has less control over the actions of personnel at an independent agency, it may be difficult to maintain a coordinated relationship over a period of time.

Putting aside some of the drawbacks of a house agency—such as attracting top personnel, coordinating with other company marketing departments under one roof, and realizing that there may not be financial savings with an in-house agency—let's take a look at what it takes to set up and operate an advertising agency within an advertiser's company.

Position of the House Agency Within the Overall Structure of the Company

There are three key questions to decide. Who does the head of the house agency report to? At what level in the company's organization should the house agency be placed? Should it be high up near the chief executive or at a lower level, closer to operating divisions?

Depending on the policies of the parent company, the functions of the house agency with respect to other departments within the company, and the officer to whom the head of the house agency reports, there can be major differences in the effectiveness of a house agency.

Generally speaking, the agency itself would probably have a name different from (yet related to) that of the parent company in order to distinguish it from an advertising department. It might also be incorporated under that name and operated as a separate entity, with its own staff, accounting department, bank account, operating policies, and plans. The head of a house agency might be known as the advertising manager, or if the house agency is in fact a separate, incorporated entity, the head person could be the president of the agency.

Whatever the title may be, that person would normally report to the chief marketing officer of the parent company. Assuming that the house agency will work closely with other departments of the parent firm, keeping it separate from other marketing functions may be best in order to obtain more varied and objective approaches. In that case, the head of the house agency would be better off reporting directly to top management, perhaps the chief executive officer.

Reporting to the Marketing Director

If the primary purpose of the house agency is to increase sales of company products, the house agency should report to a director of marketing operations. This will enable the marketing director to aid in the coordination of product advertising with other marketing elements for those products, since supervision of the products comes under the marketing banner. The marketing director is also capable of controlling and evaluating the efforts of the house agency better than others in the company, since he or she is trained and experienced in marketing and responsible for sales of the products being advertised.

Reporting to the CEO

There are some companies whose advertising is devoted not to promoting the sale of particular products, but rather to developing favorable brand images and attitudes toward the parent company. Large oil companies, for instance, spend millions of dollars a year informing the public of their environmental efforts and unique manufacturing techniques. If a firm's advertising efforts are of this type, it might be desirable for the house agency to be outside the marketing chain of command, reporting directly to the CEO.

A disadvantage with this arrangement is that the CEO may have little or no experience in the management of advertising. This places a greater burden of responsibility and accountability on the person running the house agency.

There is also the possibility that personal selling is the dominant element in the marketing program and the role of the house agency is primarily that of being an aid to the sales force. Advertising in such an instance may be designed to get leads for the salespeople or build sufficient awareness of the company or its products so that the salespeople can gain easier access to prospects. In that case, it would be desirable to have the house agency report to the company's sales manager.

One problem to watch out for is that many times the interest of a sales manager is in the sales function rather than in the advertising function. And the performance of the sales manager is more likely to be judged in terms of sales effectiveness than in terms of advertising effectiveness.

Organizational Level of the House Agency

At which level does advertising decision making take place? If decisions are made high in the company structure, the house agency function would be considered centralized. If the decisions are made lower down the corporate ladder, close to the operating units, the house agency would be considered decentralized.

Centralized Agency

If a firm's advertising efforts are corporate campaigns not focused on particular products, a centralized house agency offers the advantage of substantial specialization. Because centralized advertising pools total advertising resources and demands, it is feasible to retain full-time specialists in areas such as sales promotion, copywriting, research, and package and display design. These specialists would then be available as needed to work on problems in various operating divisions.

Controlling the activities of a centralized house agency is facilitated because it is centrally located and responsibility is easily pinpointed.

Decentralized Agency

Decentralizing the house agency brings it in closer contact with other marketing decisions concerning company products. This should lead to better-informed advertising decisions and better coordination of advertising.

Starting and Staffing the House Agency

The head of the house agency is responsible for building an effective structure and operating it as if it were an independent ad agency. If the agency is small, as many are, the internal organizational problems will also be small. Many house agencies are one-person operations, in which case all responsibilities are borne by that one person.

As a house agency's responsibilities increase, so will the need for staffing up. The staffing can be done in a number of ways: by function, product, geographic location, and customer.

- The functional method divides the work by specialty. For example, the agency might hire a media specialist and a creative director, both of whom would contribute their specialized skills to the advertising programs of all products or services advertised by the parent company.

- The product method gives responsibility for all advertising of a particular product or service to an individual or group of individuals on the house agency staff.

- The geographic method divides the efforts of the house agency along geographic lines. The company's total distribution is divided into a number of subareas and each of those areas is assigned to a person or group in the agency who supervises all advertising activities for that area. This can be an effective marketing method if there are important geographic differences in consumer characteristics or product usage.

- The customer method is used when a product has distinctly different classes of customers and each class requires different advertising approaches. In this case, it might be desirable to assign advertising responsibility for each customer class to a different member of the agency staff. Selling products for both industrial and consumer use and marketing products through, say, the medical profession as well as directly to the public through mass advertising are examples of why a house agency might assign the work to staff members on the customer method.

The number and qualifications of house agency employees depend on the amount of operational work to be carried out within the agency.

Basically, the same steps involved in establishing the type of business structure (sole proprietorship, partnership, limited partnership, corporation) that would be taken in setting up an independent agency should be taken here. The house agency may also be established as a department within a company that advertises.

The legal and accounting aspects of setting up a house agency operation will be easier, since the parent company is likely to have staff accountants and attorneys or attorneys on retainer. If the parent company is in good financial standing, getting loans and establishing credit will be easy for the house agency.

The physical facilities within the parent company offices should, of course, be large enough to house the staff required—and the offices should be located close to other departments within the company that the agency will be working with regularly. Furnishings, equipment, and supplies would be the same as if it were an independent agency. If furnishings, typewriters, and certain supplies are available from the parent company, substantial savings can be realized.

Establishing relationships with suppliers will be easier, since the house agency is "part of" the parent company which may already have credit with those same suppliers.

Agency Recognition

Without agency recognition, the house agency will not be able to receive rebates on media commissions, thereby defeating one of the reasons for having a house agency in the first place.

For an advertising agency to receive recognition, the media generally require that it be an independent company, servicing a number of different clients without control or ownership by a medium or client, and that it have the financial capacity to meet its obligations to media sources.

In the case of a house agency, the media will often overlook the fact that the client controls the agency, especially since house agencies have been accepted entities for many years. They will also overlook the control factor and grant recognition if the media budget is substantial, if the house agency is incorporated, and if the agency has the necessary financial requirements. It will also help if the house agency places advertising for more than one product for the parent company or handles other accounts outside the parent company.

Once a house agency receives recognition from one or two publications or broadcast companies, other media sources will fall in line so as not to lose out on the potential business.

Staff Specialists Versus Outside Specialists

Unless a house agency has sufficient work to keep an artist or copywriter occupied full time, it may be more economical to purchase the services of free-lance specialists on a job-by-job or hourly basis—for the same reason that ad agencies do not own printing plants, video and film facilities, or photography studios. If you are not going to use the services of full-time employees, it does not pay to employ them full time. Remember, there are payroll-withholding regulations, pension and profit-sharing plans, medical and dental insurance programs, office needs, vacations, sick days, and other factors to consider when you have full-time employees.

If a house agency's requirements are large enough economically to justify staff specialists, there are other considerations affecting the choice of inside versus outside employees. The major advantage of having staff is not only the economy, but the added control over the advertising process they provide. This is especially true for an agency requiring large amounts of specialized or technical advertising materials such as brochures, literature, and sales aids.

Offsetting the advantage of greater control is the difficulty a house agency may have in attracting high-caliber personnel. The best copywriters and designers, for example, are usually attracted to the better, larger, independent agencies in which both the prestige and salary are high. High-caliber employees like the greater variety of work offered by an independent agency. The house agency can counter these disadvantages by offering higher salaries and better company benefits, and by delegating more responsibility to house agency personnel.

Dealing with Other Company Departments

The house agency of a major advertiser will rely heavily on assistance from other departments within the company. It will also be required to coordinate its activities with those of other departments and possibly share specialized personnel with those departments.

Keep in mind that the house agency probably does not have authority over the other departments and vice versa. As a consequence, all parties must rely on their influence or persuasion to accomplish their goals. Since the agency will usually be in the position of requesting help rather than supplying it, it is in the interest of the house agency to take the initiative in forming effective relationships with other departments.

The departments that a house agency will have to deal with may not all necessarily be involved with the marketing function. For example, a legal department may give advice on advertising claims, a product development group might provide technical product information to the copywriters, the production departments might provide cost and distribution estimates, and accounting may supply cost measurements.

Gaining the willing cooperation of these departments, depends, in part, on well-developed personal relationships. It also helps when requests are made in a clear, concise manner with adequate justification of the need. It is also important that the relationship not be abused by requests for assistance that are unnecessary.

In dealing with other marketing departments of the parent firm, the emphasis will be on coordination of activities rather than on assistance.

Coordination of advertising activities with other marketing activities is heavily dependent on clear, two-way communications. Here is where the advertising plan comes in. The plan is the basic sourcebook describing what the house agency intends to do and why. It is not sufficient, however, to simply send a copy of the plan around to other marketing people in the company. There must be participation and communication during the preparation of the plan and intensive follow-up on its completion and implementation.

A New Breed of House Agency

If advertisers continue to lean more toward highly targeted messages and more efficiency in their advertising efforts through their own house agencies, a new breed of marketing expert may evolve from the assembly line to the house agency.

More complicated consumer and industrial markets require more sophisticated customer databases and the integration of that information into media buying and marketing decisions.

With billions of figures available from the national census, added to the already substantial output from scanner cash registers, people meters, panel diaries, syndicated studies, telemedia voice response data, and market research reports, the staff of a house agency in the years to come will have to be extraordinarily skilled at processing vast amounts of data, making sense of it, and applying it to its advertising campaigns.

And out of those oceans of numbers must come not only a better understanding of the parent company's markets but also more precise measurements of marketing efficiency.

Part 11 Action Checklist _____

- ✔ A house agency can be set up as an "independent" company (sole proprietorship, partnership, limited partnership, or corporation), or as a department within a company that advertises.

- ✔ The most important reasons for a company to create a house agency are financial savings, more creative attention, and greater control of media expenditures and operating expenses.

- ✔ The advantages of a house agency over an independent agency include not having to solicit new business, ease in establishing credit and recognition, and little or no investment in equipping and staffing an office. The two main disadvantages are attracting top personnel and coordinating with other company departments.

- ✔ If the primary purpose of a house agency is to sell more product, the head of the agency will most likely report to the parent company's marketing director. If brand and company image is the function of the house agency, the agency head would more than likely report to the CEO of the parent company.

- ✔ The staffing of an in-house agency depends on a number of factors. The functional factor concerns the need for specialized skills, such as media buying and design. The product factor involves the need for skills related to the marketing of a product. The geographic factor relates to a product that has widespread sales in markets with different consumer characteristics. The customer factor comes into play if the product requires different advertising approaches to sell to different types of customers.

✔ In order for the house agency to be an effective part of the parent company's marketing efforts, there must be coordination of advertising with other marketing activities within the company.

Part 12

Conclusions

34

Some Final Words About Creativity, the Advertising Business Today, and What the Future Holds

All ideas, good and bad, start the same way. With a blank piece of paper.

Every copywriter, art director, media planner, cost accountant, or cinematographer—in short, everyone who communicates ideas in any way, in any media—faces this blank every working day of the year. It frightens the good ones. It terrifies the great ones.

But when you take that blank piece of paper and add the 26 letters of the alphabet rearranged creatively, it's astonishing what you can accomplish. You can make people want, understand, laugh, cry, and buy.

In the hands of Shakespeare, that blank piece of paper became *Hamlet*. In the hands of Irving Berlin, it became "White Christmas." In the hands of Walt Disney, it became a mouse named Mickey. And in the hands of Bill Bernbach, it became one of hundreds of truly great advertising campaigns.

Once that piece of paper is filled with creative thoughts, it can put you behind the wheel of a new car. It can tell you how to settle your upset stomach or where to save money on a new pair of shoes. It can demonstrate how to get rid of those hard-to-remove stains, even give you a whiff of the latest perfumes.

It's been said that half the money spent on advertising is wasted on people who have no interest in what is being advertised. The trick to being successful in the advertising business, of course, is knowing which half.

Increasingly, advertising's influence in society has grown from being merely a reflection of our culture to actually becoming a part of it. Its power lies in its ability to create demand for consumer products, which encourages spending, which creates jobs, which encourages more spending.

Today, advertising itself makes news. Articles have been written about the merchandising of products tied in with singing and dancing animated raisins. The sales of these products in one year alone were twice that of the raisin market. When large companies fire their ad agencies, the stories often make front-page news. Some newspapers, like *USA Today* have reviewed television commercials along with TV and Broadway shows, books, and movies.

Advertising today is hip and upbeat and with it. Advertising today has almost become entertainment. You can hear people humming the tunes of current jingles. Politicians use the tag lines of commercials in their speeches. Comics do parodies on advertised products. "Infomercials" and "advertorials" are represented as programs in the TV listings. If you know what the latest ad campaign for Pepsi-Cola or McDonald's is you don't need to know about what's going on in Poland, because people aren't talking about Poland as much as they are about some ad campaigns.

As we rapidly approach the twenty-first century, you might ask the same questions that have been asked for generations: Does advertising really work? Will we need it 20 years from now? Put away your crystal ball. The answer is *yes!*

As the cost of advertising space and times goes up, forcing advertisers to use less of it to get their messages across, it falls on the advertising business to find innovative, creative forms to execute those messages with maximum effectiveness. We must continue to explore the technologies of database creation, polling and market research, sampling and couponing, satellites and cable, interactive telephones and television, electronic publishing and computer graphics—as well as all the technologies yet to be discovered—and apply what we find to making our ads better targeted and more effective.

Even as you read these words, new markets are developing, as are innovative and effective new ways to reach them.

What will be the most significant changes in advertising 20, 30, or 40 years from now? There will probably be 200-channel interactive cable TV systems that will let viewers select the very program they want and purchase products from every country in the world, without ever leaving the house. Every home may have the television-telephone, eliminating the need to ever visit grandmother, while giving the fax machine a run for the money. And a typical grand prize in a sweepstakes at Burger King may be as high as a billion dollars.

But whatever the future holds for us, one thing is certain. All ideas, good and bad, will still start the same way. And advertising will still be around to communicate those ideas—even though the paper to write them on may no longer exist because we were not environmentally responsible and killed off all the trees. And voice mail, which already is replacing paper, will probably also be replaced with some new technology.

Far off in the future, it's even possible that radio and TV sets, newspapers and magazines, and billboards and specialty items will all be recycled into spaceships traveling to Venus. And that a new advertising idea for a product will originate in one advertising person's mind and travel from there to the minds of every person on earth who is remotely interested in such a product, without even the flick of a switch. Buy don't get excited. That idea is sure to come to your mind courtesy of a sponsor.

Glossary of Media Terms and Frequently Used Abbreviations

Media Terms

Adjacency: A program or time period that is scheduled immediately preceding or following a scheduled program on the same station. See *Break Position*.

Advertorial: A type of advertising message (commercial) that is presented in an informative "program" format that often features dramatization. Advertorials generally are from 5 to 30 minutes in duration and can be much longer. They are most often used on cable TV. Sometimes also referred to as *infomercials*.

Affiliate: A broadcasting station, usually independently owned, in contractual agreement with a network in which the station grants the network an option on specific time periods for the broadcast of network-originated programs. See *Network Affiliate*.

Agate Line: A newspaper space measurement that measures ¹⁄₁₄ of a column inch deep, so that in one column inch (1 inch deep by approximately 2 inches wide) there are 14 agate lines.

Age/Sex Populations: Estimates of population, broken out by various age/sex groups within a county.

315

AM (Amplitude Modulation): The transmission of sound in radio broadcasting in which the power (amplitude) of a transmitting wave is changed (modulated) to simulate the original sound.

AM-FM Total: A figure shown in market reports for AM-FM affiliates in time periods when they are simulcast.

Announcement: An advertising message (commercial) in broadcast media. Announcements can be up to 5 minutes in length but are generally of 60, 30, 20, or 10 seconds duration.

Area of Dominant Influence (ADI): An exclusive geographic area, consisting of sampling units in which the home market television stations receive a preponderance of viewing. Every county in the United States (excluding Alaska and Hawaii) is allocated exclusively to one ADI. See *TV Market.*

As It Falls: A method for simulating media plans in test markets.

Ascription: A statistical audience survey technique that allocates radio listening proportionate to each conflicting station's diaries as calculated on a county basis. The technique utilizes up to four TALO (Total Audience Listening Output) surveys from the previous year. Diary credit is randomly assigned to a station based on its share of total diaries in the county.

Audience: A group of individuals or households that are counted in a broadcast audience according to one of several alternative criteria.

Audience Composition: The demographic profile of audiences of a particular advertising medium.

Audimeter: An electronic recording device attached to TV sets in sample households of A. C. Nielsen. It records set usage and channel tuned, on a minute-by-minute basis.

Audit Bureau of Circulations (A.B.C.): An organization that was formed by and run by print media, advertisers, and advertising agencies for the purpose of auditing the circulation statements of its member magazines and newspapers.

Availability: The commercial time available for purchase by an advertiser in a program or between programs on a radio or TV station or network. Also referred to as *avails* for short.

Average Audience: In broadcast, the term refers to the number of homes (or individuals) tuned to the average minute of a given program. In print media, it refers to the number of individuals who read all or part of an average issue of a given publication.

Average Quarter-Hour Persons: The estimated number of people who listened at home or away to a particular station for a minimum of 5 minutes within a given quarter-hour. The estimate is based on the average of the reported listening in the total number of quarter-hours the station was on the air during a reported time period. This estimate is shown for the Metro, TSA, and ADI, where applicable.

Average Quarter-Hour Rating: Refers to the average quarter-hour persons estimate expressed as a percentage of the universe. This estimate is shown for the Metro, TSA, and ADI, where applicable.

Average Quarter-Hour Share: The average quarter-hour estimate for a given station expressed as a percentage of the average quarter-hour persons estimate for the total listening in the Metro within a given time period. This estimate is shown only in the Metro.

Away from Home Listening: Estimates of listening in which the person keeping a diary indicates the listening done away from the home, either in a car or someplace else.

Barter: Usually refers to the acquisition of commercial time from broadcast stations in exchange for merchandise or services. Can also pertain to the acquisition of print space, outdoor space, promotions, or advertising in other types of media in exchange for merchandise or services.

Billboard: In broadcast, free air-time given to a sponsoring advertiser. In outdoor media, an advertising structure. .

Black-and-White Page: A print media advertising page that uses no color. Abbreviated as B/W.

Bleed: In print media, a page on which the ink of the copy and/or illustration extends (bleeds off) the edge of the paper into the trim space of the page (that is, the part of the paper which is trimmed off in the binding process). Publications will usually charge a premium for bleed ads.

Brand Development Index (BDI): A numerical display indicating the geographic or demographic areas of a product's strength or weakness.

Break Position: A commercial aired between programs as opposed to within a program. See *Adjacency.*

Broadcast Coverage Area: The geographic area within which a signal from an originating broadcast station can be received.

Bulk Contract Rate: A newspaper advertising rate discount offered on the basis of agate lines purchased during a given time period (usually one year). There are decreasing line rates on some predetermined scale (1000 lines, 2500 lines, etc.).

Bus Cards: An advertising unit inside or outside a bus.

Bus Shelters: A shelter for bus riders located at scheduled bus stops the side panels of which are used as advertising units. Not available in all cities.

Busorama: An advertising unit within transit media.

Cable TV (CATV): Community Antenna TV provides special lines rented by a firm to a household either to bring in outside television stations, with a clear picture, and/or to provide special programming on a direct hook-up.

Car Card: An advertising unit within transit media. See *Bus Cards, Taxi Cards.*

Cash Discount: A discount granted by the media to an advertiser for prompt payment (within 10 days), usually amounting to 2 percent of the net amount due.

Chain Break: The time between network programs when a network-affiliated station breaks away and identifies itself.

Circulation: In print media, the number of copies sold or distributed by a publication. In broadcast, the number of homes owning a set within a station's coverage area.

In outdoor, the number of people passing an advertisement who have an opportunity to view it.

Clearance: The broadcast stations that carry a given network program.

Clock Spectacular: An advertising unit within transit media.

Closing Date: The final date when all advertising materials must be received by a publication in order for an advertisement to appear in a particular issue. These dates are often "extended."

Combination Rate: A special rate for advertisers using both morning and evening editions of a newspaper, more than one zone of a newspaper, or more than one vehicle in a group of publications.

Condensed Radio Market: Usually a small to middle-sized radio market. Most are surveyed only once, in the spring. The Metro and TSA sample objectives are considerably less than those for Standard Radio Markets and an abbreviated version of the Standard Radio Market Report is produced.

Conflict: Two or more broadcast stations using the same or similar slogan, program, personality, or sports identification in the same county or listening area.

Consolidated Metropolitan Statistical Area (CMSA): Defined by the United States Government's Office of Management and Budget: a grouping of closely related Primary Metropolitan Statistical Areas.

Continuity Discount: A rate discount allowed an advertiser who purchases a specific schedule within a series of a publication's issues.

Controlled Circulation: The circulation of a publication that is sent free and addressed to specified individuals.

Cost per Thousand: The cost per 1000 individuals (or homes) delivered by a medium or media schedule.

County Size: Designation of a county into one of four categories as defined by A. C. Nielsen on the basis of population.

County Slogan Edit Listing: A county-by-county listing of stations whose signals penetrate a county. Includes each station's call letters, slogan ID, city and county of license, exact frequency, and network affiliation(s).

Coverage: The percentage of persons (or homes) covered by a medium.

Cume Persons: The estimated number of different persons who listened at home and away to a station for a minimum of 5 minutes within a given daypart. Sometimes referred to as *cumulative, unduplicated,* or *reach* estimates. This estimate is shown in the Metro, TSA, and ADI.

Cume Rating: The estimated number of cume persons expressed as a percentage of the universe. This estimate is shown for the Metro only.

Cut In: The insertion of a commercial, at the local level, into a network program.

Daypart: The days of a week and the portion of those days for which broadcast listening estimates are calculated (e.g., Monday–Sunday 6 a.m. to midnight, Monday–Friday 6 a.m. to 10 a.m.).

Daytime: In broadcast, the daytime hours of programming, usually 10 a.m. to 4:30 p.m. EST.

Delayed Broadcast (DB): The term given to a network TV program that is delayed for airing at a different time in a given market.

Demographics: Statistical identification of human populations according to sex, age, race, income, etc.

Demographic Editions: Special editions of publications directed to specific audience types.

Designated Market Area (DMA): See *TV Market.*

Discrete Demographics: Uncombined or nonoverlapping sex/age groupings for listening estimates (e.g., men and/or women 18–24, 25–34, 35–44) as opposed to "target" group demographics (e.g., men and/or women 18+, 18–34, 18–49, 25–49).

Drive Time: The morning and afternoon hours of radio broadcasting. Morning Drive: 6 a.m. to 10 a.m.; Afternoon Drive: 3 p.m. to 7 p.m.

Duplication: The number of individuals (or homes) exposed to more than one advertising message through a media schedule.

Effective Reach: The number of individuals (or homes) reached by a media schedule at a given level of frequency.

Effective Sample Base (ESB): An estimate of the size of simple random samples that would be required to provide the same degree of statistical reliability as the sample actually used to produce the estimates in a report.

Efficiency: The relationship of media cost to audience delivery. See *Cost per Thousand.*

Electronic Media Rating Council (EMRC): An organization that accredits broadcast ratings services; performs annual audits of the compliance of a service with certain minimum standards.

Ethnic Controls: Arbitron Ratings placement and weighting techniques used in certain sampling units to establish proper representation of minority populations in the Metros of qualifying Arbitron Radio Markets.

Exclusive Cume Listening: The estimated number of cume persons who listened to one and only one station within a given daypart.

Expanded Sample Frame (ESF): A universe that consists of unlisted telephone households. These are households not listed in current telephone directories because they have either requested their name not be in, or they did not get listed because of the date of their telephone installation and the date of the telephone directory publication.

Exposure: A person's physical contact (visual and/or audio) with an advertising medium or message.

Fixed Position: In broadcast, a commercial unit purchased with nonpreemption guarantees. In print, position guaranteed to the advertiser in specified issues.

Flat Rate: The nondiscountable rate charged by a newspaper for advertising.

Flighting: In broadcast, scheduling a heavy advertising effort for a period of time, followed by a hiatus, then coming back with another schedule at the same, higher, or lower level.

Flip: A computerized edit procedure that assigns aberrated call letters to legal call letters, or the AM designation of a set of call letters may be changed to an FM designation, e.g., WODC-AM flips to WOBC-FM and WOBC-FM flips to WOBC-AM.

FM (Frequency Modulation): A clear radio signal, without static or fading, that results from the adjustment of the frequency of the transmitting wave to the originating sound.

Four-Color Page: An advertising page that utilizes three colors as well as black. Abbreviated as P 4-C or 4-C P.

Franchise Position: A valued position because of editorial adjacency, program value, or geographical location.

Frequency: The number of times individuals (or homes) are exposed to an advertising message.

Frequency Discount: A rate discount allowed an advertiser who purchases a specific schedule within a specified period of time.

Frequency Distribution: The array of reach according to the level of frequency delivered to each group.

Fringe Time: In TV, the evening hours that precede and follow primetime, usually 4:30–7:30 p.m. and 11 p.m.–1 a.m. EST.

Gatefold: A folded advertising page which, unfolded, is bigger in dimension than the regular page.

Gross Rating Points (GRPs): The sum of ratings delivered by a given list of media vehicles.

Group Quarters: Residences of all persons not living in nuclear households. The population in group quarters includes: persons living in college dorms; nursing homes; military facilities; rooming houses, hospitals and institutions.

Hiatus: A period of nonactivity.

Hi-Fi: Advertising on a continuous roll of paper that is fed into and becomes a preprinted insert in a newspaper. The completed advertisement, usually run on a heavier-than-newspaper stock and in full color, resembles a wallpaper pattern.

Home Market Guidelines: The criteria by which a radio station with multi-city identification can be reported home to a metro area. Also known as *Multi-City of Identification.*

Home Number: A unique four-digit number assigned to each household within a county being sampled.

Homes Using TV (HUT): The percentage of homes using TV at a given time.

Houseperson Time: The midday hours of radio broadcasting: 10 a.m.–3 p.m.

Identification (ID): In broadcast, a commercial that is not over 10 seconds long (visual) and 8 seconds long (audio).

Impressions: The sum of all exposures.

Independent Station: A broadcast station not affiliated with a line network.

Index: A percentage which relates numbers to a base.

In-Home Readers: Those persons reading a publication in their own home.

In-Tab: The number of usable diaries actually tabulated in producing a ratings report.

Issue Life: The length of time it takes a magazine to be read by the maximum measurable audience.

Junior Panel: A scaled-down version of a 24-sheet poster.

Lead-In (Lead-Out): A program preceding (or following) the time period or program being analyzed.

Line Networks: TV signals transmitted over telephone lines from one station to the next.

Listed Sample: Names, addresses, and telephone numbers of selected potential diary keepers derived from telephone directories.

Little U.S.: A method for simulating media plans in test markets.

Make-Good: In broadcast, a commercial position given in lieu of the announcement missed due to the fault of the station or network. In print, the free repeat of an advertisement to compensate for the publication's error in the original insertion.

Market Totals: The estimated number of persons in the market who listened to reported stations, as well as to stations that did not meet the minimum reporting standards, and/or to unidentified stations.

Media Objectives: The statements of action required of media to fulfill marketing needs.

Media Strategies: The media solution used to fulfill the media objectives.

Mention: The number of different diaries in which a broadcast station is mentioned once with at least 5 minutes of listening, in a quarter-hour.

Merchandising: Promotional activities that complement advertising and that are provided free or at nominal charge by media purchased for advertising.

Metro Totals and ADI Totals (Total Listening in Metro Survey Area or Total Listening in the ADI): The Metro and ADI total estimates include estimates of listening to reported stations as well as to stations that did not meet the minimum reporting standards plus estimates of listening to unidentified stations.

Metropolitan Statistical Area (MSA): As defined by the U.S. Government's Office of Management and Budget: a free-standing metropolitan area, surrounded by nonmetropolitan counties and not closely associated with other metropolitan areas.

Milline Rate: In newspapers, the cost per agate line per 1,000,000 circulation.

Minimum Reporting Standards: The mimimum group of listening households or individuals of a particular radio station needed to qualify for various Arbitron projections and ratings.

Monopole: In outdoor media, an advertising structure on a single, high pole.

Multi-City of Identification: A multi-city identification, with the city of license required to be name first in all multi-city identification broadcast announcements, according to FCC guidelines. Also known as *Home Market Guidelines.*

Network Affiliate: A broadcasting station, usually independently owned, in contractual agreement with a network in which the station grants the network an option on specific time periods for the broadcast of network-originated programs. See *Affiliate.*

O & O's: The stations owned and operated by the networks.

One Percent (1%) TALO Rule: An Arbitron radio procedure that establishes a cut-off point for resolving conflicts. The cutoff is one percent of the previous year's TALO by county, by station. All potential conflicting stations are analyzed to determine whether they qualify for conflict resolution. If only one of the two or more stations potentially in conflict receives one percent or more of the mentions in that county, then that station will receive credit for the contested entries in that county. If two or more of the stations potentially in conflict receive one percent or more of the total mentions in that county, each is considered in conflict.

Open Rate: The maximum rate charged by publication—its rate for one insertion.

Out-of-Home Readers: Those people reading a publication outside of their own homes.

Painted Bulletin: An outdoor advertising structure on which an advertisement is painted directly.

Participation: The purchase of an individual announcement within a network broadcast; the purchase of an in-program spot announcement in a local program broadcast.

Passalong Readers: Readers of a publication which they or other members of their household did not purchase.

Penetration: The proportion of persons (or homes) that are physically able to be exposed to a medium.

People Using Radio (PUR): The percentage of people listening to radio at a given time.

People Using TV (PUT): The percentage of people watching TV at a given time.

Point-of-Purchase Display: An advertising display at the place where consumers purchase goods or services (e.g., counter card at a retail outlet).

Porta Panel: A mobile poster panel that is wheeled to a given location (e.g., a supermarket parking lot). Sometimes referred to as a *triangle sign.*

Poster Panel: An outdoor advertising structure on which a preprinted advertisement is displayed.

Preemption: The displacement of a regularly scheduled program, or announcement, on a broadcast facility by the station or network.

Premium: In media: payment for an advertising unit which because of its position in a publication or on a broadcast, commands a special higher rate. In surveys: a token cash payment most often mailed with diaries to households participating in a survey. A premium is usually sent for each person in the household 12 years of age or older. The amount of the premium may vary.

Primary Market Area: A geographic area defined by a publication or broadcast station.

Primary Metropolitan Statistical Area (PMSA): As defined by the U.S. Government's Office of Management and Budget, a metropolitan area that is closely related to another.

Primary Readers: Readers who purchased a magazine or are members in a household where the publication was purchased.

Prime Access: The half-hour immediately preceding primetime television in which local stations were originally charged by the Federal Communications Commission to broadcast programs in the interest of the local community.

Primetime: In TV: a 3-hour time period (Monday–Saturday) and 3½-hour time period (Sunday) designated by a station as its highest viewing time, usually 8–11 p.m. (Monday–Saturday) and 7:30–11 p.m. (Sunday) EST.

Psychographics: A term identifying personality characteristics and attitudes that affect a person's lifestyle and purchasing behavior.

Pulsing: A flighting technique that calls for a continuous base of support augmented by intermittent bursts of heavy pressure.

Quintile Distribution: A display of frequency among audiences grouped into equal fifths of total reach.

Radio Market Report (RMR): A syndicated report for a designated market. Also known as SRMR (Standard Radio Market Report).

Rate Base: The circulation of a print vehicle upon which advertising space rates are based; it may or may not be guaranteed by the publication.

Rate Holder: A unit of space or time, usually small, that is used to maintain or establish a contractual agreement over a period of time.

Rating: The percentage of individuals (or homes) exposed to a particular TV or radio program, usually in a quarter-hour period. See *Average Quarter-Hour Rating* and *Cume Rating.*

Reach: The number of individuals (or homes) exposed to a media schedule within a given period of time. For broadcast: each county in which it has been determined that the signal for a specific station may be received.

Readers per Copy: The number of individuals reading a specific issue of a publication.

Rebate: A payment to the advertiser by a medium when the advertising schedule exceeds the contractual commitments originally agreed to and the advertisements earn a lower rate.

Retail Trading Zone: A geographic area around a central city.

Roadside Signs: A type of outdoor advertising medium (billboard), usually not a specific size, owned by the property owner and leased or sold exclusively to an advertiser. The advertiser generally must arrange for the message to be painted on the board.

Roll-Out: A method of marketing in which an advertising campaign is expanded into progressively more markets over a period of time.

ROP (Run-of-Press/Paper): A position request to run an advertisement anywhere in the publication.

Rotary Display: The purchase of painted bulletins whereby the same advertisement is periodically rotated to predetermined new locations (usually rotated on a monthly basis).

Scatter: The purchasing of broadcast announcements in many different programs.

Sets in Use: The number of sets turned on at a given time. See *Homes Using TV.*

Share: The percentage of individuals or homes listening to a specific station at a particular time.

Sheets: The number of pieces of paper needed to cover a poster panel area.

Short Rate: In print media: the dollar penalty an advertiser pays for not fulfilling space requirements that were contracted for at the beginning of a given contractual period, usually one year. The penalty is the difference in rate between the contracted rate and the actual earned rate.

Showing: Gross Rating Points within outdoor advertising. The number of posters displayed on different vehicles within transit media.

Simulcast: The simultaneous broadcasting of one station's total (100%) uninterrupted broadcast flow by another station without any variation.

Slogan Identifier (ID): An alternate station name used in place of, or in addition to, call letters, exact AM or FM frequency, truncated AM frequency, city, county, network, program, personality, or generic format descriptor.

SMSA: Standard Metropolitan Statistical Area. See *Metropolitan Statistical Area.*

Special: A broadcast program that is not a part of the usual programming offered by a station or network.

Spectacolor: An advertising insert in newspapers, similar to Hi-Fi, but trimmed at the correct place.

Split Run: A scheduling technique whereby two different pieces of copy are run in the circulation of a publication with no one reader receiving both advertisements.

Sponsorship: The purchase of more than one announcement within a broadcast program allowing advertisers to receive bonus time via billboards.

Station Information Form: A computer-generated form that lists essential station information. Used for verification in broadcast surveys.

Station Reach Listing: A county-by-county listing of stations that can be received in a given county. This listing is based on a previous survey history and is updated periodically with any changes in power/antenna height, etc.

Survey Area: See *Total Survey Area.*

Syndication: A method of placing a broadcast program on a market-by-market basis.

Tabloid: A newspaper smaller than the size of standard newspaper, usually 5 columns wide by 13 to 16 inches deep.

Target Demographics: Audience groupings containing multiple discrete demographics (e.g., men and/or women 18+, 18–34, 18–49, 25–49) as opposed to discrete demographics (e.g., men and/or women 18–24, 25–34, 35–44).

Taxi Cards: An advertising unit on top of, inside of, or on the back of a taxi cab. See *Bus Cards, Car Cards.*

Technical Difficulties (TD): Time period(s) of five or more consecutive minutes, in a quarter-hour, in which a broadcast station has technical difficulties including, but not limited to, times it was off the air or operating at reduced power.

Tolerance: The range of error, plus or minus the reported number, in audience research for any medium.

Total Audience Listing Output (TALO): The number of diaries in which a station is "mentioned" in a market, a county, or another designated geographic area; a county-by-county printout showing the stations that are mentioned in the in-tab diaries and the number of mentions for each station; can be used to rank stations, to calculate weekly cumes and raw bases.

Total Survey Area: In radio, the area in which radio signals from an originating market can be received.

TV Market: An unduplicated television area to which a county is assigned on the basis of highest share of viewing.

UHF (Ultra High Frequency): The band added to the VHF band for television transmission—channels 14–83.

Universe: The estimated total number of persons in the sex/age group and geographic area being reported.

UUUU: Unidentified; listening that could not be interpreted as belonging to a specific broadcast station in a given survey.

VHF (Very High Frequency): TV channels 2–13.

Viewers per Set: The number of people viewing or listening to a program in each home.

Frequently Used Abbreviations

AAAA	American Association of Advertising Agencies
A.B.C.	Audit Bureau of Circulations
ADI	Area of Dominant Influence
AQH	Average Quarter-Hour
AM	Amplitude Modulation
ANPA	American Newspaper Publishers Association
ARB	American Research Bureau
CATC	Community Antenna TV/Cable
CMSA	Consolidated Metropolitan Statistical Area
CPM	Cost per Thousand
CRMR	Condensed Radio Market Report
DM	Direct Mail
DMA	Designated Market Area
DST	Differential Survey Treatment
EMRC	Electronic Media Rating Council
ESB	Effective Sample Base
FCC	Federal Communications Commission
FM	Frequency Modulation
FTC	Federal Trade Commission
GRP	Gross Rating Points
ID	Slogan Identifier
MG	Make-Good
MRS	Minimum Reporting Standards
MSA	Metropolitan Statistical Area
PBS	Public Broadcasting Service
PMSA	Primary Metropolitan Statistical Area
POP	Point of Purchase
PPDV	Person per Diary Value
PPH	Persons per Household
QM	Quarterly Measurement
RMR	Radio Market Report
ROP	Run-of-Press/Paper

ROS	Run of Station
SOL	Slice of Life (Commercials)
SRDS	Standard Rate and Data Service, Inc.
SRMR	Standard Radio Market Report
TAB	Traffic Audit Bureau
TALO	Total Audience Listening Output
TD	Technical Difficulty
TSA	Total Survey Area
UHF	Ultra High Frequency
VA	Value Added
VHF	Very High Frequency

Glossary of Printing and Mechanical Production Terms

What's in a word? In previous chapters we have used a number of words and terms relating to the printing and graphic arts industries. There is nothing like the precise word to help provide the ultimate in clarity—but it also helps a lot to know what the words and terms mean. Hopefully, this compendium of words, terms, and definitions will be of help to you in speaking the language of advertising.

Antique Finish: A paper with a random finish caused by felts used in the papermaking machine.

Basis Weight: The weight of one ream (500 sheets) of paper, cut to the size that is the industry standard for that grade (17" × 22" is the basis size for bonds and writing papers).

Benday: A method of laying tints (composed of dots, lines, and other textures) on negatives, metal prints, or copies. Ben Day was the name of the inventor of the process.

Bleed: Extension, frequently 1/8th of an inch, of the print area of an image past the trim line of the finished printed piece.

Blind Embossing: A technique in which a raised design is created by pressing a sheet of paper between a die and a counterplate. No ink is used.

Blue Print: A sensitized photographic paper yielding a blue and white print upon development; also trade name for a stained blue unburned print on metal.

Bond: Paper characterized by a rough, nonglare surface that accepts both printing and writing inks. High-quality bonds are made from rag fibers and exhibit a characteristic snap or "rattle" when shaken.

Border: A finishing line or design on a mechanical or plate.

Brightness: A measure of the light-reflecting capability of a given sheet of paper. Not necessarily related to color or whiteness.

Burnishing: To rub the plate or mechanical with a plastic or polished steel burnishing tool to darken the printing area of the plate, by spreading dots, or hold type firmly down on an art board.

Camera-Ready Art: All elements of an advertisement or piece to be printed, set in correct size, mounted in proper place (including headlines, copy blocks, and screened prints); keylines showing size and position of halftones or four-color photos to be stripped in; spot color elements mounted on acetate flips, properly registered over the black copy and marked for screen percentages and color.

Cibachrome: A color print made directly from a color transparency without an internegative.

Coated Paper: Paper having a woodpulp or rag base, coated with clay composition on one or both sides.

Cockle: A wavy or puckery paper surface, with a feel and look similar to that of early pole-dried papers.

Color Correction: Changing of color values in a set of separation negatives to compensate for errors of lights, filters, ink, or operators.

Color Filter: A colored substance such as glass, dyed gelatin, or colored solution, used to absorb certain colors and transmit others.

Color Guide: Graphic instructions for color rendering or placement.

Color Keys: Transparent color proofing films. When laid over the paper stock on which a job will be printed, they produce an effect close (but slightly darker because of the film) to that of the finished printed piece.

Color Print: A photographic print in color, such as Type C and Dye Transfer.

Color Proofs: Proofs of color plates combined and registered.

Color Proofs Progressive: Single proofs of each plate of a color set, and combined proofs showing result of each successive color printed and assembled in printing sequence.

Color Separation: Separation of colors in negatives: made by means of color filters; and in plate making: by means of drawing upon the plate with acid-resisting paint.

Color Transparency: A photograph in color or transparent film. Can be a 35mm slide, 2¼", 4 × 5", 8 × 10", or larger.

Combining/Combination Plate: Halftone and line work combined on one plate and etched for both halftone and line depth. Replaces need for double-burning.

Connected Dot: Halftone dots in negative or plate which are joined together.

Contacts: A general term applied to any photographic images made in a vacuum or printing frames by direct contact—as opposed to enlargements or reductions where there is no direct contact.

Continuous Tone: Photograph or illustration composed of gradient tones from dark to light. For printing, continuous tones are screened to produce a halftone dot pattern.

Contrast: The quality of an illustration possessing a wide difference in tone values. One in which the highlight and shadow tones are strongly in evidence.

Copy: The original, be it photograph, drawing, painting, design, object, or anything that is in process of reproduction for printing purposes. Also refers to headline and text of an ad and text of a collateral piece.

Copy-Fitting: The procedure used to measure the amount of space that a given amount of typewritten copy will occupy when set in type. It serves to determine, in advance, the correct typeface, size, and line width needed to fit copy to layout or layout to copy.

Cotton Content Paper: Paper that is at least 25% composed of cotton rag or cotton fibers. Standard increments for cotton content are 25%, 50%, 75%, and 100%.

Counter: The counterpart of the die in embossing and other production techniques. The die presses against this surface, which may be flat, raised, or recessed, depending on the process.

Cover Stock: Heavy paper used for covers of printed pieces, business cards, presentation folders, etc. Generally has a weight of 65 lb. or more.

Coverage: Usually refers to the amount of ink or color covering any specific area.

Crop: To cut off an edge or trim.

Crop Marks: Points indicated on a mechanical, plate, or printed piece outside the image area that show exactly where the piece is trimmed.

Cut Size: Refers to paper cut for convenient use on small printing presses. The largest cut size is 17" × 22"; most common are 8½" × 11" and 11" × 14".

Dandy Roll: A cylinder used in papermaking to form a watermark in the sheet as it is being formed. Also used to produce a wove or laid effect.

Debossing: The same as embossing, except that the design is pressed down into the paper, rather than raised.

Deckle-Edge: An untrimmed, feathered edge on the sheet of paper, created during manufacturing.

Definition: The degree of sharpness of a negative or print.

Density: The opacity of a halftone dot or solid subject on a film which will not permit the passage of light.

Die: A plate or cutter, generally made of copper, brass, or steel, into which an image may be carved, machined or etched. Used in diecutting, embossing, and hot foil stamping.

Diecutting: Mechanical press operation in which a die with a sharp cutting edge is used to punch out of a sheet of paper.

Dimension Marks: Points indicated on a copy outside the area of the image to be reproduced, between which size of reduction or enlargement is marked.

Dimensional Stability: The ability of a sheet of paper to maintain its exact dimensions under various printing operations and changes in humidity.

Dots Halftone: Minute, symmetrical individual subdivisions of printing surface formed by halftone screen.

Double-Burn: Exposing two or more negatives onto an offset printing plate so that one overprints the other; for example, a line of type printing on a screened background without a white patch or mortise-type area in the screen.

Drop Out: When the highlight dots of a halftone are etched away, they are said to be "dropped out."

Duotone: A two-color continuous tone reproduction from artwork.

Duplicate Seps/Plates: Film separations or plates made from the same negative as the original, etched and finished in the same manner.

Emulsion: The dull side of a negative or positive. It is a soft finish and can be easily damaged, scratched, or scraped if not handled properly.

Engraving: A printing operation in which an image is etched into a printing plate. The plate is inked and wiped clean, leaving ink only in the image areas. When paper is pressed against the plate, it is displaced slightly into the recessed areas, picking up the ink and forming an embossed effect.

Enlargement: A reproduction larger than full size of copy.

Envelope Conversion: A method of producing envelopes, in which the paper is printed first and later cut and folded into the desired shape.

Etching: Chemical or electrolytic disintegration of metal, also the trade name of a printing plate in which the picture or design in positive or negative form is incised by the action of acid. The process of corrosion or disintegration of metal when subjected to the action of an acid bath.

Fake Color: The process of creating a multicolor effect from a black-and-white piece of artwork.

Felt Side: The "top" side of the paper sheet as it is formed in the papermaking machine. It is usually the side that is preferred for printing.

Fine Line: A thin black finishing line enclosing the image on a plate. Also called *hairline*.

Fine White Line: A thin groove, tooled or etched into the printing surface of a plate. Also called *hairline white*.

Finished Art: A camera-ready pasteup of artwork, including type, photos, line art, and any other elements to be incorporated into the printed piece.

Flat: Trade names for metal, film, or the glass on which a number of halftones or line negatives have been stripped or printed or etched. The appearance of a picture that is lacking in contrast or one possessing a very narrow or limited range of tone values is called flat.

Flat-Bed Press: A printing press containing a flat metal bed on which forms of type and plates are locked for printing. Usable only for letterpress printing.

Focus: The point in the camera at which the converging rays of light passing through the lens from the original, coincide to form a sharp image.

Foil: A film-like material that ads a metallic sheen or color to paper, through a technique called hot stamping.

Font: All the characters of one style of type.

Form: The assemblage of plates or of type and plates, that constitutes the unit that occupies the bed of a flat-bed letterpress (or the cylinder of a rotary letterpress) is called a form. This term is not commonly used in connection with gravure or offset printing. In gravure printing, the parts that are to fill a printed sheet are combined into a unified whole on the printing cylinder, and so the printing unit is designated a cylinder. In offset printing, elements that are to fill a printed sheet are combined into a single unit, which is called the plate.

Four-Color Process Plates: Same as the three-color process with the addition of a gray or black plate.

Frisket: A paper mask used to cover up dead metal or bearers when proofing.

Fuzzy: The appearance of a proof due to a slurred impression. The appearance of a picture that lacks sharpness. The appearance of a halftone or irregularly etched dots.

Gallery: That part of an engraving plant used for making photographic negatives, etc.

Grain Direction: The direction in which the majority of fibers in a given sheet of paper lie. Long-grain paper are those with the grain running parallel to the long edge of the sheet.

Gray: A term used to express the appearance of a picture lacking in brilliancy or rendered wholly in middle of low tone value.

Gripper: The area of a sheet of paper used by the press to hold the sheet in position.

Halftone: Reproduction of continuous tone images by means of a screen that converts the image into a pattern of tiny dots.

Halftone Dot: An individual point of formation in negative or plate, characteristic of the halftone screen.

Halftone Negative: A photographic negative made by photographing a copy through a halftone screen.

Halftone Outlined: A halftone with the background outside of the object entirely cut away, leaving a definite edge without shading or vignetting—a silhouette.

Halftone Outlined and Vignetted: A halftone in which part of the background is cut away and part vignetted.

Halftone Screen: A grating of opaque lines on glass, crossing right angles, producing transparent square apertures between intersections.

Halftone Vignetted: A halftone on which one or more of the edges is cut away and part vignetted.

Hand Press: A proofing press operated by hand.

Hard Vignette: One not softened off to the point of invisibility, but exhibiting a delicate but definite printing edge.

Highlight: The light areas of a tone copy. The smaller disconnected dots of a halftone. Abbreviation for highlight halftone.

Highlight Halftone: A plate made from a halftone negative wherein the highlight dots have been so exposed and etched that they will not print on the metal.

Hot Stamping: A production process that uses heat and pressure to transfer foil to a paper's surface. The stamping die, foil, and paper are pressed against a hard, flat surface; if an embossing effect is desired, a relief counter is used.

Ink Absorption: The extent and rate by which a printing ink penetrates a sheet of paper.

Ink Holdout: The measure of the paper surface's resistance to ink penetration. The more resistant the surface, the more the ink dries by oxidation rather than absorption.

Insert: Term applied to an advertisement inserted into a publication or mailer.

Intaglio: A printing method in which the paper receives the image through direct contact with a heavy metal plate that has print areas recessed below the level of the nonprint area. Engraving is a form of intaglio.

Laid: A paper pattern intended to resemble the texture of handmade paper. The laid side of the sheet has relatively more texture than does the other side.

Layout: A designer's concept of how an advertisement, piece of collateral, sales promotion item, or other type of advertising material will look when completed.

Letterpress: A method of printing in which raised metal is inked and then pressed against the printing paper.

Line Art: Artwork (solid black image on a white background) suitable for photographing to make printing plates.

Line Conversion: A method of reproducing a continuous tone image using a screen that breaks the image into a line or texture pattern. By comparison, a halftone is a dot pattern.

Line Copy: Any copy suitable for reproduction by a line plate; copy composed of lines or dots as distinguished from one composed of tones.

Line Drawing: Same as line art. Can be a brush or pen drawing in which all elements are of full strength of medium use. A drawing free from wash or diluted tones.

Logo: A unique trademark, company name, or device used for graphic identification in advertising and collateral materials.

M Weight: The weight (in pounds) of 1000 sheets of a paper cut to the size being shipped.

Magazine Standards: Individual specifications for the making of printing plates to conform to special printing requirements of publishers.

Make-Ready: The preparation and application of underlay or overlay for proofing or printing. Term for the sheet with complete underlays and overlays in position.

Mark: A logo; a graphic extension of a company's visual identity.

Masking: The operation of protecting or blocking out on a copy proof, plate or metal print, a definitely outlined area.

Middle Tones: The various values of a copy ranging between highlights and shadows.

Minimum: Size of plate, negative or color separation, below which, cost of manufacturer remains fixed.

Moire: A formation of undesired symmetrical patterns produced by conflict between halftone screen and lines or dots of copy. As when making halftone from halftone proof or from steel engraving.

Monarch: Executive size stationery, 7¼" × 10½", used with a Monarch envelope.

Monotone: Black-and-white copy or its photographic counterpart.

Negative: Reversal of values, the white being rendered black and vice versa. Also contraction of photography negative.

No. 10: An envelope measuring 4⅛" × 9½" designed for a twofold, 8½" × 11" sheet of paper.

Offset Lithography: A printing method using a plate with an image area treated to attract ink and repel water, and a nonimage area in which the reverse is true. The inked image is offset onto an intermediate blanket which, in turn, prints the image on the paper.

Opaquing: Protecting a photographic plate or transparent medium with a thin coating through which light cannot penetrate.

Outlined Halftone: A halftone from which the screen surrounding any part of the image has been cut away. A silhouette.

Overlays: Part of make-ready always used in printing vignettes.

Pastel Leafing: A hot-stamping process that transfers a soft, pastel foil to the paper's surface, usually used in conjunction with embossing.

Perfect Bind: Also called patent bind or adhesive binding. The process involves cutting the folded gutter edge of each printed signature, roughing it, and applying an adhesive that holds signatures and cover together. Frequently used on telephone directories.

Plate: Any piece of material (steel, brass, aluminum, paper, and others) bearing in relief or incised into its surface a picture, design, or other device from which impressions are to be made by a printing operation.

Plate Making: Etching visual elements into a variety of materials (steel, brass, aluminum, paper, and others) which may then be inked.

PMT: Photo Mechanical Transfer. See *Velox* and *Stat.*

Porosity: The measure of a sheet of paper's permeability to air. Relates to the degree of ink penetration the sheet allows and its drying ability.

Primary Colors: In gravure printing they are referred to as yellow, red, and blue, instead of yellow, magenta, and cyan (blue-green).

Process: The number of colors involved in a reproduction such as four-color process and three-color process.

Process Colors: A combination of colors printed one directly over the other to produce additional colors.

Progressive Proofs: Known as Progs. A set of proofs of color plates showing each color alone, as well as in combination with each succeeding color in printing rotation.

Proportion: The relationship existing between the different dimensions of a single object of copy, or the relationship existing between any dimension of object or copy and the corresponding dimension in enlarged or reduced size.

Proving or Proofing: Proving is taking an impression of the plate on paper, after the plate has been inked up; a finished proof is one taken by overlay or underlay; a flat proof is taken of plate with all waste metal on. Proofing also refers to checking of typeset copy for accuracy against original manuscript, grammatical errors, and typos.

Ream: 500 sheets of paper.

Register: Correct relative position of two or more colors when printed from color plates. "In register" indicates a proper fit. "Out of register" indicates the opposite.

Register Marks: Guides on plates to aid in obtaining register during manufacture and proofing.

Repros: Sometimes called "slix." An abbreviation of reproduction proofs and refers to a proof of type taken on enameled or other coated paper to ensure the highest quality in the final reproduction.

Rotary Gravure: The rotary principle is employed for all sheet-fed gravure and rotogravure printing. For gravure printing the entire surface of the printing cylinder is the single printing plate. Separate plates cannot be affixed. The printing cylinder and the rubber impression roller rotate against each other and bring together the inked incised image and the printing paper.

Rotary Letterpress: The rotary principle is employed for some letterpress printing. The printing plates are curved to conform to the arc of the printing cylinder and separate plates may be affixed in position on the cylinder. The printing paper is carried on another cylinder. By rotating against each other, the cylinders bring together the inked relief-plates and the paper.

Rotary Offset: The rotary principle is employed for all offset printing. The offset process employs a single plate curved around the printing cylinder. The printing cylinder rotates against a cylinder that is girdled with a flexible blanket and transfers the printing design to the blanket. The blanket cylinder then rotates against a cylinder that carries the paper, and presses the printing design into the paper. Thus, three rotating cylinders are employed in offset printing.

Saddle-Stitching: A binding method whereby cover and forms are assembled by inserting one into another and held by staples driven through the center fold.

Scanner: An electric eye device that scans color artwork and photographs electronically for the purpose of separating the colors into a color separation. Scanners are also used on printing presses to adjust register and ink viscosity or strength.

Scotchprint Proof: A semi-transparent proofing paper adhered to plastic with a glossy, hard surface which makes it more desirable than regular repro proofs. A direct negative can be contacted from a Scotchprint proof.

Screen: A fine dot or line pattern used to print gradations of tones of black and colors. The term is used to denote the particular ruled screen to be used for halftone reproduction. Screens are ruled for practical purposes from 65 to 300 lines to an inch. The coarser rulings are used for plates to suit the conditions of newspaper printing, and the finer ones for the higher printing requirements. The numbers between are more generally employed to meet intermediate conditions. The character of the paper and press work, and to a certain extent the nature of the copy, determine the selection of the most suitable screen to be used in each instance. A screen can also refer to sensitized glass, either wet or dry, used in the camera for photography. Also a printing plate.

Screen Value: The number of lines or dots per square inch on any halftone, tint, or four-color separation.

Screened Print: A positive or negative print (any size) of artwork output on a coated or photographic paper in a fine dot or line pattern for the purpose of reproducing the artwork in graded tones of black and colors. Sometimes referred to as a velox.

Shadow: The part of a picture obscured by lack of illumination. The darker areas of any copy.

Side-Stitching: A binding method whereby forms are gathered and stapled together after which the cover is applied with adhesive.

Silhouette: A halftone from which the screen surrounding any part of the image has been cut away or etched away.

Silk Screening: A printing method in which ink is pressed through a silk screen and masked to form an image on the printing surface.

Sizing: Substances such as starch added during papermaking to improve the printing qualities of the finished sheet. May be added either to the pulp from which the paper is made or to the dry web of newly formed paper.

Snappy: A term describing a brilliant picture of wide contrasts and wealth of middle tones.

Stat: Short for photostat. Same as *PMT* or Photo Mechanical Transfer. Also see *Velox.* A one-step method of making a positive or negative print (any size) of line or screened art on photographic paper, eliminating the need for a negative.

Stripping: The handwork of combining two or more pieces of negative or positive film into one unit so that a contact film of the entire page can be made or the stripped-up film can be put directly into the form of plating.

Substance Weight: The weight of 500 sheets of paper in a standard size. Weights for bonds and other writing papers are based on 500 17" × 22" sheets. Also known as *Basis Weight*.

Swatch Book: A book of samples of various weights, colors, and finishes of paper.

Thermography: A mechanical process in which a raised image is formed on a sheet by dusting the paper with a resinous powder while the ink is still wet, then baking it, causing it to fuse and harden.

Tint: A reduction or percentage of a solid color.

Tint Block: A solid plate to be used in printing a light flat color.

Tip-On: A method of attaching fractional-page inserts for a signature for binding. Normally, all signatures and inserts are gathered and bound flush at the top. If a fractional-page insert must position elsewhere on the page (such as a business reply card insert), it requires a tip-on.

Two-Color Process Plates: Two halftone plates made at different screen angles from monochromatic or colored copy by the photomechanical separation of colors by etching, to reproduce the copy when the plates are printed in two contrasting colors.

Typeface: A given design of printed letters, numbers, and punctuation marks. Hundreds of typefaces are in existence.

Typography: A style or arrangement of printed letters; design using type elements.

Vellum: A smooth, nontextured paper finish.

Velox: See *Screened Print*.

Vignette: Gradually shaded off edge, from dark to light, as on a photograph or engraving. A halftone with the background setting blending into an invisible finish, due to the gradual reduction in the size of the dots of the background as they approach the printing edges.

Wallet Flap: Full-length rectangular flap used to close an envelope.

Watermark: A permanent, integral pattern in a sheet of paper created during papermaking.

Web: Paper or other stock from the roll in a printing press; the full length of paper contained in a roll of stock as it passes through the press.

Wet Printing: A term applied to one color following another immediately in printing color plates, i.e., one impression is made upon another before the ink has time to dry.

Wire Side: The "bottom" side of paper as it is made, which may show a pattern formed by the screen that carried the paper pulp.

Wove: Any paper that shows no laid or chain lines.

Glossary of Computer Terms

To the uninitiated, the lingo surrounding computer systems is like a foreign language. The following common computer terms and definitions will help you better understand what computers are about and teach you how to speak "computer."

Acoustic Coupler: A telecommunication device for transmitting data from one computer to another using standard telephones. A type of modem.

Applications Software: Programs used to perform specific tasks on the computer, such as word processing or accounts payable.

ASCII: The American Standard Code for Information Interchange. This code is widely used to represent numbers, letters, or characters in a computer's memory and to transmit them from one computer to another. ASCII assigns a unique binary number code to each character.

Backup: To make an extra copy of software or data in case the original material is lost.

Baseline: The line upon which upper-case and most lower-case characters sit.

BAUD: A measure of the speed of data transmission, equal to one signal per second, between computers or between a computer and a peripheral.

Binary: The "base two" numbering system used by all computers to store and represent information and instructions. The binary system represents all letters, numbers, and characters as combinations of the numerals one and zero. This is because an electrical circuit has two states: on and off.

Bit: Short for "binary digit." This is the basic unit of information in all computer systems. Each bit has a value of either one or zero. All data is made up of combinations of bits.

Booting: A computer's start-up procedure.

Buffer: A device that temporarily holds information in memory until another (usually slower) machine such as a printer can use it.

Bus: A circuit or pathway used to transmit information in a computer.

Byte: A string of bits (usually eight) that represents a single character. Combinations of bytes are used by computers to represent words or numbers. The storage capacity of computers is measured in bytes (64K = 64,000 bytes).

Central Processing Unit (CPU): The part of a computer that carries out data manipulation and controls the sequence of operations performed by the computer.

Character: A single letter, number, symbol, or space. Requires one byte of computer memory.

Chip: An integrated electronic circuit etched on a wafer of silicon.

Circuit Board: A plastic board with chips mounted on it, connected by imprinted circuits. Circuit boards can usually be easily removed or added to computers.

COBOL: The Common Business Oriented Language. A computer programming language that reads like standard English. Programs written in the same version of COBOL can usually be transferred from one computer to another.

CP/M: A common operating system.

CPS: Characters per second.

Crop: The technique of trimming the edges of an illustration in order to fit it correctly and artistically within a given space or frame in the computer layout.

CRT: Cathode-ray tube. A device like a television that displays information in the computer.

Cursor: A small dot, line, or square that shows where the next character will appear on a computer screen.

Database: A collection of structured information on a specific subject or related group of subjects (such as a mailing list) that can be accessed by a computer.

Diskette: See *Floppy Disk*.

Display Type: Type larger than 14 points generally used for headlines and bold copy.

Documentation: The instructions for using a computer or software.

Dot Matrix Printer: A printer that forms characters by printing tiny dots to form letters or numbers.

File: A collection of records or information such as a word-processed letter or a budget stored by your computer in one place.

Floppy Disk: A flexible plastic disk coated with magnetic material on which data is recorded and stored.

Flush Left (Ragged-Right): Flush left is a paragraph setting in which text abuts the left margin and has a ragged right margin—sometimes referred to as "left" or "left justified."

Flush Right (Ragged-Left): A paragraph setting in which the text abuts the right margin and has a ragged left margin—sometimes referred to as "right" or "right justified."

Font: In desktop publishing font has the same meaning as typeface. A font is a set of characters with the same basic design, such as Helvetica and Times.

Format: Format refers to the overall ordering and layout of material. Paragraph formats usually include margins and tab settings. Character formats include font, type style, font size, and other style attributes.

FORTRAN: FORmula TRANslator. A computer programming language originally designed for scientific and mathematical uses, but now common in computer systems for business.

Hard Copy: Printed output from a computer.

Hard Disk: A rigid version of a floppy disk, made of aluminum and used for storing large amounts of data.

Hardware: The physical devices that constitute a computer system.

Input/Output Devices: Devices that can send messages to and receive messages from a computer.

Integrated Circuit: A chip of silicon with thousands of interrelated electronic circuits etched onto it.

Interface: Software or hardware used to connect devices that cannot be connected directly.

Internal Memory: The storage facilities in a computer system where programs and data are held while being worked on.

Joystick: A lever that controls movements of a cursor on a screen.

Justify: To fit a line of text to a box or column width so the text will have uniform left and right margins.

K: A kilobyte (sometimes used to mean simply one thousand). As a measure of a computers memory, 1,024 bytes.

Kern: Kerning adjusts the amount of white space between letter pairs.

Keyboard: The typewriter-like device that allows you to enter information into your computer.

Lap Top: A portable, battery-operated computer that folds down for convenient transportation.

Laser Printer: A printer that uses a laser to print.

Leading: In computer terms, the measurement of space occupied by a line of text measured from baseline to baseline. A leading value includes the font size plus the space between lines.

Letter Quality: Printers that produce printouts as good as an office typewriter.

Light Pen: A small pen-like input device used to point out choices on a computer screen.

Local Area Network (LAN): A group of microcomputers closely linked together to be able to share information, programs, and peripheral devices.

M: Megabyte. Equal to 1,024,000 bytes.

Mainframe: A large commercial computer.

Menu: A list of program functions from which a computer user can choose what to do.

Microcomputer: A complete personal computer system built around a microprocessor.

Microprocessor: A central processing unit on a single integrated circuit chip.

Minicomputer: Or "mini." A computer of moderate price and size. Bigger than a personal computer, smaller than a mainframe.

Modem: Acronym for MOdulator DEModulator. A device that lets you link one computer to another computer over a telephone line.

Monitor: A televison-like screen that displays data.

Mouse: A palm-sized device used instead of a keyboard to move the cursor and as an electronic pointer.

MS-DOS: A common operating system.

Operating System: A group of programs that are used to operate the whole computer. Any application software must be written for a specific operating system, such as CP/M.

Peripherals: Hardware devices that are external to the computer, such as printers, modems, and monitors.

Personal Computer: A small computer capable of the entire range of computer functions, inexpensive enough for an individual or small company, but large enough for professional or business applications.

Plotter: A printer that produces lines, curves, and characters by moving a pen and/or the paper.

Printer: A device that prints out hard copy.

Program: A series of precise step-by-step instructions that tell your computer how to accomplish a specific task.

RAM: Random Access Memory. The kind of computer memory available to the user, most often in a small computer.

Read: To retrieve information from a computer memory.

Records: In database programs, individual collections of related information. In database programs, records are organized into *files.*

Resolution: The precision of representation, which determines the accuracy of reproduction and distinctness of visual elements. For printer output and computer screens, resolution is defined in dots per inch (dpi). The more dots per inch, the finer the resolution.

ROM: Read-only memory. A type of memory already built into a computer, used for permanent storage of program instructions. ROM cannot be altered or added to by users.

Software: The general term of all computer programs, as opposed to the actual physical devices, or hardware.

Stand-Alone: A self-contained machine.

Telecommunications: The process by which computers can be linked to other computers using telephones.

Terminal: Usually a display screen and keyboard connected to a computer system. A terminal is used for entering and retrieving data, programs, and instruction.

Tiling: The process by which a document larger than the paper to be printed on can be broken into sections the size of the paper, and then assembled.

Widow: A single word or hyphenated portion of a word which makes up the last line of a paragraph. A widow which is carried to the top of a new column or new page is called an orphan.

Winchester Disk: Another term for a hard disk; an information storage device with a very large capacity.

Window: An area of a computer screen that displays an application in addition to the main program being worked on.

Word Processing: An application that serves as an electronic typewriter with a built-in memory and other added functions.

Index

Note: An *f.* after a page number refers to a figure.